T0128542

Heading North

A Narrative

DONALD R. BELIK

authorHOUSE®

AuthorHouse™
1663 Liberty Drive
Bloomington, IN 47403
www.authorhouse.com
Phone: 1 (800) 839-8640

Published by AuthorHouse 05/14/2020

ISBN: 978-1-7283-6176-5 (sc)
ISBN: 978-1-7283-6175-8 (e)

Library of Congress Control Number: 2020908827

CONTENTS

PART 2
Unsettled Years

PART 3
Michael's Journals

AUTHOR'S NOTE

A lot of time has passed since the events rendered in this book have occurred. Dialogue and events are accurate to the best of my recollection. I have strived to bring forth an honest story as vividly as possible given the time span of fifty years. Naturally, I cannot be certain that every quote is entirely accurate or that my interpretation of events will be in exact agreement with those of others involved.

PREFACE

One evening while I was sitting at the dinner table with my friends during one of our fishing trips, one of us mentioned an old fishing story. While we sat in discussion, a question was asked: "Does anyone remember the year that happened?" Not one of us could pin it down. Remembering what happened just a year or two ago was hard enough. We all agreed the story's events had taken place many years ago, but we could not put a date to it. We asked Michael if he might have this story in one of his journals. He said, "Maybe!"

Michael had kept journals for many of the years we came north fishing. I told him he should author a book based on them. "There must be enough material in those journals," I told him. He looked at me with piercing eyes, befuddled, and said, "I'm not writing no book." Well, that was final enough! But what about someone else? When I mentioned it, everyone thought it to be a great idea. What a neat way to preserve some of our stories. The thought entertained us for the rest of our meal, but in the end, nobody volunteered.

All through that evening and into the early morning, the idea about drafting a book kept going through my mind. Even weeks after that trip, the daunting task kept resurfacing in my thoughts. The material was all there. All that was necessary was to organize it and write it down. I finally succumbed to the idea that it might not be that difficult of an undertaking. I admitted to myself that maybe I could write it. I decided to try it. If a simple narrative of events could be documented, we would not have to take our stories to the grave.

For most of us, the grave was getting nearer and nearer. We were all over seventy or pushing it. Except for me, everyone was retired. For the past fifty years, we have all been engaged in a friendship ritual—a coming together for one magical week of fabulous fishing, eating too much, drinking what is desired, and good old camaraderie that has stood the test of time and distance. Embarking each year from the same town toward the same destination hundreds of miles away, our resolve to maintain this legacy has been, and is still, strong.

Since our first trip up north in 1967, we have amassed a rich and plentiful collection of fishing stories. Most of the stories from our earlier years have been penned from memory. None of us had the foresight to document or keep a small diary of what took place. Even photos were pathetically omitted by all of us. We simply ignored the fact that at some time in our lives, we would cherish the possession of even one photo. Michael, on the other hand, realized we were letting something special slip through our ever-declining memory. So, in our latter years, Michael started keeping his journals. I am thankful to have them, as it made writing about those years easier and more complete.

Over the years, not everyone made every trip. School, careers, military obligations, and personal affairs all played a part in our ability to do what we wanted to do. Conditions and positions in which we found ourselves dictated our lives. There was not one of us that managed to make every trip, but nobody was keeping score. We respected each other's privacy enough not to engage in any critical conclusion of each other. Each year, those that made the trip were rewarded with lasting memories, and those that did not were always invited back without question or hesitation. I consider myself to be one of the lucky ones to be associated with a bunch of guys that grew up together and, over many years, have continued to get together as part of a lasting friendship.

Doug is a PA in Fairbury, Nebraska, and still practices. Rick is a software engineer that owns his own business in Washington State and is retired. Michael worked for the State of Nebraska Workforce Development team and is retired. Terry is a construction engineer and lives in Washington State and is retired. Jim is a civil engineer that owns his own business out of Columbus, Nebraska, and is retired. Wayne worked for the Burlington Northern Railroad in Lincoln, Nebraska, and is retired. Leonard owns a farm in Prague, Nebraska, and is retired. I still work as an application engineer for Goodyear Tire and Rubber Company out of Lincoln, Nebraska.

Thanks to Michael's journals, some old pictures, and a lot of soul searching, I was able to reconstruct a time line as accurately as I could. Here you will find stories of some of our most treasured memories, from our first trip north in 1967 to our fiftieth year in 2017. The narrative describes our experiences as seen from my perspective.

PART 1

WHAT A GREAT IDEA!

CHAPTER 1

September 16, 2017

M y alarm went off at 5:30 a.m. Normally on a workday, I liked to snooze a couple of times before dragging myself out of bed to take a shower and head to the office. This morning, however, was different. My morning procrastination was absorbed by a strong urge to meet the day willingly and without delay. After weeks and months of planning, the day had finally arrived. My life would take on a whole different meaning for the next couple of weeks. It would be filled with camaraderie, good eating, and—hopefully—good fishing.

Soon my fishing friends and I would again be united to see the most beautiful Bottle Lakes. It is hard to describe this piece of paradise nestled just twenty miles north of Park Rapids, Minnesota, among tall pines, colorful maples, and the beautiful white clump birches. Crystal-clear water, fresh air, foggy mornings, and crisp and cool evenings awaited us. If that didn't get us pumped up, there was nothing like sitting over one of Michael's early-morning breakfasts or experiencing one of Michael's great evening dinners.

The year 2017 marked our fiftieth anniversary heading north. We had been talking about this milestone for many years, and now the time had arrived. How could the years have gone by so fast? Our first fishing trip in August 1967 started out as just an idea of us getting together for one last time after our graduation from high school and before we all set out to find our own way. That one trip made such a vivid impression on us that for year after year, we would find a way to traverse the same landscape, going back to the same destination to experience heaven on earth once again.

CHAPTER 2

Prague, Nebraska, 1953–1963

A ll of us can trace our roots to one small town: Prague, Nebraska. Prague is located within a small farming community situated among the hilly farm fields of Saunders County in southeastern Nebraska. Homesteaders migrated into this community by taking advantage of the great Homestead Act of 1862. Those settlers who were willing to carve out a new beginning for themselves received a 160-acre tract of land. It came with a promise of finding a new life and a fresh start.

Prague owes its beginnings to the railroad. The railroad needed a halfway station along its line that ran from Ashland, Nebraska, to Schuyler, Nebraska, and that prompted the Lincoln Land Company to purchase a 160-acre land tract from one of the early homesteaders and build a station. The town was platted in 1887 by Lincoln, and they started selling lots in hopes of attracting families and business-minded entrepreneurs to raise a village in support of the station. By the end of 1887, a general store, a hardware store, and a saloon had opened for business. A prosperous lumber yard started in late 1887. In October 1887, the first train arrived. A post office was established in December 1887. In 1888, the village of Prague, with a population of about two hundred, was incorporated.

The newly incorporated small farm community started to grow immediately. In 1900, the population of Prague was 324. Census records from 1930 showed Prague had risen to its all-time high of 421. A variety of stores, businesses, and services that catered to the agricultural nature of the economy were started. In addition to the already established business district, a meat locker was built. There was a mortuary. A Ford dealership thrived—the largest in southeastern Nebraska. The growing town started a bank and a drug store. Prague was the home of the first hospital in Saunders County. It lasted until 1953, when the building was converted to a parochial school for kindergarten through eighth grade.

Most of the families that set roots in and around the town of Prague had a strong Catholic heritage. My family was no exception. I would be part of the first kindergarten class to attend the new parochial school. The year was 1953. As luck would have it, my mom and dad decided to get me started in school at the early age of four. The price I paid for this early entry into the school system was a lack of maturity, both socially and physically. I simply needed to be kept back one more year. However, my life would have been quite different if they had kept me back. I would not have gotten to know Jim, Doug, or Mike, and certainly not Rick, who is over two years my senior. Because of my parents' decision, I was lucky enough to get into the same class and thus nurture a friendship that lasts to this day. Consequently, through them I got to know Wayne and Terry.

CHAPTER 3

Learning How to Fish

I grew up on a small farm located just half a mile from the township of Prague. Homesteaded by my great-grandfather and passed down from generation to generation, Dad's eighty-some-acre farm bordered the town of Prague to the north. The farmstead had a house, a barn, a crib, a chicken coop, a garage, three outbuildings, and a pump house. It was my home until 1967.

My father had three abstractions: music, farming, and fishing. He was preoccupied with those activities to the exclusion of anything else. Number one on the list was his music. Everything else took second fiddle. He was a Czech musician who consumed as much of his time as he could allow—and then some. He arranged. He composed. He performed. Most notably, he played a button accordion. I must say that his talent with the button accordion had no equivalent, and his style was unmatched. He was well known in the Czech community for his playing ability and devotion to Czech music.

His second love was farming. Dad did his best to raise his family on the small homestead, which had been handed down to him at an early age. Eventually he had to submit to the escalating cost of running a farm and supporting his family, and he did what a lot of farmers did: he took a job to help supplement his income. However, Dad still found time for his music, worked a full-time job, and farmed the land that he loved. It was a large undertaking of responsibility that demanded a great deal of respect.

Dad's third love was fishing. His eyes lit up just talking about fishing. Dad taught me how to fish at an early age, and we would go almost every weekend to a nearby lake, a sand pit, or the great Platte River. I developed a passion for the sport. I grew to love how purely simple fishing can be. I grew to love the peace and quiet I found every time we went fishing.

Most of our outings favored the Platte River in search of carp. Seeing the river from the road or through a window from a car cannot compare to standing on the river's sandy bank and gazing out at the movement of the water, which followed a wandering course that appeared to be in disorder and agitated. Pockets of turbulence caused by the uplifting of water by some hidden obstruction beneath resembled pots of boiling water. My first experience at seeing the river's turbulent unrest was scary. However, with a few outings under my belt, it didn't take long for me to admire the river with its impressive, tall cottonwood trees; the repetitive muffled sounds of the running water; the vast expanse of exposed sandbars; and all the auditory sensations associated with it. Even now while fishing the river, I will catch myself just staring across the expanse of sandbars in an almost calming awareness while listening to the water flow its course. It attracts and holds my interest, demanding complete attention. Whenever I fished the river, very seldom did I ever take my eyes off it. It is that serene and beautiful.

There is nothing like fishing the Platte River for carp. For me it is the ultimate fishing experience. Dad and I also enjoyed fishing the Platte River bottom sand pits. The Platte River valley itself has a very unusual characteristic. It is mostly composed of the sorted sediment of gravel, sand, silt, and clay deposits that flowed into the basin during the ice ages from eroded rocks originating in the Rocky Mountains. Over time, as water carried the rocks downstream, they broke up into sand and gravel, which helped to form the Platte River bottom.

The extraction of the sand and gravel from the river bottom formed the sand pits. Large pumps were used to remove the aggregate from the ground. After a separation process, high-quality sand was then sold to concrete manufacturers. Because the water table on the river bottom was remarkably high and normally followed the river's water table, the hole that was made from the extraction of the sand and gravel quickly filled up with water, forming the lake, which is known as a sand pit. They were deep, were mostly clear, had sandy bottoms, and were full of fish of varied species. Bass, crappies, bluegills, carp, and catfish could be caught. Dad taught me how to fish for all of them.

CHAPTER 4

A New Fishing Buddy

Dad and I often would go to the Platte River or fish some of the sand pits found around the river's valley. A river or sand pit fishing adventure normally lasted all day and was reserved for a Saturday or Sunday afternoon. Sometimes during a weekday, in the evening, Dad and I would go and fish some of the local farm ponds in the area. We could go on short notice and not have to drive far to spend just an hour or two fishing. Most of the time, these small farm pond lakes would hold bluegills and a good quantity of bullheads.

One of those ponds was located about a mile just south of Prague. We fished this pond often. The pond was formed by a county road built across a deep creek bed that ran through the property of old Tom Cizek, another Czech whose family had settled near the Prague community. Since the county road formed the dam, anyone could fish the lake from off the face of the dam. However, since most of the surface water existed on old Tom's property, Dad got permission to fish the backwaters of the lake, which were filled with abundant trees and stumps. Most of the banks of the old creek bed still existed and were never destroyed when the dam was built. It was not unusual to find a spot at water's edge that simply went straight down fifteen feet. If we found an old tree stump or dead tree next to the bank, chances are there was deep water close by—a prime location to swing out the cane pole.

One day Dad and I were fishing at Cizek's pond when I noticed Jim Musilek walking down the opposite bank, looking for a place to fish. Jim was one of my classmates at parochial school. He was carrying a cane pole very much like what Dad and I were using. I looked around to see if there was a car parked on the road. To my surprise, there was not, and I wondered how he'd gotten there. I told Dad, "That is Jim Musilek on the other bank."

Dad said, "That is Leonard's boy. If we would follow the creek bed north, eventually we would end up on Leonard's farm." We decided he must have walked in. I continued to watch Jim, and when our eyes met, we shared a wave.

The next day at school I approached Jim and asked him about fishing at Cizek's. He answered, "I go there all the time. Did you catch anything?"

I replied, "Just a couple of bullheads." As conversations go when people are of an early age, we didn't talk long.

As Dad and I continued to fish Cizek's that summer, we saw Jim more. He was always by himself. One day Dad offered to drive Jim home instead of leaving him to walk back. During that short trip home, Dad asked Jim if he would like to come fishing with us sometime. His answer was a definite yes. Dad arranged it with Jim's parents, and the next Sunday I had a new fishing friend.

Over that summer and into the summers that followed, Jim and I became good fishing buddies. Jim came fishing with Dad and me whenever he could. We fished the sand pits and the river, as well as the lakes around Prague. We gathered worms together and seined for minnows. In some ways, fishing with Jim made me a stronger person. I honestly believe Jim could have grown up to be a mountain man if he had been born 120 years earlier. The more we fished together, the more I realized Jim showed little fear about anything. He didn't mind fishing by himself or camping overnight by himself. Later, when he could drive, he would go to the river and set bank lines and then check them at night by himself.

Jim's grandfather taught him how to trap. During his grade school days and into high school, Jim ran trap lines by himself, mostly for muskrats and beavers. Occasionally he would get a mink. That meant walking on ice to set and retrieve the traps. Jim used to describe to me how he chopped holes in the ice next to dens just to set the traps. I am deathly afraid of ice. To this day, I simply cannot walk on ice. I do not care how thick it is.

Jim showed me once what it took to set a beaver trap. It scared the crap out of me. I cannot even set a mouse trap without cringing, let alone a beaver trap or a muskrat trap. He did that on the ice in the middle of winter, usually in the dark, all by himself. He learned how to skin and stretch all his own furs and made some good money selling his pelts.

Since Jim grew up on the farm, he learned how to drive early on. He would take one of his father's old beater cars and drove himself out to check the traps in the morning before school started. Then, after supper in the evening, he would check his traps again, usually by flashlight, all by himself. I mean, really! What drives a young boy to do that, other than his total control over fear-inducing situations and his love of nature? He simply was fearless. When I talk to him today, he tells me, "Being fearless had nothing to do with it. I just love to trap." His love for the sport took the fear right out of it. For me there was no way I would have even considered it.

Jim became one of my best friends. Throughout grade school and into high school, we hunted, and we fished together whenever we could. During the spring, summer, and fall, there were few weekends when we didn't go fishing somewhere.

CHAPTER 5

On Common Ground

During my childhood years and throughout my high school years, no family, other than my own immediate family, has had a greater presence in my life than the Musileks. The Musilek clan seemed to be all over the place. In my class alone, there were three first cousins: Jim, Mike, and Carolyn. One class above, there were two more first cousins: Rick and Leo. Rick and Carolyn were brother and sister. One class below me, there was another first cousin—Pat. Pat and Mike were brother and sister. Just two years below me was another first cousin—Connie. Connie and Jim were brother and sister. I get confused just writing about it.

What started this composite of related parts can be traced back to Jim's grandfather, old man James Musilek. He had five kids. There were four girls and one son. Leonard Musilek was the youngest of the brood and the only boy. He decided to farm the family homestead after his return from WWII. The Musilek homestead lies about one mile east of Prague. The four girls, along with Leonard, all got married about the same time just after WWII and started having families all about the same time. That just happened to be about the same time my parents decided to start their family. Prague's contribution to the baby boom generation was underway.

From 1953 to 1963, all of us baby boomers attended the same parochial school. In the fall of 1963, Jim, Michael, and I entered Prague High School along with thirty other classmates. It was the largest incoming class in Prague High School history.

Douglas

I first met Doug Ruzicka during my sophomore year in 1964. Doug and his parents moved into Prague that summer, and he promptly fit right into our class. Doug was very much into high school sports. Unlike me, who was pathetic in those activities, Doug was a particularly good athlete. My getting to know Doug occurred not through high school sports participation, but through outdoor sports: hunting and fishing. It didn't take long for the both of us to realize we had those common interests. Ironically, it was not fishing that bonded our friendship, but hunting, which just happened to be Doug's favorite outdoor sport.

When I found out Doug loved to hunt, it didn't take us long to get together on a Saturday or Sunday, after a fresh snowfall, and walk down Cottonwood Creek for a few hours of rabbit hunting. Cottonwood Creek had an ample supply of quick and jittery rabbits, and man did they make for some good eating. Another one of our favorite spots was the railroad track that ran into Prague. The ditches and land next to the track were never cleaned out and provided us with good rabbit hunting. It was tough walking through the dense undergrowth, but the struggle was worth it. There were a lot of fat rabbits in those groves of thickets and bushes.

We also loved to hunt pheasants and quail. In the sixties and seventies, Prague sat right in the middle of pheasant heaven. There were so many in southeastern Nebraska, owing in large part to the abundant safe habitat our lands provided during that era. A big part of the habitat can be attributed to the farmers planting milo as part of their crop rotation. Milo fields were everywhere, and the pheasants loved milo. The crop was a large part of their diet and provided the birds good protection during the winter and during the hunting season. Obtaining permission to hunt the fields was not that difficult, since most of the farmers around the town knew us. Fortunately for the pheasants and the quail, I could not hit the side of a barn, so my bags were very few. Doug, being a crack shot, normally hit everything he shot at.

Those kinds of outings lasted well into the late winter months. Our hunting adventures during winter days required us to do more walking in fields that were already harvested and usually snow packed. But the birds were there, hiding among the foxtail and cornstalks. There were times I got the shit scared out of me while walking down a corn row covered with snow when a pheasant would flush out of the cornstalks right next to me. It really was a thrill I will never forget.

Doug and I did more hunting than fishing while we were in high school. However, we did manage to wet the line at times during the summer school breaks. A few times, Jim, Doug, and I would set out to the river to set some bank lines or sneak into a sand pit for a chance at some catfish. Doug became one of my best friends in the short three years we spent in high school.

Rick

Rick Shimerka was one of those kids that lived in town that I really did not get to know until later in my high school years. Rick was one grade ahead of me and because of that was more than two years older. My social interaction among the students in grade school was confined to my own classmates, and I had few opportunities to really get together with the kids that lived in town. I got to know Rick on a more personal basis through my interaction with his cousins Michael and Jim. During our senior year at Prague, Rick was already into his first year at the University of Nebraska. Rick was one of those all-around great people to know. He was smart, assured, and never self-centered. Rick has a personality that just makes folks feel good when he is around.

Michael

Michael Pabian: A jock. A sportsman. A culinary artist. A classmate. A friend. Michael and I went to school together from kindergarten through high school. The enormous difference between Michael and me was his athletic ability. He was bigger, stronger, and older than I was. It was that same age difference that kept defining me as less mature than most kids in my class. When it came to athletics, Michael excelled.

Michael's parents ran the Pabian Produce and Meat Locker in Prague. Since Mike lived in town and I lived on the farm, a strong bonded friendship did not develop between us until we were well into our high school years.

In fact, we didn't have that much in common during grade school except for our love of baseball. Even that sport was a bitter pill for me to swallow because of my age difference. I continually got bounced around between two different age groups. Michael continued with an older age group and became a formidable player at catcher and a good batter.

Michael's excellent work ethic led right into high school. Football was Mike's strong sport. Even though he participated in basketball, baseball, and track, Mike excelled at football. He was fast and solidly built with a sturdy foundation. Mike played center, which is one of the toughest positions to play in football. Just as with playing catcher in baseball, he met that challenge with quickness and pure strength.

Michael was part of the Musilek clan; his mother was a sister to Jim's Dad, Leonard. This was an important relationship as it relates to Doug and Jim. Jim didn't continue going to Prague Public School but went to Bishop Neumann during his sophomore year in 1964 when the Catholic high school opened in Wahoo, Nebraska. That was the same year Doug came into our class as a sophomore in Prague. Since Doug and Mike lived in town, their friendship formed almost immediately. One of Michael's favorite outdoor activities was hunting, so their friendship was further strengthened by their common love for that sport. It was inevitable, then, that Doug would come to meet Jim through Mike or me. By the time our senior year came around, Jim, Doug, Mike, and I shared many good times together hunting and fishing whenever we could.

The bond Doug and Mike developed for themselves is still close to this day. I consider myself lucky to have become good friends with both. Some of the best times in my life took place in high school during our senior year together. We had so much fun.

By 1967, the great bond between all of us had formed through the outdoor sports of hunting, and fishing, which we all loved. Mike, Doug, Rick, Jim, and I spent as much time together engaged in those two activities as circumstances would allow.

CHAPTER 6

The Summer of 1967

When the summer months of 1967 arrived, Rick had just finished his first year at the University of Nebraska, and during the summer he would help his Dad run their family business. The rest of us graduated from high school in May and were looking for summer jobs. Doug and Jim landed jobs in North Bend, Nebraska, working in a trailer home manufacturing facility. Mike worked for his Dad in Prague at the meat locker. I managed to land a summer job working for the soil conservation service in Wahoo, Nebraska. Our adult lives started that June; it was unknown to us what the future would bring.

No one's path forward was clearly defined that summer except for Rick's and Mike's. Rick had already committed to the University of Nebraska. Mike landed a scholarship to Doane College, now Doane University, to play football. Mike had developed himself into a formidable football player. He was lucky enough to be part of the great Doane College Tigers undefeated teams of 1966, '67, '68, and '69. Those teams had an unbeaten streak of thirty-five games, which was all part of a thirty-eight-game win streak. Doane's success drew the attention of *Sports Illustrated*, who wrote a feature on the Tigers in October of 1969, when the unbeaten streak was the longest in college football. What an honor for Michael! Doug was undecided as to what he wanted to do, and Jim wanted to become a civil engineer.

I had in mind to pursue a career as a forest conservation officer. When my folks and I checked into it, we found out that the University of Nebraska didn't have a course of study for that degree. They did, however, have a course of study in association with the University of Missouri. The degree required the last two years to be completed in Missouri. The first two years would be at the University of Nebraska. This was something I was not prepared for. Out-of-state tuition was out of the question for me, as money was tight. It affected our decision-making process. So my parents and I decided that I would go for one year to UNL for general studies and register as an undeclared freshman—a major mistake for myself for years to come. It was unclear to me at the time that I needed a set direction and not some undecided course that would lead me to total failure in the upcoming years at UNL. My unclear path was set. I was going to UNL starting in September.

CHAPTER 7

What a Great Idea!

That summer in 1967, mixed in with our own jobs, we fished, we camped, we played cards, and we just hung around when we could. One night, while we were playing cards, Rick mentioned the idea that we should all get together before the summer ended and do something special. Maybe we would get away for just a few days as a kind of bon voyage for all of us, but what would we do? Michael suggested a fishing trip somewhere. Mike said that his family and another family used to head north into Minnesota on a fishing trip when he was younger. My head started spinning at once about the prospect and thought the whole idea highly imaginative. For me, a fishing trip to Minnesota was so farfetched I would have never given it a thought. My folks took us on vacations, but seldom outside of the state of Nebraska. At that time, fishing in Minnesota was only something I heard or read about. We all looked at each other with excitement but also skepticism. Rick and Mike decided they would investigate it further. I left that night expecting nothing and never gave the idea a second thought.

In the town of Prague in 1967, there were three bars, a produce and meat locker, a grocery store, a lumber yard, two gas stations, a bank, a post office, a national hall, a Catholic hall, a John Deere dealership, a small department store, a mortuary, two churches, a high school, a parochial school, and one drug store. That single drug store was a local hangout for a lot of the teens in town. It was a place to sit and have some ice cream, play a jukebox, play cards in one of the four booths in the back, or even buy some fishing equipment. Rick also knew that the owner of the store, Otto C. Matous, and his wife used to do a lot of fishing in Minnesota. Rick and Doug contacted Otto and told him about our plan to go on a fishing trip into Minnesota. They asked him, "Where would you suggest we go?"

His answer to them came straight away: "The Park Rapids area of Minnesota."

Ironically, Mike was checking with his parents at the same time, and he found out they also used to go to a resort north of Park Rapids.

With two references already given to us, we were ready for a meeting to discuss the trip in further detail. We all sat down one evening and discussed what Mike and Rick had found out about the Park Rapids area of Minnesota. Both Otto's and Mike's families had stayed at a fishing resort. For me the word "resort" normally was associated with an expensive stay. However, after discussing the cost issue, we decided that if we split the cost equally, with no questions asked, it might not be that bad. But, regardless of our speculations, we needed to know what the cost would be. Finding that out required some investigation. Rick decided he was going to contact the Park Rapids Chamber of Commerce for any brochures they could send us about fishing opportunities in that area.

Rick pulled out a map of Minnesota. Some quick measurements on the map showed the drive to Park Rapids to be about five hundred miles one way as the crow flies. We all thought it to be a far piece. How were we going to get there? If we decided to make the trip, none of us had a car, and nobody's parents were going to let any of us use their car for a trip that far out, no matter what. We decided to figure out our transportation issue after we found out what our costs would be.

We were fortunate to have Rick as part of our band, as he was not one to be deterred. If it had not been for him, I doubt our little adventure would have ever made it out of Otto's drug store. But as it was, Rick did send a letter to the Park Rapids Chamber of Commerce, and about two weeks later, I got a call from Rick asking me to be at his place the coming Friday night. He had finally received his package. I remember being extra excited after that call. I hoped that, after Friday night, we would at least know our cost. I knew of nobody living in Prague at that time that had been born with a silver spoon in his or her mouth. It was the most important piece of information we needed.

CHAPTER 8

The Bottle Lakes

F riday night arrived none too soon. I could hardly wait for seven. Once everyone arrived, it was time to open the package. Rick had every right to open the package before we even assembled that night, but he did not. He was considerate enough to wait until we were all together. I can only imagine how hard it must have been for him to keep from breaking down and letting his inquisitiveness rule.

We gathered around the kitchen table, the rather large bulky package in front of us, unopened. It was time for the unveiling. With great anticipation from us all, Rick opened the package and dumped the whole contents on the table. Out flew dozens of brochures. Some were printed on just single leaflets. Most were folded into three sections that opened into single 8½" × 11" brochures. Each of us started grabbing, anxious to see the contents and get an idea of what we were facing.

As we were reading the brochures, we noticed some differences that caught our attention. Most of the brochures were from resorts. A few were from rental properties, which would have required us to stay in the town. At once we declined to even consider those, and they were promptly set aside. Some were from hotels in town. Those found the "dead pile" right away. Some of the brochures offered a community complex resembling a hotel found on the resort property that offered little privacy. We didn't want to have anything to do with that. Those also made it to the dead pile. After sorting the unwanted items, we decided to separate out only the resorts that offered lakeshore cabins. Out of the original bunch, we narrowed it down to somewhere around thirty.

Okay, now what? We were stuck rummaging through that pile for the longest time, unable to figure out how to move forward and arrive at a choice. Rick then came to the rescue! He suggested we sort from highest price to lowest price first, set aside the ten brochures for the cabins with the lowest cost, and go from there. Our most important criterion was that the cabin have no more than two bedrooms. We didn't need three bedrooms. Nobody was modest in those days, so sleeping two to a bed was no problem. The rest would get the floor or sleep on a couch. Each one of us grabbed a brochure and found out the price. We wrote down the cost on a small piece of paper and set it on top of the brochure and then set it aside. When we were done, the pile ended up sorted neatly in rows with, a price set on top. Then we sorted them all from highest cost to lowest cost. It didn't take long to see the results. We removed all the brochures except the ten cheapest and sent them to the dead pile. Finally we were getting to the bottom of this. In front of us was one brochure that we would eventually decide upon.

We looked at the price range of the bottom ten. There was not much difference from the highest to the lowest. We decided to sort by location and the resorts' proximity from Park Rapids. We just felt that we wanted as much privacy as we could get. None of us had any experience fishing in Minnesota except Michael, who remembered nothing about the lake or the resort his family used to go to. Part of our expectations about fishing in Minnesota was total isolation from the rest of the world; we didn't want the resort to be located just off a highway. Those resorts found on or close to a highway made the dead pile. We ended up with five resorts that suggested a location that was isolated and remotely located.

We were down to five. We started scrutinizing them. We looked at everything from price to the quality of the pictures they presented in their brochures. They were all similar. Finally, and very scientifically, we decided upon the brochure that had the most pictures of fish displayed on the front. That brochure belonged to Home Bay Resort located on Bottle Lakes in Hubbard County, Minnesota, twenty miles north of Park Rapids. Of course, we questioned ourselves. We took second and third looks. However, the result was always the same: Home Bay!

All Home Bay cabins were single multibedroom units. There were no joined cabins. The brochure showed them to be found right on the lakeshore. There were eight units to choose from. Some had three bedrooms; some had two. There was only one cabin that had a single bedroom; it was just a one-room cabin. Only a couple of the larger cabins had a bathroom. A community bath was available for the rest of the guests. The cabin came with one boat. If we wanted a motor, it would be separate. There was bait on site, which at the time didn't mean a thing to us. What bait? The only bait we ever used were small creek minnows and worms. Even night crawlers were not plentiful in Prague.

Finally, we had our destination and we had our resort. We started working on the cost. The cabin we were after had two bedrooms and was just at $200 for the week. Dividing that by five, and it was $40 just to sleep. That was nothing to sneeze at. Today we spend $200 on one visit to the grocery store. In the late sixties, that was a lot of money. The motor would be $50 for the week. The old phrase "they will nickel and dime you to death" came to mind starting with the motor. That was it for the resort costs.

We started considering the other costs we would incur: food, gas licenses, bait, and, of course, our alcohol. Food was hard to consider, since not one of us went to the grocery store and bought food for our family. That was Mom and Dad's job. We figured we could get by on about $75 for the week.

Gas was easy to figure out. The average gas mileage on a car in the sixties was about twelve to fifteen miles per gallon. Gas was cheap then; twenty-five cents per gallon was the norm. So we figured gas would cost us around $30 for a thousand-mile round trip. In addition, we would have to pay $7 each for a seven-day nonresident fishing license. We eventually figured on about $100 each to make the trip. That seemed doable to us "not-so-grown-up men" sitting around a kitchen table. At least now I had something to talk about when I asked Mom and Dad for permission to go. But we still had one question that needed answering: how were we going to get there?

CHAPTER 9

Leo

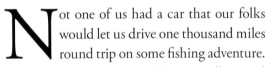

Not one of us had a car that our folks would let us drive one thousand miles round trip on some fishing adventure. That was out of the question. What were we to do? We were all excited about the possibility of getting to experience a Minnesota fishing trip, but at the same time, it seemed silly for us to build up our expectations without knowing whether we could get there. This one issue loomed big for us. We had no solution. We left that evening excited but fraught with uncertainty. Unbeknownst to us, Rick had an idea.

Leo Tepoel is another first cousin to Jim, Rick, and Mike. Leo's Mom also was a sister to Leonard. Leo was the oldest of all the cousins and just happened to be born the same year as Rick. Leo and Rick were classmates, and they were both members of the 1966 graduation class from Prague High.

Leo's Dad operated a large farm with a lot of land. It makes sense, then, that Leo became somewhat of a gearhead. For him, the mechanics of vehicles came easy. Since Leo's interest was primarily cars, it stood to reason that Leo owned one of his own, which he did, and Rick knew it.

I never came to know Leo like I did the other Musilek cousins. Sometimes when I was asked to go hunting with the guys, Leo would come along, but those times were very few. I cannot remember Leo ever coming along with us for a weekend of camping and fishing. However, he did like to fish.

Rick's idea was simple. He would ask Leo whether he would be interested in a fishing trip up north with all of us and ask him if he could drive. Leo understood our dilemma and, faced with an exciting proposition like fishing in Minnesota for a week, did not hesitate to accept.

CHAPTER 10

The End of August 1967

Yay for Leo! Rick gave me a call one night and told me Leo would be driving us up. Until that night, I still felt our little adventure would not take place. Rick said he was going to write to Home Bay and ask to rent a two-bedroom cabin for some time in late August. That would put six in the cabin, and we would then need an extra boat and motor. Instead of dividing by five, we would now divide by six. Could six of us get into Leo's car with all our junk?

It came time to break the news to Mom and Dad. They normally would never prevent me from doing something fun with my friends. They knew the guys I spent time together with, and they knew we were all respected in the community. And we were. None of us were rowdy bullies. Sure, we each had our run-ins with suspect behavior and sometimes making some wrong character decisions, such as getting caught for being a minor in possession of alcohol or getting a speeding ticket. What teenager did not? But we never purposely got into fights; nor did we ever go looking for a fight. We were not reckless and didn't have a defiant, careless disregard for danger. We all understood the consequences of such foolhardy behavior. When I asked for permission to go, they didn't hesitate.

We talked about the price and the way we would deal with the costs. I told them about our meetings and explained that we thought each one of us could do the trip for $150. We had thought $100 would do it, but I wanted to get an extra $50 out of the deal just in case. I didn't mention anything about alcohol, but they knew what that was all about. So it was a go for me. I just had to come up with $150, and then the last piece of the puzzle would have to fall into place: Rick getting the cabin booked and then finding out the date we would leave.

Rick wasted no time. He received the news we were all waiting for. Another meeting at Rick's house took place around the third week in July. All six of us were there: Jim, Mike, Doug, Leo, Rick, and me. We were all packed with excitement. Rick had confirmed a two-bedroom cabin for the third week in August. The cabin would cost us $220 for the week. Home Bay needed a deposit. Rick agreed to handle that for us.

The actual dates were Saturday, August 19 to Saturday, August 26. This was not good news for Michael; his football camp started the third week in August, and he knew right away he would not be able to make the trip. That was sad news for all of us. Michael was a grand member of our group, and right away I believed we were all a little apprehensive to even consider going if Michael could not come along. But Michael, being of great character, in no way wanted us to hesitate just because he could not come. We decided to continue with our plans. There would be five of us leaving for a fishing trip up north on August 19. We decided to go with the one boat that came with the cabin and rent one motor.

Leo was confident that we could pack everything into his car if we limited each of us to one suitcase and a coat. The coat could be put into a paper sack if needed. We also decided on one rod and one tackle box apiece. There would be one boat and motor ready for us when we got there. Jim and I each had one metal minnow bucket to take along.

We had two large Coleman coolers we would take, primarily to bring home fish. That was somewhat of an arrogant thought, since none of us knew anything about fishing in Minnesota. However, we were not amateurs; we all knew how to catch fish. We had all been fishing since we were young kids, but none of us had any experience fishing out of a boat. Except for Mike, our fishing experiences were limited to bank fishing and river fishing. But we were confident that if there were fish to be had, we would find a way to catch them.

Out of all the questions that merited serious discussion, none were more important than "Where were we going to buy our booze?" None of us were heavy drinkers, but most of us did enjoy beer. I was not one of them. I would drink a bottle of beer here and there, but it was not necessary for me to have any alcohol. Soda pop was just as good for me. But the consensus was that if we were going to enjoy a week's fishing in Minnesota, then by God those that wanted to enjoy drinking some beer were going to drink some beer.

There was never any issue buying beer in Nebraska if one had a few buddies that were twenty years old. However, there would be no room in the car to pack in a few cases and haul them up from Nebraska. Some other plan needed to be drawn out. First and foremost, our age needed careful consideration. Nobody in our band was twenty. Leo and Rick were still nineteen. Nebraska's buying age was twenty in 1967. Minnesota's was twenty-one. South Dakota's, however, was eighteen. We had our answer to our dilemma. We would have to buy in South Dakota somewhere and then try to get the precious cargo to the resort without incident. Out came the map!

Our plan, then, was to get as far north into South Dakota as possible without backtracking and find a larger town that might have a bar. That way we could limit the time we had to deal with the stuff before we arrived at Park Rapids and the resort.

There were very few large towns along South Dakota's eastern border. After carefully scanning the map, Milbank looked to be the town that would fit our needs. It was about as far north as one could get into South Dakota and was located right on the Minnesota border. Milbank offered us our best solution.

In 1967, most states were right in the middle of planning their interstate systems or were in the middle of constructing them. South Dakota was no exception. In 1967, I-29 was under construction in South Dakota and had been completed only about halfway north through the state. We had to route ourselves accordingly. Once we reached Milbank, we could head into Minnesota and then plan a route into Park Rapids. Coming out of Milbank, we would head for Alexandria, make our way to Wadena, and then go straight north to Park Rapids.

Our departure time was next on the checklist. Our necessity item again played a big part in our decision. We didn't want to take a chance on getting to Milbank so late that the bars were closed. There were no liquor stores scattered about like there are now, so we would really be screwed if that happened. Getting into Milbank in the evening would require us to drive through Minnesota at night, which was something we didn't want to do. We would then be forced to stay in Milbank for the night, which for us was not an option.

Our only alternative was to leave Friday early enough to put us into Milbank late afternoon and then, we hoped, into Park Rapids Friday evening. We could then spend the night sleeping somewhere in or near Park Rapids and on Saturday morning make our way to the resort. Doing some quick math, we found that the plan dictated a ten-hour drive time to Park Rapids, give or take a couple of hours. It really would depend on Leo's heavy foot. All things considered, we decided to all meet at Rick's at nine in the morning on Friday, August 18. That would allow enough time for us to pack and then be off no later than ten. We were set. If something came up or if there was a change in plans, Rick would give us a call.

I remember feeling excited but apprehensive when I left Rick's that night. There was some fear in venturing out into the unknown. I was always for adventurous activity, and this trip would most certainly be that, but a few things were weighing on my mind: I had never been in a boat, and I didn't know how to swim.

CHAPTER 11

Heading North

From our last meeting in July to the morning of August 18, I continued to work as much as I could. I still had my weekday job. I tried to land a job helping local farmers bale alfalfa on weekend days. Farmers were also hiring to walk soybeans. Another chance at some extra money were those farmers looking for help shelling corn. I received $1.25 per hour on these types of jobs and worked mainly eight to twelve hours on a weekend day. The extra money I made in that manner was put toward my goal of $150 for the trip. Mom and Dad contributed, along with my grandmother. By the morning of August 18, I had my $150.

The day before we were to leave, I started getting my fishing equipment in order. I made sure my Zebco 66 was in prime working condition. This was my first Zebco 66. Dad had bought it for me when I entered high school as a freshman in 1963. What a reel! For me it was almost unbeatable. I used it everywhere Dad and I went fishing. I caught bass, carp, catfish, crappies, and bluegills using that reel. It was easy to clean and easy to use. I do not know how many times I stripped that reel down to clean it. It always reassembled with no problem. Try that with reels now. It is impossible.

I set the minnow bucket aside so I would not forget it. I went through my tackle box and made sure I had everything in order. The only thing left to do was pack my clothes. Mom and Dad let me use their suitcase, which was of medium size. There were no backpacks or stuff bags in those days, so

I needed to pack light. My personal hygiene kit consisted of a toothbrush, a razor, deodorant, a bar of soap, and shampoo. A few T-shirts, a couple of pairs of jeans, underwear, socks, and a sweater, along with a towel, is all that went into the case. I also took along one heavy coat, packed in a sack. What weather conditions challenged us during the week, we would have to deal with. I hoped we would not have to worry about rain, as I had no rain gear. I packed a camera that had been given to me as a graduation gift in the suitcase. I looked at my stuff and tried to visualize it times four more people. I hoped Leo had a big trunk.

When I went to bed Thursday evening, I tried hard to get some sleep; however, the excitement and anticipation of the coming week allowed me only a few hours. When I crawled out of bed Friday morning, I knew I had not gotten enough. I had that dreary, sleepy-eyed feeling. I would surely feel it Saturday morning, but with a little water in my face and the morning sun heating up, I was ready to go.

Dad had taken a job working for the county and had already left with the old beater 1950 Ford. Dad was a sentimental type of guy, so he said his good luck wishes the night before. I made sure I had my billfold, and then I piled all my stuff in the trunk. Mom drove me to Rick's house just before 9:00 a.m.

I remember being the last one to arrive. The others were waiting for me before packing so we could see just how much gear we had to deal with. Michael was there to help us pack and to see us off. The coming Monday, he would leave for football camp.

When everything was laid out, into the trunk it went. I stayed a good distance away from the grumbling. Nobody would take a seventeen-year-old's advice anyway. Plus getting in the way of a bunch of cousins was just asking for trouble. "Who brought this?" "Why do we need this?" "Where should we put this?" Some stuff managed to make its way into the trunk only to be taken out again and rearranged. The coolers were the problem. They were too big. I made the stupid comment "Could we get by with one cooler?" The consensus was no.

Leo had managed to mount an overhead storage rack to his car, which came in very handy; I doubt everything would have fit otherwise. Jim wanted to take a cane pole, but that was voted down. There was no way we were going to tote a cane pole all the way to Park Rapids.

Most of the food we would need for the week we would buy in Park Rapids. Nobody brought along any food to speak of. Jim's Mom had made some sandwiches and cookies for later in the day. Those took their place in the rear window well. Douglas brought a sack of apples, which also rested in the window well. I didn't bring anything.

Regarding eating, I can remember Mom telling me when we got back from the trip that she thought I had lost ten pounds. That must have made me look very scrimpy, because I didn't weigh much to begin with.

Eventually everything got packed that needed to go. We all said our goodbyes to those that were there. I should have been smart enough to take a picture of us all just before we were going to leave. I had the camera, but it was in my suitcase, buried deep in the trunk of the car. Nobody took a picture—not even the parents that were there to see us off. What a shame! In our defense, we were all anxious to go, and all of us acted very cocky while crawling into Leo's loaded-down car. Taking pictures was the last thing on our minds.

In the summer of 1967, on August 18, we embarked together: Doug, Jim, Rick, Leo, and me on our first fishing trip up north. Unfortunately, Mike could not make it. That trip was meant to be a high school going away present to ourselves. Unknown to us all, we were setting the stage for a grand story. Little did we know that in the upcoming years we would find a way to get back together, year after year, for one week of fishing up north. For now, however, our journey was just beginning.

CHAPTER 12

North to Milbank

F inally, we were heading north down Highway 77 into Sioux City, Iowa, and then straight north to Milbank. Rick, with the map, sat in the front. Jim, Doug, and I crammed into the backseat. There was no way Leo was going to allow any of us to drive his machine, and with Rick hogging the map, the front seating arrangement was final. They were one year our seniors, and nobody was going to complain to them about seating arrangements—especially me!

The first thing we did was pony up five dollars apiece for gas; this went into an envelope Rick had already prepared. Most cars then had at most a twenty-gallon tank. Assuming Leo's car to be no different, and assuming around fifteen to eighteen miles to the gallon, filling up every 150 miles was common. It didn't take much more than four dollars to fill up the car. At every pit stop, the three of us in the rear would rotate to take our turn in the middle.

We stopped often, and not necessarily for gas. If the one in the middle wanted to relocate, then we stopped and rotated. It was a good thing we were all skinny young men. I could not have weighed more than 160 pounds. Jim was even lighter. Doug was about the same. Rick was nothing to write home about. Leo probably weighed the most out of all of us, and he was in the right place—behind the wheel.

Air-conditioning in the cars of the sixties was not commonplace. Most of the time we traveled down the road with the windows wide open.

We talked, gabbed, and laughed all the way to Sioux City. Once we were past Sioux City and found the highway that would parallel its way north along the South Dakota–Minnesota border, most of us were getting tired. I suspect lack of sleep was starting to take hold, and I doubt anyone had gotten a good night's sleep the night before. I had never traveled past Sioux City going north. I found out very quickly how boring it is. There is not much there. In fact, the whole trip to Milbank was boring, but we still managed to find something to talk about or find some insignificant situation to make fun of.

Speed limits were fifty-five to sixty miles per hour, depending on the highway we were on. The distance to Milbank from Prague was about three hundred miles. That would be about five hours if we were to average sixty miles per hour. We rolled into Milbank about three in the afternoon. Five hours prior, we were just leaving Prague. We must have been pushing it at times to make up for pit stops and going through small towns where the speed limit was drastically reduced.

There was nothing special about Milbank, South Dakota, except that it was the largest town we had seen since we left Sioux City, Iowa. Like most of the towns we had gone through, it had its share of old buildings. We skirted the town, looking for a bar. We eventually had to go into the town itself to find one. In went Rick and Leo. Out came three cases of beer. This whole beer thing was somewhat of a burdensome necessity. The only place not packed to the gills in the whole damn car was the floorboards of the backseat. In they went, forcing those of us in the back to straddle the priceless cargo.

Leo would now be forced into watching his speed. Some common sense on entering Minnesota was necessary. The last thing we needed was to get stopped for speeding. We were all eighteen except me; I was seventeen. Leo and Rick were nineteen. Since I was seventeen, if we got caught in South Dakota, Leo could have been cited for contributing to the delinquency of a minor. If we got caught in Minnesota, the situation would have been much worse. We lumbered our way onto Highway 12 out of Milbank and into Minnesota at fifty-five miles per hour, heading for Alexandria. To get there, we needed to pick up the highway out of Benson that would take us straight up to Wadena. Then Highway 71 out of Wadena would lead us straight north into Park Rapids.

If South Dakota was boring, Minnesota was anything but. I do not believe there is a three-mile straight section of road in Minnesota, owing to the endless lakes and small rivers. They aren't kidding about it being the Land of Ten Thousand Lakes. At last we were seeing some interesting scenery and not endless miles of nothing. The trip from Benson to Wadena was littered with lakes. One of the neatest things I can remember about Alexandria is seeing a huge statue of Paul Bunyan right in the middle of the town.

I was starting to get a bit disappointed at the scenery. I'd had this fantasy vision of what Minnesota looked like: endless, pristine clear lakes surrounded by tall pines and spruce trees, and the shores lined with reeds so thick one could walk on them. Where in the hell was that? So far I had not seen it. There were plenty of lakes, but most of them were void of any pines or spruces. Countless houses and cabins littered the shoreline on most of the larger lakes. Was this what we were headed for? I hoped not!

Once we got through Alexandria and were on our way to Wadena, the appearance of the landscape had not changed. We were all getting tired. I could sense it because our interaction with one another became eerily quiet. It is a good thing we were all young and in decent shape. Jim, Doug, and I were very cramped in the back, straddling the cases of beer. I can remember falling asleep at some time during that stretch only to wake up as we were going through Wadena.

An interesting thing happened to me while I was trying to bring myself back to reality. I remember opening my eyes and glancing out the window at nothing but pine trees. "So, this is where they are," I told myself. Rick was mumbling something about it being only forty more miles. It was not pitch dark yet, but it was late evening. We were all at our best attention during this last stretch into Park Rapids. Leo must have felt a great deal of pride in getting us there without incident and without a speeding ticket.

CHAPTER 13

Park Rapids, Minnesota

T he road to Park Rapids from Wadena was lined with pine trees. We could make out a few lakes along the way, but it was impossible to see them clearly because of the dense pines and early evening darkness. The landscape had changed in appearance since we'd left Alexandria. It started looking more like what I thought Minnesota should be. The pines eventually gave way to flat, open countryside. Out in the distance, we could see the Park Rapids water tower confirming our arrival. It is hard to describe what it felt like when we realized we'd made it. It felt as if a big load had been lifted off our shoulders. It was 9:00 p.m.

What a neat town! There were plenty of cars and boats from all over the country converging on Minnesota's prime exhibit of fishing heaven. Main Street was wide enough to allow parking in the middle—something we were not accustomed to seeing. It was also a good four blocks long. This was truly a tourist-oriented town, as neat and clean little shops existed side by side up and down the street.

We drove around for some time, trying to decide what we were going to do for the night. Leo must have been exhausted, and the rest of us were pretty shot. Plus, we needed to get some food into us. The sandwiches and cookies had been consumed long ago, along with Doug's apples.

Somehow we managed to get ourselves mixed up in a car jam on Highway 10, heading east. It was close to nine thirty, and the traffic was bumper-to-bumper. The neat little shops on Main Street gave way to more local support businesses, such as grocery stores, gas stations, boat stores, outboard motor shops, lumber yards, and a bowling alley.

Jim suggested we check out the bowling alley. We could hang out there for a few hours. We strongly needed to get out of the car and stretch our legs. Food was becoming a necessity for us, plus it was an opportune time for a piss call. Bad decisions are usually spawned from lack of sleep or exhaustion. However, before we left the car, we needed to cover the goods in the backseat. We pulled out a couple of coats and draped them over the precious cargo.

Lucky for us they had a small grill that served hamburgers and, to our liking, pizza. We ordered a couple of pizzas and enjoyed some time away from the car, just hanging around in the bowling alley. We must have looked like some vagabonds without a destination. In today's world, we would not have lasted one hour in any town. Some freaked-out individual would have called the cops, and they would have been on us at once. However, in 1967, we managed to not attract too much attention, and when midnight rolled by, we made our way back to the car.

CHAPTER 14

The School Bus

The temperature certainly had dropped since we left Milbank. We all realized right then that we would not be experiencing any of the ninety-to-one-hundred-degree days that were common in Nebraska during the summer. What we really needed right now was sleep. The lack of it was causing us some irritation, and in a few minutes, this caused us to make some bad decisions.

We drove around for some time until we found an unsecured area where we could park the car for the night and get some sleep. In that area, we noticed a school bus. We could not tell whether it was abandoned or whether this spot really was its assigned parking spot. At that moment, it didn't matter to us. If we could get into that bus, we could stretch ourselves across a couple of seats and get a few hours of sleep. Who should care? We were not going to hurt anything or vandalize anything; we just needed to sleep. Rick and Leo checked it out and found the rear escape door to be open. In they went. Jim and Doug followed. I decided to stay in the car. I sprawled out on top the cases of beer. I was able to stretch my legs a little and still sleep rather comfortably. I fell into a deep sleep, ignorant of what happened around two thirty in the morning.

I must have been dreaming! My eyes opened to the swirling colors of red, white, and blue. That could only mean one thing—a cop car! "Christ Almighty, now what?" I lay there wondering what was going down with the other guys. I could not hear much except some mumbling. I didn't dare peek up. I only knew that the next thing I would experience would be a flashlight shining into the car. I kept waiting for that flashlight, but it never came. "Are they getting arrested? Jesus, if they are, what about all this beer we have in the backseat?" There would be no explaining that to any sheriff in Park Rapids.

The whole ordeal was taking forever. Then, just like that, it was over. The swirling lights stopped, and the car drove off. I finally got myself straightened up in the backseat just in time to see all four of them walking back to the car. When everyone got settled in, I was waiting for some explanation. I thought we would have to follow them to the station. "What happened?"

Jim and Doug only looked at me. Leo cranked up the car, and Rick was jabbering something like "Let's get the hell out of here. That was a close one!" Everyone looked as though he had seen a ghost.

Finally, they all started talking profusely at once: "I was lying there when suddenly I saw this flashlight in my eyes." "Did you hear the pounding on the rear door?" "Good thing they didn't check out the car." "It could have been worse." "All I could think of was the beer in the car." "Did you sleep at all?"

Finally, I interrupted their continuous gabbing and asked again, "So what happened?" From what I could gather from their gibberish, the sheriff was making his rounds and noticed someone rummaging about in the bus. He investigated, caught them in the bus, and ordered them out. Some sly talking and quick thinking prevented him from searching the car, in which case we certainly would have been taken to the slammer—and there's no telling what would have happened to us then. The cop got an earful listening to the guys' explanation. Rick told the sheriff, "We are only in Park Rapids for a fishing trip and arrived too early to check in to the resort. We were in search of a place to sleep until the morning. The bus was open, so we crawled in." The sheriff didn't see much point in escalating the ordeal. After a small reprimand, he suggested the park area if we wanted to wait out the night. Thank God it was 1967. In today's culture, we would all still be in jail.

We decided to head for the park. It was around four early Saturday morning. The surrounding features of the park were obscured, as if that mattered to us at all. We were all shot. Getting some sleep was still our priority, but that was impossible in the car. We were sick of the cramped accommodations and longed for a place to just lie down and stretch our legs. Time crept by slowly. Eventually the light of dawn exposed the layout of the park, and by 6:00 a.m. we were ready to get going—but going where? It was still too early to head to the resort.

We all got out of the car to stretch our legs and talk things over. The morning air was cool and was a welcome replacement for the stale air in the cramped car. I can remember a slight hint of motor exhaust in the air. It was not overwhelming, but I could smell it.

There was a public outhouse nearby, and relieving duties took priority. We wandered about the park for a time, enjoying the fresh morning air that, for me, still held the hint of exhaust. We felt we were getting a second wind.

CHAPTER 15

Home Bay Resort

F eeling energetic, we decided to just drive around and check out Park Rapids. We wondered what the day would bring us. We were only a couple of hours away from checking into Home Bay. As good Catholic boys would do, we decided to go look for a Catholic church for tomorrow morning's Sunday church service. We drove up and down some of the residential streets until we hit upon a sign that directed us to the one Catholic church they had in town. We made note of the service times.

Once that was settled, we could not hold back our excitement and decided to go find Home Bay Resort on Lower Bottle Lake. Rick brought out the map and the brochure that had been sent to him. On it were some directions showing where the resort was located on Lower Bottle Lake. We needed to head back up Highway 10 and find St. George Road just east of Park Rapids.

We had been up for almost twenty-four hours now with minimal sleep. We must have all looked like derelicts, but it didn't matter. The sum total of our weeks of planning would soon be upon us. It was an anxious time. We headed east down Highway 10, again facing bumper-to-bumper traffic. I wondered what was up with it. It was slow moving, and I know Leo was not a fan of slow moving.

There it was—the sign for St. George Road. Soon we were heading north along a two-lane paved road. The directions on the brochure indicated that we needed to look for a Home Bay sign. Okay! We could do that. We drove and drove. Everybody's anxious eyes were glancing all around. There were a few lakes in view, but nothing big. We didn't know whether we would need to turn left or right, so our eyes remained fixed on any road turnoff we passed. Still no sign! Up ahead we approached what looked like a large road to the right. We could make out many signs nailed to the trees, but no Home Bay sign. When we got right up to the turnoff, however, we noticed this old, dilapidated sign that hung cockeyed with painted white letters against a blue background: "Home Bay."

Leo turned right onto the unpaved road. The surface was hard-packed sand and clay. It was a wide road lined with dense undergrowth mixed with clump birch and pines. True to form, like all Minnesota roads, it was very curvy. A distracted driver would have an accident in no time around some of those bends. We were really getting deep into wherever we were going.

Around one of the bends, the road divided. Which one should we take? All eyes were looking for signs of Home Bay. Then one of us spotted another old rickety Home Bay sign hanging from a tree, pointing to the left.

We started to see glimpses of a lake to our right as we continued down the road, and then we were there. The road split, with the entrance to Home Bay to our right. Leo entered the small access road that led right into the resort. Between the cabins and trees, Lower Bottle Lake was in view. We made our way slowly across a small bridge and stopped in front of an office. We could not keep our eyes from the lake, and I could not wait to see it in full view.

It was 8:00 a.m. We crawled out of the car, which was a welcome relief. There was not much going on in the campgrounds that we could see. We were all nervous and, at the same time, anxious to see which cabin we had for the week, to see what the boat looked like, and to meet the owners, Lou and Betty Neiman.

It was not long before a tall, lanky middle-aged man came out of the office to meet us. "You must be the boys from Nebraska," he said with a wide smile on his face. "Welcome to Home Bay. I'm Lou Neiman!" After the greetings were over, we were always known to Lou and Betty as "the boys from Nebraska."

There was a calming characteristic about Lou that we could sense right away. He wore a cap. People just did not wear caps in the 1960s. They were reserved for baseball players and coaches. The cap craze didn't catch hold until the seventies, but there was Lou with his cap, which had a John Deere insignia on it. He wore a loose-fitting one-piece dark green mechanic's overall of short sleeve design. I do not believe I ever saw him dressed in anything but that style of clothing the whole time we were there. He wanted us to meet Betty, his wife, but she was busy cleaning out cabins, which led us to our next situation we would have to deal with. Lou told us that we were a little early. Our cabin was not yet ready, and it would be early afternoon until it was. In fact, the previous week's tenants had not left the premises yet.

It was against Lou and Betty's resort rules to let any loitering occur in the resort by anyone that was not checked in. Hanging around the resort proper was out of the question. Lou explained the rules to us nicely and politely. Our only alternative was to leave the premises until early afternoon. Lou thought around one would be fine and apologized for our inconvenience. We crawled back into the car, which would be our home for another four to five hours. The thought of that was almost intolerable, but we had to do it. What was four to five more hours? After all, the car had been our home for the past twenty-four hours, and we had survived. We were so close, and yet it seemed so far.

CHAPTER 16

Mosquitoes

We thought about going to get some food for the week, but we were reserving that for Sunday, when we would figure out what we needed. Also, we had no room anywhere to pack in food for five guys for six days. We knew nothing of what would be supplied with the cabin or how big the refrigerator was. We decided to head out to St. George Road and cruise for a while.

Once back on the highway, we headed north. In a couple miles, the road curved into a small town called Deer Lane. It was a busy place for a small town. There were cars coming and going constantly, and one would certainly get himself run over if not on the lookout. There was a small grocery store and a few tourist shops and a restaurant. There was also a gas station that appeared to double as a mechanic's shop.

I felt a hunger pang again. We had not eaten anything since our pizza the previous night. After parking the car, we all decided to wander into the grocery store looking for something to help tide us over until we got settled in at the resort. After chowing down on a couple of Twinkies, back into the car we went. We decided to head back the way we'd come from. We were acting like lost rovers looking for residence.

As we went around the large curve that led out of Deer Lane, we could see the east shore of a small lake. Farther down the road, we noticed a small sign that said, "Public Access." That would mean us. We decided to turn into the very narrow pasture-like road and head down the drive until we ended up at the water's edge that was Pickerel Lake. There was a small boat launch nearby and a small clearing for parking. We could spend the rest of the time here and wait until it was time to get back to the resort. Maybe we could find a nice cozy spot to just lie down and fall asleep for a couple of hours.

We got out of the car just to look around. The lake was so clear I could hardly believe it. There were reeds everywhere along both shores as far as we could see, with a mixture of pines and birch scattered about on the banks. There were also mosquitoes. Suddenly there were thousands of them. Soon there were hundreds of thousands of them. I don't know what stirred them into a frenzy, but we were lunch for them if we didn't find shelter. Back into the car we scampered, swatting and slapping mosquitoes. I have never seen anything like it—Swarms and swarms of mosquitoes. It sounded like a high-pitched fan running close by.

The windows had been open when we first arrived. We'd left them open when we got out of the car—a huge Minnesota mistake! Once we got back into the car, Rick yelled, "Get the windows up!" Up came the windows, but it was too late. We could hear them buzzing all around us. The cab was full of hungry blood-sucking mosquitoes. We all sprang into action, declaring all-out war on the damn things. There we sat like caged animals at the mercy of the little beasts buzzing around the cab looking for a way to suck the blood out of us. The cab was full of them. They were the biggest mosquitoes I have ever seen.

The killing went on for some time. Eventually we believed that no more existed and that would be the end of them. Now we could just lie back and get some sleep. What a folly idea that was. There was not going to be any sleep for any of us. The cab would become quiet, and then suddenly we could hear it. *BUZZZZZZ!* One of the little bastards had managed to survive. We all sprang into action to find it. That was easier said than done, but eventually it gave itself away and we splattered it across one of the windows. A few minutes went by, and another one was swatted dead. This went on and on.

Finally, all was quiet. Now what? The conditions in the cab were getting stale. If one of us farted, we would have all suffocated. We didn't dare venture outside, what with the threat of getting eaten alive. Our only solution was to get out of Dodge and get back on the highway back to

Deer Lane. Getting the windows open and letting in some fresh air revived us. Is this what we were going to face for a whole week—mosquitoes? The thought of it made me want to get back to the sand pits on the Platte. I had to assure myself that could not be the case.

We stopped at the gas station in Deer Lane to use the restroom and freshen up. Then we wandered about the town, visiting some of the small stores. Time sure creeps when watching the clock. We'd had enough of this aimless drifting about, so when twelve thirty hit we decided to just take our chance and head back to Home Bay. With the way Leo drove, it didn't take us long to get there.

CHAPTER 17

Lower Bottle Lake

When we got back to Home Bay, out came a short happy-go-lucky lady to greet us. She introduced herself as Betty Neiman. She was such a friendly lady we could not help but feel totally welcomed by her demeanor. She apologized for the morning's situation, but just as Lou had done, she explained their policy. We had no problem understanding. Once we had all introduced ourselves, she told us Lou would be with us shortly and was out and about somewhere. She invited us to join her in the office for check-in. Our cabin was ready.

While we were going through the check-in procedure, in walked Lou. Right away he told Betty with a chuckle, "These are the boys from Nebraska." Betty finished out the paperwork for our check-in procedure and then left us with Lou.

The first order of business was getting our dates confirmed. Lou wanted to know whether we still planned to stay until the following Saturday morning. That was a definite yes! Next was getting our fishing licenses. Lou was a funny guy. Once he got to know us by name, we were then and forever known as "Uncle Don," "Uncle Jim," "Uncle Rick," "Uncle Leo," and "Uncle Doug." I think it was his way of breaking the ice between two people that were unknown to each other. We had to pay for the fishing licenses up front: seven dollars each. I noticed a large sign on the back of the office wall stating bait prices and gas prices. They also sold candy, ice cream bars, and bread. *Man, I could use a Hershey bar right now*, I thought. Lou also had an impressive display case that was filled with fishing equipment. We would be asking him about some of those items later.

Lou went over the resort rules and what we might expect during the week. Trash was picked up every morning. He told us about the community restrooms and said we were to have absolutely no loud parties. Lou required that any walleye or northern pike that we caught be logged in a ledger. Once the fish were cleaned and filleted properly, he would wrap the fish for us and keep them frozen until it was time to leave. Lou didn't want any frozen fish kept in the cabin. He told us he worked closely in association with the Department of Natural Resources (DNR), which was the purpose of the log. He kept track of the size and number of northern pike and walleyes his tenants caught during the season. He also told us about his rearing pond. Working with the DNR, he raised thousands of northern pike fry. The DNR hauled in minnows by the truckload until the pike reached a certain size. Then, in late September, he released them into Lower Bottle Lake. He must have been proud of his pond, as he made sure that we saw it before the week was out.

He gave us each a pamphlet from the DNR regarding daily and possession limits. We went over those differences and he made sure we understood what they meant. We were considering eating fish for some of our meals. We asked Lou about that, and he said we could eat as much as we wanted, but we could not freeze any packaged fish in the cabin. Lou said, "There is nothing like fresh walleye caught out of this lake."

Next we went over the rules concerning the boat and motor. Each one of us needed a life jacket. We didn't need to have them on but were required to have one for each person in the boat. Lou told us he would recommend wearing them. We expected nothing more from a resort owner. The last thing he needed was someone falling overboard with no life jacket around. Well, none of us had a life jacket so Lou rented one to each of us for five dollars apiece. It was at that time that he pulled out a card tab for cabin 5. Any charges we would incur would be added to the tab. The twenty-five dollars for life jacket rental went on the tab.

Lou explained to us about the gas for the motor. We would start out with a full tank. Any gas added to the tank during the week would be added to the tab. Then, at the end of the week, whatever amount filled the tank would be added to our bill. That was simple enough.

Once we got all our fishing licenses, it was time to get to the cabin. Number 5 it was. He grabbed the key and told Leo to follow us with the car. On the northern side of the resort, we followed Lou to the front of the cabin, which was facing east. My jaw practically dropped to the ground as my eyes scanned Lower Bottle Lake for the first time. It truly was one of the more beautiful sights I had ever seen. Dark greenish-blue waves were crashing onto the sandy shoreline. The lake seemed to go on forever. My eyes followed the shoreline as far as they would take me. Patches of reeds were everywhere. In the distance, the shoreline gave way to beautiful clump birch trees mixed in with beautiful maple trees. Beyond were majestic pine and spruce trees that reached out into the clear blue sky. Back on Home Bay's shoreline, five wooden boat docks stretched out into the lake. Each dock had at least two boats tied alongside it. The lake was magnificent.

Before we all got to settle in, Lou wanted to go over the operation of the motor and show us the boat we would be using for the week. We followed him up to our boat dock. I can still remember that walk. The shoreline was about fifty yards from the cabin. The first thing I noticed was how clean everything looked. There was no litter anywhere that I could see. I'm not sure that I expected anything less. A well-manicured lawn gave way to sandy shores about three-quarters of the way to the dock.

The boat was tied up toward the end of the dock. It was painted green and was all wood. It looked to be very heavy, and it sat deep in the water. I had thought the water in the sand pits was clear back in Nebraska. This water was so pristine and transparent we could see small baitfish, schools of minnows, and small perch dancing in and out of the weeds under the dock. I could only imagine at that time what it must be like to land a fish in water this clear. The weeds were visible just under the surface of the water for a considerable distance beyond the end of the dock. I wondered how deep it was out there.

Lou stepped into the boat with Leo right behind him. None of us had any problem with Leo running the boat and motor. I, for one, wanted nothing to do with it. Choke, pull the cord, throttle up a bit, close the choke, forward lever, neutral, reverse lever, kill switch to stop. Nothing to it. It fired up the first time Lou pulled the cord. The smoke billowing out from behind the motor had the same faint smell I'd noticed back at the park. The exhaust from the oil-and-gas mixture those small engines burn must linger in the air in concentrated places. I remember the park back in Park Rapids was situated alongside a large lake. There were many boats on that lake. With as much exhaust as these motors let out, it is no wonder some of the fumes drifted into the park area. Leo gave it a try, and the motor fired up with one pull, which prompted a thumbs-up by Lou. We went back to the cabin for a walk-through and we were then done with our orientation. The rest was up to us.

We were all excited to finally move into the cabin that would be our home for the next seven days. (See figure 1.) The cabin was roomy with two bedrooms, each having one double bed. Each bedroom contained a small dresser with drawers. There were plenty of hooks on the walls scattered about to hang up jackets or clothes. We had a decent-sized couch, a table with chairs, a stove for heat, and a kitchen. There was a gas cooking stove along with ample cabinets and a refrigerator. Within the cabinets were dishes, pots and pans, and all the eating utensils we would need. The whole interior was an open design, apart from the one bedroom that was sectioned off with its own door.

There were no restrooms in the cabins. We would have to make do with the community bathhouse. The interior of the cabin was unfinished. Two-by-fours were visible throughout the whole structure. The cabin was sealed off on the outside with painted pine siding. The windows were nothing fancy and could be opened when needed. There was one large window facing east where we could sit, eat, and just stare out onto the open water. Over the course of the week, I found myself doing just that—staring through the window for endless minutes, looking out over the blue water, watching the waves, the reeds, and the rest of the beautiful scenery that was Lower Bottle Lake. I could not wait to see it from the water.

As tired as we were, the urge to get out and fish was stronger than our bodies' powerful suggestions to go to bed. If I had sat idle or stretched out on the bed for just a brief time, I would have collapsed into a deep sleep from which no person, place, or thing could have brought me back to consciousness. So, ignoring sound judgment and sensible behavior, by the time 4:00 p.m. rolled around, we decided it was time to go fishing.

Our first order of business was to "figure out how to do this." We had no idea what to expect or how five of us would fish out of our small fourteen-foot boat. We decided to take only a couple of tackle boxes. Everyone had one rod and reel. We needed to take along the life jackets, which made everything just that much more constricted. The jackets were not the kind fishermen wear now. They were the seaman-orange type of jackets; they fit around the neck and were bulky. We didn't have to wear them, but with so many in the boat, we would have been foolish not to. No matter how we threw the dice, we would be cramped with five in that little green boat. (See figure 2.)

Bait! Off to see Lou. We brought along one of our old tin minnow buckets and figured we could get a couple dozen minnows and a box of night crawlers. We realized that tracking down Lou when we wanted something might require some degree of patience. He was a busy man. But lucky for us he was in his maintenance shop, which just happened to be where he kept his bait. His night crawlers and leeches were kept in a small fridge. After obtaining a box of night crawlers and some small minnows, we were ready to hit the water. Lou didn't offer any advice to us that evening. He wanted us to just get out on the water and get a feel for the boat.

We had no experience fishing in Minnesota waters. We had no experience fishing out of a boat. We had no depth finder. We didn't know where to go. Nevertheless, getting out on that lake for the very first time is something I will never forget. The wind was calm, and the sky was clear. The boat had four wood-covered seats, typical of a 1960s fourteen-foot fishing boat. Rick sat in the bow, which became his permanent seat every time he got into the boat. There was no dethroning him from that position, as it was the most comfortable in the boat. (See figure 3.) Just forward in the next seat sat Doug and me. Jim sat in the third seat, and Leo sat in the stern, determined to run the motor.

The boat was moored up to the dock with heavy-duty rope tied to the mooring cleats in the front and rear. Before we left the dock, we made sure we were all baited up and everyone was in position. Five lines hung down from five rods, with the bait just dangling above the water. Leo gave a pull, and the motor fired up. A small push away from the dock and we were making our way out to open water. The weeds and grasses under the surface gradually disappeared into the depths of the greenish-blue water. My heart was pounding with anxiety. This was my first boat ride, and it was with four other guys in an overly crowded boat. I was the only one that had the life jacket on. I was the only one that didn't know how to swim.

When we no longer could see any weeds below the surface, Leo threw the motor into neutral. It was time to get the lines in. Over the side they went, all five of them. I cannot remember what bait I was using. We had the minnows with us, but I do not believe I was in any condition to try to fish a minnow. Minnows require more concentration on the fisherman's part than I was willing to give at that time.

Our plan was to troll forward with Leo's line behind the boat on the right side of the motor. Jim, since he was sitting the closest to Leo in the next seat, would fish behind the boat on the left side of the motor. Doug and I would fish out the side of the boat, and Rick, in the bow, would have to stretch his line out to either side of us, being careful not to get it tangled into our rigs. Anyone who has tried to perform this kind of layout nonsense and catch a fish realizes right away the madness of it all. But there we were, bound and determined to make this work, not understanding right away that going forward was simply not the right thing to do.

Things got screwed up almost immediately. What we were doing was okay if we were going in a forward direction for a long distance and the depth was constant. We quickly found out that was not the case in Lower Bottle Lake, where the contour of the lake resembles a bowl. Straight-line trolling was out of the question, and Leo found himself constantly correcting his bearings just to keep us in deep water. Some of us had to extend out our rods from the boat just to keep the line from getting hung up or, worse, getting caught in the motor. Making a turn was impossible for us, and the only manner we had of going back the way we had come from was to reel in our lines, reset our bearing, and drop the lines back into the lake. Over and over this happened. Lines were getting crossed up and tangled. It simply never dawned on us that all our frustrations related to forward trolling could easily have been resolved by trolling in reverse.

Seeing the resort from the lake allowed me to admire the beautiful shoreline and beaches from a new and distinct perspective. While we were on the water, there were no obstructed views of the surrounding areas. We could see much deeper into the landscape. Beautiful colored pines and birch trees were all around us. It was hard for me to concentrate on fishing when my mind was so occupied with the lake's beauty. But given our situation at the time, a loss of concentration for too long would invite a mishap with tangled lines.

We never knew our depth except when we got too close to shore, where we could see weeds below the surface. Leo was constantly adjusting our direction to get us out of the weeds when we were too shallow, and then inevitably back into the weeds when we believed we were too deep. Leo had to be subtle about his course changes; otherwise, we were dealing with a tangled mess. The whole thing became somewhat of a chore, and the ordeal tested our limits of already strained patience, simply because we were all in dire need of sleep. However, we all remained calm and collected, and not one of us jumped to any judgment. Leo was doing his best, given the circumstance. I certainly would not have wanted that responsibility.

Since this was our first time out, we didn't want to lose sight of the cabins. We trolled Home Bay's shoreline back and forth, trying to get a feel for what it was we were trying to do. Many times, we got tangled up in each other's lines. We never fouled the prop, which was a major miracle given the number of lines we had in the water. There were fish to be had, I was sure of that, but it was not as I had envisioned it to be, where all we had to do was drop a line into the water and—bingo—fish on. Until we figured all this out, it was obvious we would have to work for any fish we would put on the stringer.

One thing we can all be proud of about our first time out is that we didn't get skunked. After a couple of hours on the lake and still no fish or even a sense of a bite, the sun started to set, and the evening was upon us. We still had not figured out the contouring of the lake around Home Bay, and with the sun's light disappearing quickly, we lost sight of the weeds. Without the weeds, it was easy for Leo to slip us out into very deep water. We had decided then and there that this was going to be our last troll before we went in, and lo and behold, Leo hooked into something. We were all so excited to see a fish being caught that we quickly reeled in our lines so as not to take a chance on getting tangled up. After a brief fight, Jim got out the net and with one scoop landed the biggest damn bullhead I ever saw. Someone shouted, "It's a bullhead!" Come on, now! That is not what we came to Minnesota for. It truly was, however, the biggest ever. I caught bullheads out of the sand pits back home that I thought were large, but they were nothing compared to the size of this thing.

That was it. Time to head back in. We were not going to deal with one bullhead at that hour, so over the side it went. Leo cranked up the motor and off we went, back to shore. There were two things we had learned that evening: One, it was not going to be easy to catch fish. Two, there was no way we could continue doing what we did with five people in the boat. Something had to change.

Back at the cabin, all priorities centered around getting some much-needed sleep. We never had thought about sleeping arrangements until now. Leo voted to take the couch. It was a big couch that would sleep one person very nicely. That left the two bedrooms. None of us were modest, so we had no problems in that regard. We drew straws: two short straws for the one bedroom, two long for the other. Rick and I landed the open bedroom, while Jim and Doug would sleep in the closed-off bedroom. It didn't take us long to hit the hay. Hunger was not the issue for us, as we were all too tired to even consider eating. Even if we did want to eat something, there was no food to be had until tomorrow morning. The evening air was cool. I slept hard that night. I could hardly believe the morning had come upon us.

CHAPTER 18

Sunday: A Change in Tactics

One thing I found out quickly was that the Musilek gene pool did not allow for any extended sleep. Rick was up at the break of dawn. Leo was already stirring in the kitchen. Jim crawled out next. Doug followed. I was down shit creek on sleeping. Man, how I could have slept for another four hours. Good, unbroken hard sleep was what we all needed; however, even lacking my usual eight hours, I felt refreshed that morning. We were all anxious to get out on the water once again. A peek outside revealed a glorious day free of clouds and wind. The lake was like glass.

Our plan for the morning included heading back into Park Rapids for 8:00 a.m. church and then heading to the grocery store to pick up some food. Going to church that morning was open to debate. All of us grew up in strong Catholic families, and the notion of allowing ourselves to skip church didn't get far. Off we went, even though we were not dressed for the occasion.

After church services, it was off to the grocery store. We bought only essential items, and those were cheap ones at that: hot dogs, plenty of bread, SpaghettiOs, jelly, pork and beans, butter, cooking oil, candy, and coffee. For breakfast we figured on coffee along with toast and jelly, or corn flakes with milk and sugar. We would have no time for lunch, as we planned to be out on the lake. Supper would be a toss-up: hot dogs, pork and beans, or SpaghettiOs, and plenty of bread. I hoped we would have some fish to eat sometime during the week. We were all anxious to get back to the resort to do some fishing.

We discussed options about our fishing situation. It was obvious that five in one boat was not going to cut it. It was dangerous and unproductive. We had two choices: rotate one man out during each excursion or get a second boat. Rotating one man out would put a manageable four in the boat at any one time. Discussions around that idea concluded it not to be a fair trade. It was fair in that everyone would take his turn, but that was not why we came. To sit out on the shoreline while your friends were out fishing was not fair to anyone, and it was not who we were. We had to think of something else.

Our second choice would require each one of us to pony up a little more money and get a second boat. Off we went to see Lou, and we told him of our dilemma. He offered us one of his older resort boats at a discounted price. We jumped on it.

Our plan was to use the motor on the first boat to propel the second boat out to a location on the lake where two guys would anchor while the other three went out with the motored boat. It seemed logical at first that our plan might work. We would all take turns in the second boat, and we would all take turns in the motored boat. When Lou mentioned the second boat, it didn't take long for us to figure out why the boat was given to us at a discounted rate. It looked older—much like the boat we had currently, but dilapidated in some respects. It was the same design: an all-wooden fourteen-foot older resort boat painted a dark green. It too sat deep in the water. Lou assured us the boat was safe and very stable. Without knowing any different, we were thankful to have it.

In hindsight, we should have gotten another motor; it would have been easier for all of us. But money took command of most decisions we made that week. If we had known the boat situation when we first set our budget weeks before, we could have planned for not one boat and motor but two.

Now that we had a plan, we needed to focus on how to catch some fish. It was obvious that what we had done the previous evening was not correct or there were no fish in the lake. Off we went to see Lou for some pointers on Minnesota fishing.

As far as fishing goes, Lou simply was a northern pike fanatic. Not only did he raise them in his rearing pond, but he also promoted catching them. We were all for that. He knew that if his guests could catch a few northerns, they would come back for more. And that is where his success in running a resort would come from—the return guests. Lou also realized we didn't have the experience to get out and troll artificial lures and spoons, especially with a resort boat, so he introduced us to a northern pike trolling rig.

As a business decision, showing us this harness rig paid him great dividends. We paid for the harnesses. We paid for the chubs that went on the harness. We paid for the gas used to pull the things. Lou got our money! In return, we might get the chance to experience what it was like to feel a hit on one of these rigs and, with some luck, catch a northern pike. If I knew then what we have come to know now, I would not have paid a nickel for that damn rig.

Basically, the rig required the use of large sucker chubs about four to six inches long. The harnesses were made of wire with a loop at one end. The loop was just large enough to attach a tandem hook at the end of it. With sucker in hand, one ran the loop end of the wire through the sucker's mouth and down through the digestive tract until it exited out the other end, where one attached the tandem hook. It was a ghastly process, but surprisingly, if one did it gently enough, the chub would stay alive for a long time. The other end had a spinning spoon attached to the wire and then another loop where one attached one's line. The whole thing was about fifteen inches long.

The chubs used for this thing were not cheap. Lou kept a good quantity on hand, as he knew we would be buying more. Chubs are a natural food source for the northern pike. If the pike were hitting, the chubs didn't last long. We were all pumped. We each bought a harness and one dozen chubs to fit into two tin minnow buckets. It was early afternoon and time for our first lot drawing. Doug and I were the first to draw our turn in the second boat. When we were all ready, off we went.

CHAPTER 19

The Heavy Green Boats

P ast the peninsula, Lower Bottle displayed its magnificent beauty in full perspective. The lake seemed to go on forever, with distant hills visible that were lined with spruce and pine trees. Just admiring the scenery took our minds off our sore hands, which ached from struggling to keep the boats together. As we motored along, a large set of reeds came into view along the south shoreline. It was a gorgeous setting that might have been carved right out of a painting. Doug and I decided that was where we wanted to sit if we could find a spot. Leo set his bearing straight for it. It took us a while to get there, going as slow as we were. That five-horsepower motor was barely enough for two boats side by side.

As we approached the reeds, we could see how far back they went and how long they stretched along the south shore. Where to anchor? We motored down the reed line, peering down into the shallow water. There were no weeds. After seeing all the weeds back at the dock, we had assumed the whole lake was full of weeds, but that was not the case. The area we were in had nothing but a sandy bottom below our boat. We thought this was as good a place as any, so we coasted to a stop. We let out the anchor and said our farewell to the other boat. Off they went to check out beautiful Lower Bottle Lake.

Leo must have enjoyed having only three people in the boat. As soon as they were clear of our anchored boat, Leo engaged full throttle. The bow rose slightly and then settled gently back into the water as the little five-horsepower Johnson pushed the boat nicely along. Doug and I watched them head down the same reed line and then disappear around the first bend. It became eerily quiet sitting alone in the middle of a strange lake in an unmotorized boat. *Now what do we do?* We had worms, six of the big chubs, and some smaller minnows from the night before.

We both decided to put on the northern pike harnesses we'd bought from Lou. I grabbed my trusty Zebco 66 rod and reel and tied on the harness. Doug was using his Mitchell open-face spinning reel mounted to a sturdy fiberglass rod, and he did the same. We each grabbed one of the big chubs and went through the ghastly process of hooking the unfortunate things onto the harnesses. Then we started casting them into the deep water. We figured it would be best to cast them as far as we could and then slowly retrieve them back to the boat. I let my harness rig settle all the way to the bottom to see how deep the water was. I had enough fishing experience to detect deep water just by noticing the angle of the line back to the boat. No doubt we were casting into deep water; the line angle was every bit of 45 degrees.

I started a slow retrieve back to the boat but got snagged in weeds. Doug also complained about snagging. So there were weeds down there. It took us a while to figure out how long to let the harness sink and then how fast to retrieve it to keep from getting hung up in the weeds. Over and over, we would cast and retrieve. After a dozen or so tries, I noticed my chub was as stiff as a board. *Well, crap!* No matter where you fish, using dead bait is a waste of time. Off it came, and I baited up with a new one. Soon Doug's chub kicked the bucket, and on went another.

It was during one of those retrieves back to the boat that suddenly my line went very tight, the rod bent, and I started pulling against something. *I'm in the damn weeds again*, I thought. Not wanting to hurt the chub, I started reeling very slowly back to the boat. I told myself, "It must be a sizable chunk to bend the rod that much." When I got my harness close to the boat I peered down into the clear water. I could just make out the biggest damn fish I had ever seen. I hollered to Doug to get the dip net. Just like that, the big northern pike let go of the chub and slowly swam off. He must have seen the boat and decided to abandon his dinner. I was dumbfounded. I had him on all that time and didn't know it. If only I would have set the hook. I could see he had the chub in his mouth. When

I pulled the chub back into the boat, it was all punctured and torn up. If that pike let me know he had grabbed the chub, I didn't know it or didn't realize it.

Disappointing as it was, I felt a little more confident that we might hook into one of those monsters and land it. Doug never did see it. When I told him what happened, he didn't say much. We sat there casting and admiring the scenery until all six of our chubs were dead. I believe the constant casting into the water may have killed the chubs. Hitting the water over and over would be like casting them onto concrete. They could not survive. We never did hook into anything or have another hit. Without chubs, we decided to use either worms or some of the small minnows with a hook and weight. Doug put on a bobber while I just let the bait sit on the bottom, a little frustrated. We sat there for another hour without any sign of a hit.

How beautiful it was out on the open water while sitting in the boat! The sky was void of clouds, and the water was calm. It was almost hot sitting in the bright sun without any breeze blowing over us. We didn't bring anything to drink—a lesson we would learn for future adventures. Alcohol was not allowed in the boats. Even if it had been, there is no place for alcohol in a boat. Lou would have kicked us out of the resort if we were to take beer on the lake. Pop or a jug of water was what we needed right now.

We wondered how the other guys were making out. There was no sign of them. The lake was not so long and wide that we couldn't make out the opposite shorelines, but seeing a small boat was another thing entirely. There we sat, stranded like castaways. We could have repositioned the boat, but we decided to stick it out until the guys came to retrieve us. We were feeling a bit frustrated.

Finally, we could see a small boat coming our way from across the lake. It had to be our guys. It took forever for them to get to us, but eventually they pulled alongside. Of course, our first words to them were "Did you catch anything?"

Their disgruntled answer echoed across the water: "No! How about you?"

We answered in disappointment, "Nothing!"

It was already late afternoon. We decided to up anchor and head back in for a break and some needed supper. Leo maneuvered his boat alongside. We locked hold and headed back to Home Bay.

I am not sure how everyone felt right then, but for me it was good to get out of the boat and stretch the legs. We still had not caught anything except that one bullhead. I felt tired, which was normal for me anyway. However, we were a band that would not give up. We were bound and determined to figure this thing out. After all, I had gotten skunked many times back in Nebraska, but then I would tell myself, "This is Minnesota. We should be able to catch something." To sum it up, we were all a little disappointed.

That evening, over a supper of SpaghettiOs, a hot dog with bread, and a beer, I told my pike story. The only thing I caught in that story was a lot of shit from everyone. "How in the hell did you not know you had a fish on? Could not you feel him on the other end?" On and on it went. By the time everyone got done riddling me, the story did seem to induce some level of enthusiasm back into us. Jim said he had felt a hit as one of his chubs came back torn up.

The guys found out that if they pulled a dead chub, it would spin like a top. Using a snap and swivel was mandatory; otherwise, we would end up like Rick, who found out the hard way. His chub croaked quickly, and before he knew it, his line was so twisted he could barely reel it in. He had to replace his line right on the spot if he wanted to continue fishing. It was clear to us that using chubs on these harnesses would be an expensive way to fish. We hoped to do better that evening.

Jim told Doug and me about some of the neat places they'd found while trolling. They had tried to control their depth by watching the weed beds below the surface just as we did yesterday afternoon. Leo would troll closer to shore if they lost sight of the bottom. When the bottom became visible again, Leo would then head out to deeper water. It was this back-and-forth tacking that guided them along. I was anxious to get out and experience trolling for the first time and to see more of Bottle Lake.

That Sunday evening, we had to get more chubs. Another dozen went into two minnow buckets. It was Rick's and Jim's turn in the green boat. We pulled them out to a location just up the shore from where Doug and

I were fishing. When we were sure they would be okay, Leo headed out into open water. We headed east to the far shoreline.

It took a long time to get where we were going. The small boat putted along, leaving a small wake as it cut through the water. Getting caught in a wind or high waves with this boat and motor would be dangerous. Eventually we got to shallow water on the east shore. Leo put the boat in forward troll, and in went the chubs dangling from our lines. I watched the spinner turn as it sank deeper and deeper. I constantly had to fidget with how much line I had out. Too much and the bait got hung up in weeds. Not enough and the harness simply stayed only a few feet below the surface. When Leo would head back into deeper water, I would let out more line.

The three of us in the boat were constantly on the lookout for shallow water. I didn't envy Leo's responsibility of running the boat. He had to watch out for our lines and keep us in some consistent depth. Slowly we were getting the hang of it, and occasionally we could all just sit back and look out over the water and admire the splendor of the lake.

By now we were all wondering what a hit would feel like. We had made satisfactory progress down the shoreline without any unfortunate mishap—except for our encountering no fish. The chub harness put a good strain on the rod already, and I started wondering to myself whether Leo might be going too fast. Leo was doing a decent job tacking in and out of shallow water, but I thought varying the speed might help. If it had been Rick or someone else on the motor, I would not have hesitated to suggest it. Not knowing Leo that well, I kept my mouth shut. Plus, I really didn't know anything about fishing like this or what was required to keep the boat in line and steady.

During the evening, we all experienced the spinning a chub does when it is dead. The damn things didn't last long. This time, thanks to Rick's experience, we all had snaps and swivels to save our line. Time went by fast, and I was surprised when it came time to get back and pick up the green boat. We removed the chubs from the harnesses and tossed them back into the lake. The chubs would eventually die once on the harnesses; there was no sense keeping them. There went six chubs without anything to show for them. There had to be a better way.

It was time to sit back and relax during the return boat ride across the lake to the south shore. Leo was doing all the work. I got to sit in Rick's throne at the bow of the boat—a rare opportunity, as if Rick was in the boat, it was off-limits. I could rest my back, which was a welcome relief from sitting on the bench. The old green boat came into view. Nothing to report from Jim and Rick. *Can this be happening to us?* I wondered. We'd gotten skunked on our first full day on the lake. That was not the way this was supposed to be!

CHAPTER 20

Monday: Changes a-Coming

That is the way it went for us using the harnesses. We went through chubs like crazy without catching one fish. We didn't have a good understanding on how to use them properly. That is really what it was all about—understanding how to do it. It was not until later in the week that we first experienced what it was like to tangle with northern pike.

That night I slept like I had never slept before. When morning came, I was well rested and refreshed. It was time to get a shower and clean up. Sleep and a shower—the best remedy for frustration there is. My normal breakfast meal that week was toast with jelly and coffee. It was decided that breakfast would be everyone for himself. We never did have a community breakfast of eggs, bacon, toast, and coffee for two reasons: nobody wanted to cook, and we simply were not willing to tap into our fishing time. Fishing time to us was precious.

Monday we decided to fish the way we knew how to fish, which drastically changed our ability to catch fish. For whatever reason, Leo decided not to go with us. I believe he just wanted to get back into Park Rapids and explore the town on his own. With Leo gone, we could manage four in a boat and keep the older green boat docked. Our plan was to find some weeds, anchor next to them, and fish deep alongside the weeds with night crawlers and small minnows.

We needed minnows. Lou's bait shop didn't open until eight, so we impatiently waited. Lou wanted to know how we were doing. We told him our disappointing news. His first suggestion to us was to troll backward. He said, "You can control the boat better." Next he suggested we slow things down. The bait needed to get down to ten to fifteen feet. He doubted we were trolling deep enough.

We asked him where to fish for perch. Lou told us the lake was full of perch of all sizes, including the jumbo perch if we could find them. He described them as being ten to fourteen inches in length. His eyes lit up just talking about them. He told us, "Fish the weed beds," and that was exactly what we had in mind. He said we needed small leeches for the jumbo perch and told us to fish them deep, at twenty-five to thirty feet. *Ka-chunk*, another sale! He sold us some leeches. We never did try for the jumbo perch during the whole week, and I cannot remember if we used the leeches on anything else. Lou also told us to try for walleyes toward evening in the Narrows. That evening, we would try our hand at walleyes.

There were a lot of places we could try with deep, dense weeds that disappeared into the depths. Jim wanted to head out to one spot he remembered from Sunday afternoon. Rick positioned himself at the bow, enjoying his sovereign seat. Doug decided to drive the boat. Jim and I sat where we could. We were all excited to catch anything. We were confident we could find something, considering how nice the weed beds looked and with the day being clear and calm once again. Off we went.

It is funny how much slower that boat was with four in it as opposed to three. The small five-horsepower motor was screaming, but the boat was sluggish plowing through the water. It took a long time to get where we were going, which was a hidden cove on the south shore. I remember that ride as being one of the most enjoyable. I suspect this was because we had a good plan and the morning air was as fresh as ever. We'd all had a chance to catch up on our rest. I was with my great friends, enjoying something I had never experienced before. Life was good!

Jim's cove was just ahead. Just as we entered the bay, there was a point jutting out that held many weed beds. We could see them under the surface, strung out from the shore and disappearing into deeper water. It was here we would try to anchor, positioning ourselves just out from the most visible part of the weed bed. Rick dropped the anchor as soon as

Doug stabilized the boat. Down it went and down it went! From the looks of the anchor depth and our proximity to the shore, I knew this must be one hell of a drop-off. Rick secured the anchor, and Doug sent the stern anchor down. The boat was stable apart from our squirming around, anxious to get some lines in the water.

Our technique was simple: put on a worm or a minnow and drop it over the side with a small split shot about two feet above the hook. Let the whole thing go to the bottom, and then reel up a few cranks. We fished right under the boat. Jim and I would do the same thing fishing under the pumping platforms in the sand pits back in Nebraska. It was highly effective there. It was just as effective here.

We all started catching perch, one after the other. Most were little guys that sometimes swallowed the hook—an occupational hazard for the small perch. It was impossible to retrieve the hook without hurting the perch once they swallowed it. Those that did ended up as seagull food. Sometimes one of us would hook into a nice-sized perch, every bit of eight to ten inches—not the jumbo perch Lou had told us about, but good eaters. Sometimes we had to catch a dozen small ones for one worth keeping. It didn't matter to us. Finally, the action was quick, and there is absolutely nothing like catching a fish in Minnesota's clear waters.

A word about the seagulls. To this day, they never cease to amaze me. It is not that the gulls continually glide above our boat and dive down when one of the unfortunate perch ends up on top the water. Nope! They just suddenly appear from out of nowhere, and only when there is a flopping fish on top the water. Otherwise they are not to be seen, except far in the distance, sitting on the water or gliding the thermals in the air. It is just as much fun to watch them as it is to be fishing.

The whole thing with the gulls started when one of us would have to rip the hook out of a small perch and toss him overboard. The unfortunate fish would try to head back down to the privacy of the weed bed but eventually would surface in a dying attempt to rekindle some life into its body. I'm not sure what attracts the gulls. Maybe they can see the unfortunate fish flopping on top of the lake or can hear the fish splashing on the surface of the water. Whatever instinct it was, it didn't take long before a seagull came along, setting up his approach. Normally the gull would make a few practice approaches while gauging the wind and the size of the fish, and, I suspect, trying to figure out his chance of carrying out the task.

The best is when there is competition between two or more gulls going after the same fish. Those that hesitate will lose out in this kind of competition. Once the gull has everything set up, he makes his last approach low and slow. Without breaking flight, he extends his bill, picks up the fish, swallows the fish whole, and then heads off a small distance. He eventually lands in the water to digest his dinner and clean himself off. What a wonderful bird, the seagull! They must have eyes like eagles. The whole time we were out there, if the perch bite was on, those clever birds were right there with us.

Not all of us were fishing minnows. It dawned on us after catching dozens of these perch that the bigger ones were feeding on minnows instead of night crawlers. Before long, all of us were fishing small minnows. The action was so fast we were running out of minnows, so we tried to save our minnows if they flopped off in the water while we were landing a fish. Many times we would catch ourselves reaching over the boat to save the minnow. Dead or alive, the minnow was the bait to use.

Besides perch, occasionally someone would tie into a nice-sized bluegill. What a joy it is to catch bluegill! They fight like the devil. They are thick in the shoulders, and what a beautiful color they have. I should say they are my favorite panfish to catch besides crappies, and they are very tasty. Speaking of crappies, I thought we might tie into a crappie or two fishing, as we were, with minnows, but there were none to be had.

When we exhausted our supply of minnows, we were just into the afternoon hours. It was time for us to head in and check out the fish-cleaning house. Back at the dock, it took two of us to haul in the stringer of fish.

When we got back to camp, Leo was still gone. We manhandled the stringer up to the cabin, and after we retrieved a couple of butcher knives, off we went to clean our catch. Jim was a master at using a knife. He had along his skinning knife, which was very thin and sharp. Jim, being a trapper, knew how to handle it. We didn't know how to fillet fish. Lou, however, made sure we did before the week was over. For this stringer of fish, it was off with the heads, clean the guts out, then skin them. We had a nice assembly line going. These fish were destined for the frying pan.

Lou must have been keeping an eye on us, for as soon as we left the cleaning house, he was checking on us. He wanted to know what we had caught, how we had caught them, and what bait we had used. Lou was adamant that nothing was to be frozen without having been checked in. We assured him these fish were going to get eaten. Those that didn't would get checked in. He was okay with that. He asked us what we used for flour. We told him we used flour. He suggested we try cornmeal. My family ate a lot of fish, but Mom never tried cornmeal. That was doughball stuff. We confessed that none of us had ever tasted fish made that way.

CHAPTER 21

The Narrows

"The Narrows" is a local name for a small inlet connecting Lower Bottle Lake to Upper Bottle Lake. It is very narrow, very deep, and is a no-wake zone. It was also a local hot spot for walleyes. When we still had Lou's attention, we asked him about the Narrows and walleye fishing. We had not seen the Narrows yet and wondered where to go after we got there. Lou told us about a large body of reeds just to the left as we went through into Upper Bottle Lake. He told us, "Anchor just off the reeds in shallow water. Get there about six and fish till dark. Use night crawlers or leeches." Lou, however, preferred a jig with a minnow. In fact, during the week, as we watched Lou fish and talk about walleyes, we realized a jig was all he used. Lou had an ample supply of jigs in his office that he strongly recommended. After we took the fish back to the cabin, off we went to get a jig. *Ka-chink!* Another sale. More SpaghettiOs and hot dogs for supper.

Where was Leo? After supper, off we went to get some walleye minnows. Lou called them fatheads. He also had shiners, which were more expensive; but for now, we opted for the fatheads. A couple dozen minnows went into the tin minnow bucket. Lou told us of a trolling-style minnow bucket that was available if we were ever interested in getting a different minnow bucket. They were designed to stay afloat and not sink like our old tin double bucket. Lou said he might see us out there, as he was going fishing that evening. He wanted to catch a walleye so Betty could fry it up for him. Lou had a way of getting us pumped up. We were determined to beat him out there.

This was our first trip to the Narrows and our first attempt at catching walleyes. Getting to the Narrows required some time. It took about twenty minutes to make the trip. The reed bed Lou had told us about was clearly visible as we entered the narrow corridor that connected Upper Bottle to Lower Bottle. Once through the Narrows, Upper Bottle came into full view. It was a magnificent sight void of houses or cabins as far as we could see down the shorelines. It was not until years later that we started to fish Upper Bottle with any enthusiasm. We found Upper Bottle to be a fabulous fishery. Years later, when we started using depth finders, we discovered that overall it was much shallower than Lower Bottle. For now, our first attempt at walleyes found us all very much excited and very much inexperienced. We were all unsure of ourselves as to how to fish for these guys. Where was Lou so we could watch him?

We anchored just off the reeds, in water where we could still see the weeds under the surface. Our limited experience had shown us that once we lost sight of the weeds, the deep water was close by. The Narrows were no different. Down went both anchors.

The Narrows were well protected from wind. In fact, the only wind that is not good in the Narrows is that which blows from the north. Prevailing winds in late summer are from the south, so water conditions in the Narrows were normally gentle to very still, especially toward the evening hours. We found this to be the case in most of our trips to the Narrows. Very seldom over the years was it impossible for us to sit next to those reeds opposed by high waves and blowing wind.

Over the side went the minnow bucket secured to the boat with a rope. I attached the jig head Lou had sold me and put on a minnow. Lou had showed us how to hook the minnow through the lips. In all my years fishing with Dad, never did I see him hook a minnow in that manner. I was always taught to hook them just below and behind the dorsal fin. Jim, to this day will not hook a minnow through the lips if he is not trolling them. Jim was also not fond of using anything artificial. So there was no jig for Jim—just a minnow and a hook taken down to the depths with a weight. Doug and Rick resorted to the jig tipped with a minnow. The minnows were close to two to three inches long. Together with the jig, the whole combination made a heavy bait.

Out across the water the minnow-tipped jig flew, peeling out line from my Zebco 66. It hit the water with a good plunk and down it went, and down it went, and down it went. How deep was it here? Finally, the line slackened, showing that the bait had finally made it to the bottom. The other guys did the same.

I would consider myself an impatient fisherman. My first reaction was to start reeling in at once instead of letting the bait sit on the bottom. *It must be very deep over there*, I thought. Soon the line angle was straight down below the boat, and then up came the jig and minnow. Well, that was not exciting. Out it went again. Down and down it went until I had a slack line once again. This time I let it sit for a bit and then began a steady retrieve. I had the same unexciting result. The other guys were not having much success themselves, except for Jim, who kept his bait out there, fishing a tight line; the rest of us just kept casting out and retrieving back.

Yeah! We heard a motor in the distance and then saw Lou coming through the Narrows. Lou's boat had a 9.5-horsepower Johnson on it, and it screamed. We were very jealous of his ability to get from one place to the next in little time. His boat was aluminum and of a newer design, and I suspect it was much lighter than our heavy wooden boat. He slowly made his way past us and anchored into deep water just in front of the reed bed. The two boats were in talking distance, which was good for us, because soon we were going to get a lesson on how to fish these jigs for walleyes.

When Lou would talk to one of us, he would call us Uncle Don or Uncle Rick. Somehow, we were all his uncles. When he talked to all of us at once, it was usually "fellas." The first thing he asked us was "Hi, fellas, how's fishing?"

That was our cue! We asked him, "How do you fish these jigs?" He smiled and was ready to demonstrate.

Lou told us to just cast the jig and minnow and let it go down to the bottom and let it sit for just a bit. Then we were to reel up the slack line and slowly bring the rod tip up, moving the jig along the bottom. We would reel up the slack line again and let it sit. Then, after ten to fifteen seconds, we were to do the same thing. We would just keep doing that until we were ready for another cast. Lou said most of the hits would occur just as we were moving the rod tip up, while moving the jig on the bottom, or just after the jig stopped moving.

We started doing what Lou told us. Most of our attention was on Lou himself. We watched him closely as he practiced what he had just preached. Fishing that slowly was not something that came easy for me. We all started to get the idea, but what we needed now was a bite.

Sometimes one of our lines would become very heavy. We would not feel a bite, but lifting the rod tip felt quite different. It felt very much like the hit I had Sunday afternoon from the big northern. Then whatever we had hooked onto suddenly released. We thought it to be weeds at first, but we then thought maybe that is what a walleye hit feels like. None of us knew the answer until Jim decided to check his line. As he lifted his bait out of the water, attached to it was the biggest crawdad I had ever seen. Those were the culprits—giant crawdads. This lake had giant crawdads in it. We could have saved it and eaten it if we wanted to. The damn thing had its claws latched onto the poor helpless minnow and would not let go. The minnow was a mangled mess.

This kind of shit was right up Jim's alley. He didn't throw it back but let it run loose in the bottom of the boat. There's nothing like knowing there is a giant crawdad walking around in the bottom of the boat, waiting to latch onto my ankle. Before we pulled up anchor that evening, there were five or six of those damn things loose in the boat. They gave me the shivers.

The crawdads were a nuisance. We lost more minnows to crawdads than we did to fish. Lou had the same problem, so it was nothing we were doing wrong. They were something we had to deal with. We quickly realized about how long we could let the jig sit on the bottom before one of those creatures attached itself to the minnow. It was not long at all—two or three seconds at the most. It would have been nice to find out what an actual bite felt like.

I don't believe any one of us caught a walleye that first evening, not even Lou, but I do remember my first bite—one that I can honestly say was a hit. I was retrieving as Lou demonstrated when my line suddenly just peeled out. Of course, I was not ready. The sudden run by the fish caught me off guard, and before I could set the hook, the fish was gone. That was two times I had missed a fish: the northern that I didn't set the hook on and a walleye hit that caught me off guard.

Before we knew it, the light left us, and we were sitting in the Narrows in almost total darkness. Lou pulled up anchor just a few minutes before, and we could hear him screaming down Lower Bottle Lake back to the resort. Curse that 9.5-horsepower motor anyway! We, on the other hand, had a long trip ahead of us and a long time to get there. Up came both anchors. Doug fired up the Johnson, and we were off. Lower Bottle Lake looked quite different at night, when we could barely see the shoreline. We all hoped we knew where we were going.

Being in a small boat at night with three other guys on an unfamiliar vast area of water is scary business. Stupid me, not knowing how to swim, immediately put on my life jacket. *Why didn't we leave earlier? Why didn't I try harder when I had swim lessons years before?* I hadn't learned a thing from those lessons. Luckily, there was no danger from high waves and the sky was clear. We just hoped we didn't run into something. We knew the general area of Home Bay, so Doug guided us slowly toward the southern shoreline, where we could make out some lights. The one dangerous area was a shallow, flat peninsula that almost cuts the lake in half. The DNR had positioned low-water danger buoys all around the peninsula. We were on close lookout for those. We knew that if we could find one of those buoys, Home Bay was just on the western side of the shallow water.

It seemed as though we were in that boat for a long time. Rick, in the front of the boat, had a flashlight. He was looking for a buoy or the south shore reeds. The sound of that five-horsepower motor was solitary except for the wake caused by the boat. Finally, one of the buoys came into view, warning us of shallow water ahead. Which buoy was it? We knew we had to keep left to get around the shallow water. Slowly we veered left until another buoy came into view, then another, and then nothing. We felt we must have reached the southern end of the danger zone. To our surprise, we found we would have had to go a good distance more to the east and then south to miss the shallow water entirely—something we would try to remember the next time we got caught out on the lake in total darkness.

To the right were three large lights we could see in the distance. Those were Home Bay's shore lights, which Lou kept on during the night. With the danger zone passed, we headed for those lights. Before long, Home Bay came into view and we headed for our dock. We had no fish to clean tonight. We went back to the cabin for a snack and then hit the hay for another night.

Leo was back, and we told him of our little adventure to the Narrows. If we had been frustrated the previous night, we were the exact opposite tonight. We were filled with enthusiasm and proud of ourselves for figuring out a way to catch some fish. Tomorrow was another day for exploring the waters of Bottle Lake. Leo was going to be with us, so we were back to toting the other boat around. After a long day, finally, we got more of some much-needed sleep.

CHAPTER 22

Tuesday: A Crappie Story

*U*p at the crack of dawn! For Christ's sake! What is with these Musilek cousins anyway? Do not they ever sleep? Didn't they realize that sleep was the cure-all for everything? Somehow they had all missed that lesson. What I would not have given to sleep till noon!

Jim and I drew the second boat on Tuesday. We had to decide where we wanted to fish. The other three guys decided to do exactly what we had done yesterday—fish just off the reed beds with minnows and night crawlers. During our breakfast of toast and coffee, Jim and I discussed our options for the day. Jim had mentioned an old tree that was sticking out of the water way up on the eastern shore of Lower Bottle Lake. Jim had been in the first boat Sunday when they noticed the tree while pulling the northern harness. It was sitting just off the weed lines in deeper water. Our limited knowledge of Lower Bottle had shown us that the body of water was void of tree habitat. This one tree trunk sticking out of the water was certainly out of the ordinary. This would be as good a place as any to try to catch a few of the famous Minnesota slab crappies we'd heard about.

We took along the second minnow bucket with about three dozen small minnows and a box of night crawlers. It seemed like we were always going to the east shoreline when we wanted to fish. We attached the two boats together, and off we went for the long journey across the lake. At least we were getting familiar with the lake's shoreline, which would help us out in case we got caught out after dark as we had the previous night.

Identifying just a few landmarks along the south shoreline would make us more comfortable when on the lake. The entrance to Hoosier Beach, the buoys outlining the shallow water peninsula, and the south shoreline reeds were all good waypoints for us when on the water.

When we arrived at the east shore, we continued to move north until the tree was visible. It was just a tree trunk about twenty inches in diameter. It stuck out of the water about three feet and was in deep water about thirty yards from shore. It was an odd protrusion that we felt was alien to the lake. We were not that familiar with the natural features of Lower Bottle, but we were almost sure that this might be the last submerged tree trunk to exist on this lake and perhaps Upper Bottle. The weather was clear, and the wind was not blowing hard. There was a little chop on the water, but nothing that would prevent us from fishing this area. We could see the tree disappear into the depths of Lower Bottle. We didn't believe there was enough anchor rope to reach bottom, so we didn't even try. Plus, just in case there were some fish around that tree, we didn't want to scare them off.

We decided to tie up to the tree. We wondered what was down there. Was this tree trunk still attached to the bottom? As the other guys left us to explore another part of the lake called the Pork Barrel, one of the most bizarre afternoons Jim and I ever experienced on Lower Bottle Lake was about to take place.

The first thing we needed to know was our depth. I decided to attach a bobber to my line and continually run the bobber up the line until the weight touched bottom. When the bobber would not right itself, we would know the depth. I lifted my hand straight up and the rod straight up as high as I could with the bobber at the rod tip. I still could not see the weight. Then I stood up in the boat, which added another five feet. I could barely make out the weight still dangling below the water line. We figured it to be around twenty feet deep. There was no way I could fish that deep with the bobber we were using. We didn't know about slip bobbers at the time. I set the bobber so my minnow was just dangling at the water line while I was standing in the boat with my rod tip and arm straight up. I figured that if I had to land anything, we could net the fish just below the water. I attached a minnow and let the weight take the minnow down into the depths until the bobber stopped its descent. There it sat, at about fifteen feet. Jim was a little more daring and was always willing to stretch the limit. He decided to set the minnow just a couple of feet deeper.

Minutes went by. Nothing happened. I decided to check the minnow and make sure it was not dead—part of my impatience displayed once again. Into the reel came the slack line until the bobber hit the tip of the rod. To get it in the rest of the way, I had to raise the rod and my hand at the same time, standing up in the boat. I could see the minnow struggling to swim just below the water. Good! It was still alive! Down it went. Jim always displayed a tremendous amount of patience when he fished. Very seldom did he check his bait. Occasionally he would move the bobber a couple of feet, but only after sitting in one place for the longest time.

Jim's bobber went down. Excitement at last. Seeing a bobber go down in that clear water is the greatest rush a fisherman can experience. Jim raised his rod to set the hook, but there was nothing there. *Damn, what could that have been?* Up came the whole thing. The bait was gone. Another minnow was attached and sent back down. It was not long before down the bobber went yet again. This time Jim waited a couple of seconds longer and up came the rod. This time he set the hook into something. Up came a small perch. Well, that was not what we were here for. There had to be crappies down there somewhere, huddled up against the tree trunk. Jim baited back up, and down it went.

Jim had two or three more hits before I had my first. My bobber dived under the surface, and I watched it go deeper and deeper. Then I raised my rod into something that felt strong. I struggled to keep the fish from wrapping itself around the tree. Up came the bobber to the rod tip. I still had about twelve feet of line in the water. I raised my hand and my rod tip up. What I did not consider was the bend in the rod. The bend kept the fish from coming to the surface, where Jim could get a net under it. Jim yelled out, "It is a crappie!" I stood up on the bench in the boat, which allowed me to get the fish up another two feet—a dangerous maneuver, but it worked. It was just enough that with a little hand pulling on the line from Jim, we netted the crappie and brought it on board.

We stared at the enormous crappie. It was the largest crappie I had ever seen. Everything was big in this lake: big bullheads, big northerns, and now big crappies. This crappie was different from those we caught back home. The colors were dark, and the mouth not as big. The body was much

wider. It was a beautiful fish. On the stringer it went. I was so excited that
I had trouble baiting back up. Down went the minnow for another chance
at these monster crappies.

Jim and I traded hits back and forth, but we landed no more crappies.
We told ourselves there had to be more than one down there. We caught
a few perch and a couple of bluegill. We were starting to understand one
neat feature about Minnesota fishing in this manner: we never knew what
we were going to hook into. When that bobber went down, it could be a
perch, a bluegill, a bass, a crappie, a walleye, or even a northern pike. That
was what made it so much fun for us. Fishing this lake the way we were
doing it now, anchored with just a minnow on a bobber—what a thrill!

Jim's bobber went down yet again. This time it was different. Jim
yelled, "This one feels better." I noticed his rod bent more than usual. Jim
had to do the same thing I had done. He raised his rod tip and his hand
straight up just to get the fish closer to the surface. It was another crappie.
I grabbed the net. Jim could not get the fish any closer to the surface no
matter what he did. There it was, just a couple of feet below us. I grabbed
the line with one hand and the net in the other and pulled the fish up.
Into the net it went, all in one swoop. More times than not, treating a
crappie like that at the boat will result in losing it. Luck was with us yet
again. It was another exceptionally large crappie. Looking at Jim's crappie
on the stringer next to the one I had caught, we saw that they could have
been twins.

We sat there getting hits occasionally for at least another hour, but no
more crappies. It was midafternoon when the other boat came back for us.
Rick, Doug, and Leo told us about the Pork Barrel, which just happened
to be on the other side of the reeds close to where we were anchored. The
Pork Barrel would become one of our go-to places to fish in the future.
When we lifted our stringer of fish, they noticed the crappies right away.
They were unmistakable among the perch and bluegills. The guys could
not believe their eyes when they saw the size of those crappies; they were
every bit of sixteen inches. We tied up to the other boat, and Leo started
to make his way back to Home Bay.

That evening we decided to eat fish for supper. What a treat that was
for us! After cleaning what we had caught that afternoon, along with what
we already had in the fridge, Rick and Jim started cooking them up. The

aroma of pan-fried fish filled the cabin. I personally had never experienced the taste of fish that good. Perch and bluegills, along with our crappies, made it to the frying pan. With bread, chips, and a beer, we ate like kings that night. Lou would freeze what was left over and record the catch.

It might sound odd to hardy Minnesota fishermen as to why catching just two crappies that afternoon became one of our most cherished memories fishing in Lower Bottle Lake. We simply shake our heads in disbelief every time it comes up. For Jim and me, it was magnificent. Why would catching just two crappies be so grand an accomplishment for us? This is simply because, over all the following years of fishing Lower Bottle, we never caught another crappie. Never! We tried and tried without success. It was only when we started fishing Upper Bottle Lake that we realized the real crappie fishery was there and not Lower Bottle. Yet on our first trip to Park Rapids in 1967, fishing out of Home Bay Resort on Lower Bottle Lake, Jim and I decided to go out and catch crappies on that Tuesday afternoon. We knew nothing about the lake, such as where to go and how to fish it. We were not able to buzz around here and there looking for them, yet we caught two, just by chance. Those two crappies meant more to us than most of the fish we took from the Bottle Lakes over the years. I wish like hell I had taken them home to be mounted, but we didn't know the significance. We never gave it a thought.

Our plan for the evening was to head out to the Narrows and give it another try. We needed to start earlier, since both boats were going. Leo and Rick drew the wooden boat. That meant Doug would have to run the motor. When we went for bait, Lou told us of a weekly tradition they held at the resort every Wednesday afternoon. It was a get-together for all the resort guests for some treats and soft drinks that started at 3:00 p.m. Everyone was welcome, and the event was held just off our cabin, number 5, on the grassy beach.

Since we had to tote the other boat, our trip to the Narrows that evening was slower and took more time. It was later in the evening before we got both boats anchored. We wasted no time in getting our jigs and minnows out. It didn't take long before the crawdads were at it again. Damn those things. They were a problem for us. Jim started his collection in the bottom of the boat again.

What was different this evening from last evening? The walleyes were hitting. Doug landed the first walleye we caught on the Bottle Lakes. It was the first time I had seen a walleye. The eyes were the most magnificent distinguishing feature on that fish. They were like glass. We could see the reflection from their eyes well below the surface of the water as Doug guided the fish into the net. We were all so damn excited we could hardly contain ourselves. I cannot remember how many we caught that night, but we kept at least six. There were many we threw back, considering them to be too small. That was a tough thing to do considering this was our first night experiencing a walleye bite. The action was quick and exciting. We all had our chance to experience a walleye hit or, better yet, to catch one. Too bad Lou was not with us that night; he would have been proud.

It was getting dark again, and we remembered our last trip going back to Home Bay in total darkness. This time it would be much slower with two boats. We decided to get going a little earlier. Doug managed to guide us toward the south shoreline without incident. Down the shoreline we went until we could see the floodlights from the resort. A direct line toward them guided us into Home Bay. Piece of cake!

Lou had given us a brochure on filleting fish. None of us knew how to do it, so Jim took the lead in that regard and cleaned up the walleyes for us. Tomorrow we would take them to Lou.

CHAPTER 23

The Pork Barrel

It was hard to believe it was already Wednesday. The time had just flown by for us during the last few days, and we still had not caught a northern pike. In the many years that followed, nothing was more disheartening to us then seeing the time fly by so fast. I would find myself wishing that time could just stand still during our week of fishing and allow our trip to last a little longer.

After breakfast, we decided to get with Lou and have him freeze our fish. This is a process that I must take some time in describing, as I'm not sure all resort owners went through the methodical kind of procedure Lou did just to make sure everything was on the up-and-up with the DNR. In some manner, I am sure Lou was protecting us in his own way, and at the same time he was making sure we understood that if we fished in Minnesota, we had to follow Minnesota rules. Lou also had a set of rules not just for us but for everyone that stayed at his resort. Lou kept track of every northern and walleye taken by his resort guests. When he brought out his record book, it was as good as any orderly accountant's book. Entry after entry reflected an overall account of past and present resort guests regarding their fishing success. Every fish that Lou ever wrapped up and froze went into that book, and that included panfish.

The whole wrapping process took place just next to his office. Lou would try to match up the two fillets that represented one fish and get a weight on them. Next, he would take those fillets and wrap them up with freezer paper making sure he wrote on the package the species and the weight. After all the fish were wrapped up, into the office we went to make the entry into the record book. Each wrapped package needed to have a license number on it and the name of the person holding that license.

We had five licenses between us. We just needed to make sure we were dividing up the fish equally so that no one person's license was on all the packages. In that manner, we could not go over our limit in possession, which was really the whole purpose of this. Lou didn't care if only one of us caught all the fish. His concern was to make sure we had the license numbers to reflect the possession limit.

Into the record book each individual fish went, regardless of the package size. The line item would list the fisherman's name, license number, weight of fish, species of fish, and date caught. Lou only needed the game fish—such as walleyes, northern pike, and bass—to be individually recorded. Panfish could go into the book as a single line item, such as "ten perch," "six bluegills," etc.

Our plan for the day was to go back across the lake to the Pork Barrel and pull chubs with the wire harness. Leo wanted to try it again since they'd had a few hits the day before. Off we went. It was another beautiful day with the sunshine glistening off the water, making me glad I had sunglasses on. We dropped off Rick and Doug where we had caught our panfish last Monday. We were sure they would get into them again. I almost wished we were doing the same thing, as we were sure of ourselves fishing in that manner and were by that point thinking, *Screw the northerns.*

"The Pork Barrel" was a name given to a small lake within the Bottle Lakes acreage. It was only fifty to one hundred water acres in size, but accessing the area required some finesse. The entrance to the area was very shallow. I doubt it was more than one to two feet deep at its shallowest point. The shallows were filled with reeds, which helped identify a boat channel in and out of the area.

Following that channel did not guarantee a smooth ride in. Raised boulders and rocks were ever present, and hitting one of them might have resulted in a busted prop. Leo had to disengage the lock catch and raise the motor slightly while negotiating the boat through the small corridor. Once we were through the shallowest part of the corridor, Leo could safely let the motor down and lock it in place.

The Pork Barrel was protected on three shorelines by raised hillsides filled with pines and clump birch. The reeds and wild rice that grew in the shallows protected the area from waves caused by westerly winds that would blow across the main lake. The area was normally tranquil even on high-wind days. Where the name "Pork Barrel" came from is anyone's guess.

Once inside the Pork Barrel, it became evident that this little gem of water acreage should be full of fish. There were reeds all around it, along with large areas of lily pads. The water was as clear as could be. We could see long, stringy clumps of weeds rising from the depths of the water all around the Pork Barrel. Lou had suggested back-trolling to slow us down and allow the bait to run deeper. Yesterday Leo had decided to give it a try with Rick and Doug. Today we would do the same thing. Back-trolling was the answer, as Leo had no trouble dictating his direction and speed. In went the unfortunate chub. I secured the bow seat, assuring me of a comfortable afternoon.

The Pork Barrel was not very deep. We figured it was about fifteen feet max. Most of the trolling we did was concentrated in the center of the area. If we drifted away from center, we would get hung up on a weed called "cabbage weed" that we could see rising from the depths. The cabbage weed was nothing like any weed I had ever encountered. It had thick stems with wide leaves attached to the stem that resembled cabbage leaves, giving the weed its name.

When we reached one end of our troll, we would reel up, turn the boat, and start again. Back and forth we went. The day before, Leo had told us they were getting good hits but could not get a hook into them. We were experiencing the same issue. I can remember my first northern hit. I felt a good thump on the rod tip. Lou had told us to let the rod tip go forward and not set the hook right away. I let the northern or whatever it was take the rod tip forward, and when I was fully extended, I reared back to set the hook. I felt a great resistance against the rod, but then everything let loose. When I reeled in the harness, the chub was ripped to hell.

That happened more than once for all of us. We were feeding the fish chubs. We had some theories as to why this was happening: the rods were not stiff enough or we were not setting the hook hard enough or we were not letting them take it long enough. Not too many of the chubs made it off the harnesses, so it was not that the northerns were stealing the bait; they were ripping up the chubs. None of us considered that maybe the northerns were too small. Before long we were out of chubs and again had no fish to show for it. The next evening, we would figure it out.

I did manage to get one about halfway to the boat before he spit the bait out. They were real fighters, and I could feel the whole body twisting and turning as it tried to free itself from the hook. In my mind, at that time, I felt my rod was not stiff enough to bury the hook.

Since we had run out of chubs, it was time to get back and pick up the guys in the other boat. We needed to get back to the resort, as 3:00 p.m. was quickly approaching. We didn't want to miss the get-together party with the other guests Lou had told us about. I think we were all getting just a bit frustrated regarding these northerns, and the chubs were costing us a lot of money. The day was not a total bust, as Rick and Doug had some fish on the stringer—but no northerns.

Back at the resort we could see the guests starting to mingle just in front of our cabin. We just joined right in. Lou and Betty had chairs and picnic tables all set up. They laid out a tasty spread of lemonade and various sorts of pastries. Lou had a golden retriever that did some tricks for the guests. One of the best I can remember was his grabbing a treat from his nose. Lou would command him to sit and then put a treat right on top of his nose. That dog would sit there motionless until Lou gave the command. The dog would then toss the treat up in the air and catch it. It was the cutest damn thing I ever saw!

Mostly, everyone introduced themselves and then just resorted to small talk, which is something young boys just out of high school have no desire to partake in. We stayed just long enough to not be rude and then went back into the cabin. There we pondered our plan for the evening over a late supper of nothing other than SpaghettiOs with some cut-up pieces of hot dogs mixed in and bread.

CHAPTER 24

Bullheads

I'm not sure who suggested it, but we did settle on a plan for the evening. When we were planning this trip to Minnesota, we were told stories about the exceptionally large bullheads one could catch in Minnesota. During our first time out on the lake the previous Saturday, Leo caught the largest bullhead I had ever seen. For sure they were in this lake. We knew bullheads liked to feed at night. Our plan was to head to an area of the lake that was free of weeds and reeds. We wanted to bank fish, so the shoreline needed to be accommodating to allow us to run the boats ashore without much hassle. The perfect place, we figured, would be the peninsula by the Narrows. We would beach the boats and bank fish for bullheads. The area was vacant of any residents, and in our minds, we would not be trespassing on anyone's property. We felt we knew the lake well enough to not get into trouble during the night. Tonight was bullhead night.

Darkness didn't fall on the Bottle Lakes until well after eight. We sat around and played cards until it was time to get going. I must say I felt some anxiety on the upcoming trip. I was not a fan of being in a boat at night. I had learned that on the first night trip back to the resort from the Narrows. There is something scary about moving ahead and not seeing where you are going—especially on an unfamiliar lake. One or two trips from the Narrows did not qualify us as being familiar with the lake. I did make sure I had my life jacket on before heading out. I wondered if Lou heard us take off. I am sure that if he did, he pondered where we could possibly be going at that time of night. I think we all believed him to be constantly on the lookout for us.

Towing the other boat was such a hassle for us. It took so much more time getting anywhere on the lake. However, on this trip, Rick had the idea of using one of the oars as a rudder; that way we could just tie up the one boat behind the motorized boat and just be pulled out. It worked well enough for us to wonder why we hadn't thought of that before. As we headed out into the darkness away from Home Bay's floodlights, we noticed that there were very few lights on the lake to guide us. Leo was moving along in almost total darkness, relying on his keen command of the situation.

One of our flashlights lit up the southernmost buoy of the shallow area that always caused us concern when leaving Home Bay. Once we rounded that point, open water was ahead. It would not have taken much for us to become disoriented. It was akin to being in a whiteout, except we were in the darkness at night. We spotted a couple of lights way in the distance, which we believed were coming from the eastern shore. There were two private residences on that shoreline. I hoped it was their lights we had spotted. Leo set his bearing for those lights.

All along the way, all eyes were looking for signs of reeds or silhouetted trees, which would indicate we were getting too close to shore. The last thing we needed now was to run into something simply because we got disoriented out in the open water. Leo's bearing brought the distant lights closer and closer until we realized they were, in fact, coming from the east shoreline. That was a relief. We followed the shoreline with caution, passing the residences whose lights had guided us across the lake. Once we were past the private shoreline, the eastern shore took a sharp bend to the west at the start of the peninsula that separated Lower Bottle from Upper Bottle. We had reached our destination.

The trip out took us every bit of thirty minutes just to get to the area. There was a slight breeze coming in from the south, which caused small waves to pound right into our landing zone. We used the waves to our advantage, riding them into shore until the bow of each boat hit the sandy beach. Out we jumped, securing the boats higher up on the shore. I believe we all felt like explorers running ashore on a deserted beach.

We walked inland for a short distance and suddenly found ourselves face-to-face with Upper Bottle's waters on the other side of the peninsula. There was little wind on that side, but it was impossible to fish from the bank. Back we went to try our hand at catching the famous Minnesota bullhead.

There was plenty of shoreline to fish with no hindrance except for the wind blowing into our faces. The wind was no stranger to us, as we had experienced it many times in Nebraska. We found the lake bottom to not have a gentle incline; it sloped downward almost immediately. We didn't have to cast far to be fishing in waters at least twenty-five to thirty feet deep.

I enjoyed the chance to fish from the bank once again. Fishing out of a small boat is okay, but there I didn't have the freedom to roam and move about like I did on the bank. I think all of us appreciated that chance even though it was pitch dark in the middle of the night.

The action started right away. A small piece of night crawler fished on the bottom would land us a scrappy bullhead in just a few minutes' time. Man, they were fighters, and all were just as big as that first one we'd caught back on Saturday evening. There is no mistaking the fight of a bullhead. Seldom do they make a run. We could feel their big heads thrashing about with great strength as we fought to drag them onto the shore.

One problem we had with these whiskery guys was disgorging the hooks from deep inside their gullets. Most of them swallowed the whole contents, hook and all. Disgorging a hook at night was extra challenging. We knew enough about large catfish not to stick any part of our fingers in their mouths if we wanted to keep them. We figured these large bullheads were just as bad. It is unbelievable how much force these guys can generate with their huge jaws. A good pair of pliers was mandatory just to open their mouths. Using a long-shanked hook helped, because it was then easier to grab the hook during the disgorging process. However, it was inevitable that we would ruin some hooks or cut some line. It was frustrating for us to have to waste time rigging up another hook.

CHAPTER 25

The Bat

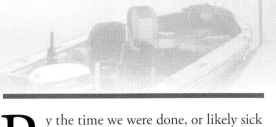

By the time we were done, or likely sick of it, we had two large stringers full of bullheads. It took two guys just to carry one stringer back to the boat and secure it. Altogether we must have had fifty bullheads packed onto those two stringers. Once they were secured, we could not miss the chance to do a little exploring.

We took what flashlights we had and started walking back into the peninsula to see what we could find. We didn't have to go far before we noticed an older style cabin just ahead, sitting right in the middle of the peninsula. The cabin was old and uninhabited. There was a For Sale sign tacked to a tree, which must have been visible from the waters of Upper Bottle. There was a screened-in porch facing to the east with a screen door that was not locked. We let ourselves in only to scout around and just explore.

Inside the porch was the main door for the cabin. It was locked, so we left it alone. With our flashlights canvassing the whole porch, a bird dived at the light and then disappeared. We heard it hit the screen. The flashlights lit up the area, but we could not find anything. Then there was another flyby. Jim yelled out that it was a bat. When I heard the word "bat," I ran out of the porch so fast I almost stumbled. I had never had an encounter with a bat, and based on my limited knowledge of those creatures, we did not want to tangle with it.

Again, this situation was right up Jim's alley. Fearful of nothing, he remained in the porch, yelling for someone to get our landing net back at the boat. Doug made his way back to the boat and brought up the net. Jim took the net, and with lights shining from outside the porch, he tried to catch the poor creature. It took him three or four swipes until the bat found himself tangled in the net. Curiosity finally got to us and we all gathered around the net to see the most mysterious of creatures up close. It was smaller than I thought and appeared not to be hurt after its ordeal. Jim wanted to put him into a box and take it back to the resort. Jim grabbed the net and carried it outside and back to the boat. We got one of the empty night crawler boxes and managed to carefully put the bat into the box. We punched a few holes into the lid and put the creature in the boat.

We were ready to get back to the resort with our stringers of bullheads. It would be a long boat trip back, and it was well after midnight. We still had to clean our catch. The wind had gone down, and a late moon was rising out of the east, which provided us with some much-needed light. It was a little tricky getting both boats back onto the water. Rick and I pushed Leo, Jim, and Doug out first. Then we pushed our boat out as best we could. Once clear of the shoreline, Leo maneuvered his boat close enough to cast us a line that we secured to the bow of our boat, and away we went, with Rick maneuvering our makeshift rudder. By the time we got back to the resort and had cleaned the bullheads, it was well after two early Thursday morning.

We left the box holding the bat in the boat the rest of the night. The next morning, we slept in. *They do sleep!* The clan stayed in bed for a few hours after sunrise that Thursday morning. I had almost forgotten what it was like to sleep later into the morning. I must say it felt wonderful. However, it was the Musilek cousins' idea of sleeping in. I was up at 9:00 a.m., dead tired. I could have slept well past noon. After some breakfast, we were anxious to find Lou and show him what we had caught the night before, not knowing what his reaction would be.

Finding Lou seemed to not be a problem, as I had thought it would be. He was always close by. Lou followed us back to the boat, and when we opened the lid to catch a glimpse of the bat, Lou about kicked us off his property. The bat had survived the ordeal, but Lou was really pissed off. He laid into us in a manner that made us feel uncomfortable, with wounded pride. We suddenly realized we had done something very stupid. His manner was that of disbelief. "What in the hell are you guys doing with that bat?" he went on. He told us to get rid of it as soon as possible. We tried to apologize and at the same time wondered what the big deal was. Lou told us, "Those bats carry disease—rabies—and most of all, are protected. They also eat mosquitoes." That is all he said. He walked off and never said another word about it.

Jim at once took the box that contained the bat close to a grove of trees and let him escape. We felt uneasy right then, and we didn't know if we could recover Lou's trust. We were taught a great lesson that morning about one of Minnesota's nighttime friends. I do not know what we were thinking at the time. I believe our not understanding Minnesota's ecosystem contributed to our misjudgment of the situation.

Back in Nebraska, confronting a bat was something that just did not happen. In fact, this was the first time I had ever seen a bat. What we learned that morning set us straight about the importance of bats to the state. They eat bugs at night, mainly mosquitoes—a lot of mosquitoes. Anything that will help get rid of the kind of mosquitoes that attacked us the previous Saturday morning is a friend of mine.

Many years later, while we were trolling for walleyes at night, things began diving by the rear boat light and then would be lost in the darkness. It happened so fast; a blink of the eye and one would miss it. They were bats attacking mosquitoes that were attracted to the light. I then remembered the lesson Lou taught us about the importance of that nighttime friend.

CHAPTER 26

Finally, the Great Northern Pike

After the bat situation, we took our cleaned bullheads up to Lou for freezing. Back at the cabin, we tried to decide what our plan would be for the day. We decided to go after panfish again, which was as much fun for me as anything. We had yet to experience the thrill of catching a northern. While we were getting bait for the afternoon, Lou told us that some people in the resort had been catching northerns in the evening just out in front of the resort. He told us we should try it using the harnesses. I think we were all thankful he was still talking to us after the morning episode with the bat. We breathed a sigh of relief that our status with Lou might not have been compromised.

It was hard to believe Thursday had arrived. Leo decided to not fish that day and left the resort once again. I wonder where he went. Nobody asked, simply because it was his car and we had no business asking. We were four once again.

That afternoon we decided to look for new areas to fish. It was fun cruising along the shoreline and looking for sunken weed beds. When we found a patch that looked promising, we would anchor just outside the weed line and fish below the boat, where we could catch bluegills and large perch. We also made our way into the Pork Barrel to try the weed beds there. There were fish everywhere in that small area of water.

At some time during that afternoon, my trusty Zebco 66 reel crapped out on me. I could not retrieve any line. Turning the handle was out of the question. I would not know the problem until I tore into it, but I was not prepared to work on the reel during the fishing trip. I knew Lou used a closed-face spinning reel, but not a Zebco. I decided to talk to him when we got back to the resort. My afternoon was over. I had no backup, and nobody else did either. It was okay with me. Watching fish being taken was just as much fun. I became the boatswain that afternoon.

While the guys were cleaning our catch that afternoon, I decided to talk to Lou. Lou was more than happy to show me the reels he used. They were called Johnson Century reels. According to Lou, the Johnson Century was the only reel he ever used. Lou took me to his office and sold me one right then. Lou told me it was the best closed-face spinning reel on the market. I handed him $13.99. My Zebco 66 had given me plenty of trouble-free hours on the lakes back home. I hoped Lou would be right about this reel.

I fell in love with the Century immediately. It fit onto my flexible fiberglass rod with no problem. It was not bulky, and it felt good when cradled in my hand and fingers. The most noticeable feature, and one that I still admire to this day, was its resistance-free casting. With a well-maintained Century reel and balanced rod, I can to this day outcast an open-face reel using the same line weight and any weight of jig. The reel had a setting that would disengage the full-time anti-reverse feature. This allowed the handle of the reel to turn backward and bypass the drag option—a setting that I always used on my Zebco reel. I would not have considered any reel that didn't offer that choice. Relying on the drag is a ridiculous way to fish when using a closed-face spinning reel. Not only do the drags not work, but if the drag is activated, the line going out tends to curl itself, and eventually the line must be replaced because of twisting.

The reel was fitted with eight-pound monofilament line. For years I used this same reel I bought from Lou in 1967. Fifty years later, it is sitting in my man cave on a shelf, still in excellent working order, along with my trusty Zebco 66. Over the past fifty years, I have used the Johnson Century reel exclusively. I must have over two dozen working reels I have collected. They are still my go-to reels regardless of what species of fish I am after. Nothing compares to the Johnson Century.

Later that afternoon, after supper, we were all excited to get out after the elusive northern pike. Rumors of northern pike being caught right out in front had circulated through the resort. We were going to give it our best that evening. When we went to get bait, Lou told us to use the harness and troll backward in a slow, steady retrieve, moving back and forth in front of the cabins. We got one dozen chubs. Lou threw in an extra and called it a fisherman's dozen. *Whoopie wow! One extra!* But that one extra meant we were back into Lou's trust. The bat situation was behind us, and I believe we all felt a little relieved about that.

Off to the boat we went. Rick manned the motor, and the rest of us staggered ourselves on the bench seats. I was able to snare the throne in the front of the boat. It was not the easiest place to fish from, since we were trolling backward. I had to fish directly behind the boat—something I was not used to doing. I liked to see the rod at ninety degrees and not directly behind me. I believe Rick realized that and decided to run the motor. Clever guy, that Rick!

We started out just as we had done all week, watching our depth using the weeds below the surface as a guide. Eventually we started using the boat docks to estimate our depth. If we got too close to one dock, we knew our bait would end up in the weeds. The next dock might dictate a greater distance away. It was this trial-and-error system that we used to map out our troll that evening back and forth in front of the cabins. It had become more of a hassle for Rick to give way to other boats then it was to regulate our depth.

We learned not to cast the chub into the water but only let it slip over the side of the boat. Then we would let out line until the chub and harness disappeared into the depths while the boat was moving. This little maneuver was easier on the chub, and at the same time we could watch the little spinner and make sure it was spinning before the whole thing disappeared. It was important to keep that spinner rotating. Any small residue or piece of weed would hamper it. We got to the point where we could feel the spinning action reverberate through the tip of the rod. If the tip of the rod stopped vibrating, then inevitably something had fouled the spinner, and back into the boat the whole thing came to be cleaned.

The past few days had given us valuable experience in trying to troll these harnesses. We already knew what a tug or a hit felt like, but nobody had been able to get a fish close to the boat to land it or see it. The only northern I had seen was the one at the beginning of the week, which I didn't even know was a fish until I spotted it. I had thought it to be weeds until it was right there and decided to let go of the chub. I was hoping for a different outcome this evening.

We must have trolled back and forth a couple of times when Rick got the first hit. I am sure his concentration was on our depth and other boats in the area, but Rick managed to get a good hook set, and the excitement was on. Rick stopped the motor, and the rest of us brought our lines in to prevent them from getting tangled. We were not going to take any chances.

I watched Rick's fight with whatever was on the other end. There was no doubt it was a larger fish. I only hoped it would be a northern. I hoped we could land him or at least see him. After a few minutes, we could see the fish from the boat. It was, in fact, a northern, and Doug managed to net it. It was a beautiful fish thrashing about in the bottom of the boat. The pike was long with broad shoulders, and teeth that demanded profound respect from anyone handling it. Finally, one of us had gotten a hook into one and it ended up on the stringer! It was every bit of four to five pounds, by our estimate.

We were all extremely excited, and kudos to Rick for landing our first-ever northern pike. For fishermen that were not used to catching northern pike, a five-pound northern was a dream catch. It is clearly understood that these rulers of the northern lakes can reach massive sizes, but to have finally had success in catching one was especially important to us.

It was not long after we started trolling once again that I felt a thump vibrate through the rod and onto my left pointer finger. This is one of the most exciting sensations a fisherman can experience next to watching a bobber go down. I tried to follow Lou's instructions. Once you feel the hit, you need to let the rod tip go forward until you cannot anymore, and then rear back. I did just that. I was bound and determined to really lay into whatever was trying to steal my bait.

When I set the hook, there was a great weight on the other end. I hollered, "Got one on!" The motor stopped, and I started what was to be my first battle with a decent-sized northern pike. It was not disappointing. I could feel his powerful body thrashing on the other end. This was the strongest fish I had hooked into during the whole trip. I would reel in some line only to have the great northern make a run. I had the anti-reverse off so I could clutch the reel myself using my right hand on the handle.

Whenever I turned the fish, I would reel in line only to be faced with another run. This happened three or four times before I could feel the fish tire out. It was then only a matter of not losing it at the boat. We were all staring into the depths of the water when the northern appeared. He took one look at the net and away he went, straight down under the boat.

Every fisherman knows about that surge of energy at the boat. It is that single moment when most fish are lost. The next time I brought him up, Jim slipped the net under him. I was lucky. Over the years, I had lost my share of fish at the net, but not this time. It was my first northern pike, and I could not have been more excited at seeing this magnificent fish. I totally fell in love with the northern pike after that experience. I could see why Lou had taken such an interest in this great fish. After I removed the hook from his mouth, onto the stringer he went. Interestingly, it was about the same size as Rick's.

That night was special to all of us. Those of us who were in the boat can all remember it fifty years later. That evening we caught a total of four northerns, all of them nice and fat and about the same size. But there was something else that made that night special. We each caught one, and we each experienced a hit or two that we missed. We lost two at the boat. We each got to experience the ferocious fight from a great northern pike, one of Minnesota's great treasures.

When we ran out of chubs, we headed back to the boat dock. Lou met us at the fish house. I am sure he was glad to see the excitement on our faces. He really talked up the catch. Lou could get us excited about catching a small perch if he worked at it hard enough; he was that good at selling his trade. It was time for Lou to show us how to clean northern pike.

The acceptable practice for cleaning a northern was to fillet it. Jim had some experience in filleting fish, as he had tried it on the nice walleyes we had caught a few nights ago. He had also started to fillet some of the larger perch we caught earlier in the week. This would be his first chance at tackling a northern. We were welcome for any help from Lou in that regard. Jim had his skinning knife that he was using all week.

Lou, however, whipped out a knife that was called a Rapala fillet knife. After our lesson, it was obvious that Jim was going to get one. The knife was sleek, thin bladed, and extremely sharp. It came with its own sheath. Lou sold them for nine dollars. They made filleting any species of fish quite easy. Back to the office we went to log our catch and get the fillets packaged and frozen. Jim bought a new knife on the spot.

When we got back to the cabin, Leo had just arrived. Leo had missed a fun time, but without another motor, whoever would have been in the other boat would not have experienced the same fortunate evening. It was hard to believe it was already Thursday night. One more day and then it would be back to Prague, where we would each face an unknown future.

I really got a good night's sleep because the pressure was off. The monkey was off our back. It had taken a long time and plenty of frustration before we caught our first northern. I am not sure what would have happened to us if we had not had the luck we had Thursday night. We might not have come back. I believe the success we had Thursday night sealed the deal for us to return in future years. It was that important to us.

True to form, we were all up early again Friday morning. This time I climbed out of the sack without cursing the Musilek clan. *Am I getting used to this early-morning wake up?* It is hard to say what I felt that morning, except that I knew it would be our last day. Perhaps our success and excitement from last night carried over into the morning. After breakfast, we planned for our last day fishing the Bottle Lakes.

CHAPTER 27

Jim's Big Northern

We could not have managed to select a better week regarding weather. We didn't have to deal with rain, and the wind was marginal. The night times were pleasant and strangely absent of mosquitoes. No wonder we ran into hundreds of thousands of the man-eating bugs on Pickerel Lake; all the mosquitoes must have hung out on that lake at the public access dock.

We were not without pests, and that included a few mosquitoes and flying bugs at dusk. However, the worst pests were the flying, biting, bloodsucking flies that seemed to constantly be around during the day—the ankle-biting ones. We called them sand flies back home. I never wore shorts and always had on jeans, but somehow they still managed to sneak up my cuffs and let me know they meant business. Anyone that has ever experienced these annoying flies know their sting. It is painful and induces an immediate reaction from any recipient that amounts to a hard slap with a hand at the source, usually around the ankle. Normally that is the only time available to kill the damn things—when they are in the process of biting. Any other time, it is difficult to swat them, as they are very quick and almost seem to learn not to stick around long. The best way to get the devils is to just let them bite and then swat them when they are concentrating on inserting their blood-sucking syringe. That is the only time they are vulnerable. That type of sacrifice requires toughness and staying power—things I lacked. Instead of sacrificing myself, I would resort to swishing them around and sometimes getting in a lucky punch.

Another interesting fact about those damn flies is that they seemed to congregate in the boat. I cannot remember them attacking any of us when we were on land or around the beach, but once in the boat, look out! They were roving vagabonds of the worst order, hitching rides at the bottom of the boat, looking for our blood. Of course, the bottom of the boat was where our ankles were, and we became easy targets for them. By week's end, Rick was bringing along a flyswatter from the cabin. The slaughter started almost immediately, as the annoying things didn't waste any time. They seemed to come out of the cracks. Once they learned not to stick around on the inside of the boat to face certain death, they flew to the outside of the boat and hung on for dear life. Rick would continue the onslaught with his flyswatter, resulting in a long trail of dead flies floating on the water behind the boat. Putting up with those bugs was a small price to pay for the honor of fishing this lake.

I managed to get into the boat with the motor on the last day along with Jim and Rick. Leo and Doug drew the short straws. The night before had been so much fun we decided that since it was our last afternoon, we would spend it trolling on the east shore. Leo and Doug decided to anchor just off the dock where we'd had so many hits last evening. If they wanted to go in, they didn't have too much distance to row back.

The day was bright and sunny. A small breeze kicked in from the south. The area we were going to was not new to us. We had trolled that shoreline several times during the week; it was the area of the submerged tree where Jim and I had caught the two crappies earlier in the week. We would use the submerged tree as a waypoint along with a boat dock to the north. We would troll back and forth between those two points. We were getting good at determining our depth through our trial-and-error method using submerged weeds. Rick manned the motor, I got to sit on the throne, and Jim was in the middle.

Running the boat backward made all the difference in the world. It allowed our bait to get down deeper because our troll was so much slower. Back and forth we went. When we made sure our bait passed the boat dock, we would reel in, turn the boat, and head back toward the submerged tree.

During one of these passes, we noticed a large school of baitfish breaking the surface right in front of our path. It was our first contact with a bait school, and it was an awesome sight. They were everywhere—hundreds of thousands of small minnows darting about as far down as we could see. Our troll would take us through the middle of the swarm.

Suddenly Jim got a hit. He let the rod tip bend down, extended his hands, then reared back to set the hook. This hook set was different. I noticed it right away from my perch. There was no give in his rod. It looked as if he set the hook into a tree stump. In fact, Jim initially thought he was snagged until the fish decided he wanted to fight. The fish wanted line—and right now! Jim was using his open-face spinning reel and had to act fast. I would not have given a plum nickel for one of those types of reels, but to each his own. He also liked to use his reel with the anti-reverse off, just like I did. At least we agreed on that little tidbit. When this fish wanted line, Jim thumbed the handle and the line peeled from the reel in a somewhat controlled fashion.

Rick shut the motor off, and we were adrift. It appeared that Jim was not gaining a foot of line. "He's in the weeds!" Jim shouted. At least that was what we thought. We didn't have enough experience to know for sure, but the lack of a tug-of-war indicated that the fish had gotten hung up on something. Jim continued to put pressure on the rod, and suddenly the fight was back on. The fish had freed himself. Another run! Then another! Back and forth they went. During this whole time, we were drifting into the north shore, where we had caught all the bullheads. We knew it was deep there, so we had time to decide what to do. Jim started to gain more and more line, and it was clear that we were going to have a net fight on our hands. If only we could see him. I managed to get into position on Jim's left with the net. Rick was ready with the motor just in case we needed to escape the north shore. Suddenly I saw a large shadow below. "There he is!" I told Jim. At least I thought it was him. What I was looking at was the top of Jim's harness that had snagged onto a significant pile of weeds. There was another large shadow a few feet from the weeds. It was the northern, dashing about while pulling along the pile of weeds. Jim was struggling against the added weight. During this time, Rick realized we had gotten too close to the shore. He fired up the motor and slowly guided us into deeper water. The struggle continued. Slowly the pile of weeds made it to the surface. I managed to get some of the weeds off Jim's line. The northern was tired and ready for the net, but the damn weeds made it difficult to get the fish up. Jim lifted his rod tip high enough for me to get most of the weeds off the trailing harness. The large northern rolled to the surface, and with one swipe, he was in the net.

What a thrill it was to see that large northern lying on the deck of the boat. He was magnificent. This northern was much larger than those we'd gotten the evening prior. The great northern pike, king of Minnesota's lakes, is a predator like none other—fearless, ferocious, and full of violent energy. They fight with high bursts of speed and unsteady swimming. It is a heart-pumping experience to fight such a marvelous fish. This one was coming home with us. We secured him to a strong stringer and could not wait to get back to the resort and show Lou.

The trip back to the resort would take us longer than this northern could survive out of the water. Along the way, we stopped a few times to let the northern back into the water for some resuscitation. We didn't have a live well; we had only our resolve to try to keep him alive. Our plan worked. When we docked the boat, we secured the stringer to the dock and watched this great fish revive himself back to magnificence, full of spunk and energy.

The other boat was already back at the dock. Leo and Doug came running out of the cabin when they noticed all the commotion. Shortly, Lou came walking out onto the dock. There was that feeling again—Lou keeping a close eye on us. To him we were strangers to Minnesota, strangers to his resort, and strangers to fishing out of a boat. He was always close at hand. At least we didn't have to run and get him. We wanted to show him Jim's northern, and his timing could not have been better.

Lou wanted to know the whole story—where we had gotten him and what bait we had used. We told him we had followed his advice: troll slowly, use the harness, troll backward, set the hook with vengeance. He never said, "I told you so," but I believe he was prouder of us than we were of ourselves. Lou never degraded Jim's catch by telling us that there were fish out there two to three times that size, or that he had caught many like that in the past. That was not in Lou's character. One of my biggest pet peeves are people that always have a better story they can tell or have a better experience regarding the same subject. Lou had nothing but praise and congratulations for us. By the time he got done with us, we were pounding our chests.

The magnificent fish did not like getting lifted out of the water. He was ready to fight all over again. Jim managed to carry him to the beach and lay him down on the green grass. We wanted a picture before we cleaned the fish, but Lou had something else up his sleeve. He wanted Jim to enter the fish in a local tournament that the resorts around Park Rapids took part in. Jim didn't hesitate to accept. To enter the fish into the tournament, we had to go into Deer Lane for an official weigh-in and fill out the registration form. Lou explained the rules to us and said we needed to keep the northern alive, as no dead fish could enter. In a hurried fashion, we followed Lou to the front of his office, where he retrieved an oblong trough that he placed in the back of his pickup and filled with water. Jim put the northern into the trough. Lou was in a noticeable state of haste. Jim and I rode in the back of Lou's white Ford pickup to make sure the northern didn't escape the trough. Leo stayed back at the cabin while Rick and Doug crammed into Lou's front seat. Off we went. By the time we got to Deer Lane, most of the water had splashed out of the trough, but we had managed to keep the northern contained, and the water around him was just enough to keep him alive.

The weigh-in location was the same store we had visited the previous Saturday. Jim lifted the northern out of the trough, and we followed Lou to the back of the store, where a large scale was located. We were all anxious to see how much this guy weighed. The owner of the store came out to greet us. Lou introduced us and asked if he could weigh in the northern for the local resort tournament. Jim placed the northern onto a curved scale. Seven pounds thirteen ounces was the official weight. Jim and Lou went into the store to fill out the entry form while we took the northern back to the pickup and placed him back into the trough. This poor guy had gone through a lot already. There was only one thing left to do before we cleaned him—get a picture.

Back at the resort, there was a set of pine trees at the end of Home Bay's shoreline. It was a picturesque location. I hurried back to the cabin to retrieve my camera, which was a simple Kodak Brownie box camera. Jim held the beautiful northern out in front of him, and I took one picture. That one picture was the only photo we had of Jim's northern, and somehow that picture survived. (See figure 4.)

After our short photo session was over, it was time to clean him. Jim's skill with a fillet knife was as good as anyone's. His experience in skinning hides during his trapping days was evident. There was no one among us better suited to fillet a fish than Jim. After we got him packaged, logged in, and set in the freezer, it was time for supper. There was one more outing ahead of us that evening before we had to pack up and head for home in the morning.

That evening I volunteered to stay back at the cabins. There was no way we were going to hassle the second boat in the short amount of time we would have out on the water. Lou wanted us to settle the bill before eight that evening. He needed the gas tank brought in before seven so he could fill it up and charge us for the gas used. The rest of the guys went out for one more attempt to catch a beautiful northern pike. They would have only about an hour of time on the water.

It was a beautiful evening with hardly any wind. I pulled out one of the beach chairs and watched the guys troll back and forth just in front of Home Bay Resort. I know they caught at least a couple of fish worth keeping, as I saw them use the net a few times. They were too far out to see exactly what kind of fish they were dealing with or how big those fish were. Just before 7:00 p.m., they trolled back to the dock. They were excited and disappointed. The disappointment came from having to come in. They said, "The pike were hitting on almost every pass." They had kept two. Fittingly, Leo had caught himself a nice pike worthy of a picture. Back in front of the pine trees, I took the only picture we had of Leo with his fish. It also happens to be the only picture we had of Leo for the whole trip. It, too, somehow survived. (See figure 5.)

Jim and Leo went to clean the fish and get them to Lou. The rest of us decided to clean out the boats—a melancholy chore for sure. For us this meant our final realization that our fishing trip had come to an end. I'm sure all of us experienced a little thoughtful sadness during those twenty minutes or so it took us to clean the boats. We were not gloomy or depressed, but we were a little somber. I cannot help believing that each one of us, during that brief time, must have wondered whether we would ever get a chance to do this again.

By the time 8:00 p.m. rolled around, Lou had topped off the gas tank of our boat, and it was time to settle with him for the week. The cabin and one boat cost us $220 for the week. Bait, gas, life jackets, the second boat, and one motor cost us an additional $175. For the week, we each paid about $79. It seems like pennies to me now.

CHAPTER 28

Getting Home

O ur plans were to be out of the resort by eight in the morning. Lou assured us he would be around to get the fish out of the freezer to pack our coolers. All that was left then was to clean up the cabin and pack our gear into Leo's car that evening. Just as the case had been while driving up to the resort, going home would require us to deal with the damn beer bottles. We had three cases of empties. No serious beer drinker in the 1960s ever threw away a case of empty beer bottles. Any case of beer, if returned with the empties, would net a small refund. We would have to straddle the precious cargo once again all the way to Milbank, South Dakota, where Leo and Rick could collect their refund. If it had been me, the first roadside dump would have received three cases of empty beer bottles.

Regarding beer drinking in the resort by us underage juveniles, none of us really believed we were pulling one over Lou. He was just too keen and smart about what happened daily on his resort. To this day, I believe he knew we had beer in the cabin but never said anything about it. That is a tribute to Lou and his confidence in us. Maybe it was only his business side that led him to turn his back. Whatever the reason, we might not have come back if Lou had confronted us in what would have certainly been an embarrassing challenge.

That evening we packed the car, defying any doubters that we could get everything into it and still make room for us. There was not one square foot of unused space available. It took us well into the evening to get everything ready and to clean the cabin. After a short night's sleep, we were up and ready to go with the car parked outside Lou's office at 8:00 a.m. We had two coolers. Our immediate concern was packing the one larger cooler with our frozen fish. After Lou brought out all the packages, there was just enough room. Lou suggested that we stop in Park Rapids and get a couple of chunks of packaged dry ice and lay them on top of the fish, which would help keep them frozen during our trip back home.

And that was it. It was time to say goodbye and thanks to Lou and Betty. We were so lucky to have met them. They made us feel welcome and secure. I still believe that Lou was constantly on the watch for us, knowing how young we were. We had no experience fishing a large body of water, which must have made him feel uneasy. That was clear on the Saturday afternoon when all five of us went fishing in one fourteen-foot boat. We never did that again.

Lou also owned his likeable personality that allowed us to admire and respect his family and his resort. After the "captured bat" fiasco, I believe we regained his trust. And best of all, he loved to fish. He taught us how to fish his beloved Bottle Lakes. How much better could we have done? We had found a beautiful Minnesota lake by chance. Lou and Betty's brochure with all the fish on the front page had sealed the deal for us. Clear water! Reeds! Beautiful trees! Isolation! Gorgeous shorelines and fish—plenty of fish! Finally, artistic charm! The Bottle Lakes embodied all that. Home Bay Resort and the Bottle Lakes were perfect for us. If God were ever to go fishing in Minnesota, I am willing to bet he would go to the Bottle Lakes. Thank you, Lou and Betty!

After one last look at the lake and a shake of hands, we jumped into the car, and off we went. All of us had mixed feelings about leaving Home Bay Resort that morning. We were excited to be heading home, but not because we were anxious to go. Driving away down the meandering unpaved road that led back to Park Rapids meant our realization that the trip we had planned months ago was over and we had pulled it off without incident. Apart from having been very tired 75 percent of the time and having spent some hard hours on the lake, the week we had spent on the Bottle Lakes was magnificent, and none of us would have changed a thing except the disappointment we felt in leaving. One week had gone by too fast. We'd all had a taste of paradise, and it was hard to leave.

Leo might not have felt the same. Something was up with Leo. He was noticeably in a big hurry to get home. After we stopped in Park Rapids for the dry ice, it was pedal to the metal all the way home. Leo's car had an exceptionally smooth ride, and Leo's reputation of knowing how to drive hard and fast preceded him, but zipping down a Minnesota highway seventy to eighty mile per hour was scary to say the least. None of us asked any questions; we just watched the landscape fly by without saying a word. Maybe Leo was just dusting off the cobwebs through Minnesota. When we had driven to Park Rapids on the previous Friday afternoon, Leo had needed to watch his speed, as we'd had three cases of untapped beer in the backseat. Going home, all we had were the empties. There were no worries with empties. After we dropped them off in Milbank, Leo decided seventy miles per hour was not good enough. I swear I saw the speedometer reach ninety at times. It had taken us ten hours to get to Park Rapids. We were going to make it home in six.

And then, somewhere between Milbank and Sioux City, one of the rear tires blew. There was a small boom like a deep-sounding firecracker. Suddenly the car started swerving, and we found ourselves at the mercy of Leo's skill and judgment on how to get the damn car stopped without killing us all. It really was a nice piece of car handling by Leo. When we stopped and checked on the tire, there was not much left. We had to remove a lot of gear in the trunk just to get to the spare tire. After about an hour, we had managed to change the tire and repack the gear. Leo must have been shaken up just a bit after that blowout. I do not believe I noticed the speedometer go past seventy during the rest of the trip.

It was midafternoon when we rolled into Prague. We cleared out all our gear from Leo's car and divided up the packages of fish equally. Jim kept his large northern. We sat around for a brief time, talking about this and that, until Leo decided it was time for him to leave. It was the last time I saw Leo. We owed Leo a great deal. If not for his willingness to drive us and be part of the week's adventures with us, we would never have experienced that trip. I believe Leo was never into the fishing thing, not like the rest of us, but we had a great deal of fun regardless. It was not long after that day that Leo joined the armed forces and did a tour of duty in Vietnam. Leo survived that tour and lives in Nebraska to this day. Our paths never crossed again.

It had taken us three months to plan our trip. We spent all of one hour together at Rick's parents' house before we separated back to our own families. We never took a picture of our return. What was wrong with us? How I wish we had a picture of our return! Jim's Mom came to pick him up, and I hitched a ride back home with them. It was over that fast.

Each one of us was heading into a cloudy, uncertain future filled with turmoil by the unpopular Vietnam War. Rick already had one year under his belt at UNL. Jim and I had orientation at UNL in one week. Doug decided to stay in Prague for a brief time, working various jobs. In a couple of years, Doug made his decision to join the navy, where he became a medic serving in Vietnam. After his tour was over, he continued his education in medicine and became a well-respected PA; he continues to practice.

Mom was surprised to see me. She was expecting a later arrival.

PART 2

UNSETTLED YEARS

CHAPTER 1

Spring 1968

I learned one thing during my first year at UNL: I simply hated to go to school. Taking business-oriented classes as an undeclared freshman was the wrong decision. I had no business being in business classes, simply because I hated business. I longed for some guidance into the career I was after. Completing that goal required two years of out-of-state study, which I was not willing to pursue. I wish I had been more proactive in that regard.

I decided I was not going to endure another year of taking business classes. Consequently, I managed to make one of the biggest boneheaded decisions of my life. I declared into teacher's college with a major in music. What a colossal mistake! It would take me three more years to realize I had major stage fright, which is something a music instructor cannot have. All that wasted time should have been funneled into a career I still considered to be my calling, but I never acted on it. When September of 1968 rolled around, I would find myself studying music.

In the spring of 1968, Jim and Rick were both pursuing engineering degrees. Mike completed his first year at Doane College playing football, racking up win after win. Doug continued to work back in Prague. Leo had enlisted in the army and was just starting his tour of duty in 'Nam.

During the early spring, talk about heading back to the Bottle Lakes inspired some interesting weekend debates. We were all up for another year up north if we could make it work. However, we all had one necessary requirement: we wanted to make sure Michael could come. It would have been unthinkable to leave Michael behind once again.

If Michael were to come, we would not be able to go in the fall or late summer. Michael was looking forward to another football season, and practice would start once again in late summer. Midsummer was out because of our jobs, which were much more important to us than a one-week fishing trip. The only other choice was a spring trip.

The more we talked about it, the more anxious we got. Time was getting short, and March 1968 was upon us before we knew it. Rick called a meeting one weekend in late March to see what kind of plan we could come up with. Planning a second trip was much easier than it had been the previous year. We knew where we wanted to go. We knew how much time it would take to get there, and we knew the route. Most importantly, we knew about how much it would cost. Since we had to watch out for summer job commitments, our trip would have to take place either the second or third week in May. Rick agreed to get a call out to Lou as soon as he could and see if we could get reservations for either of those two weeks. When we left that night, three questions loomed over our heads: (1) Which week in May? (2) Can we get reservations? and, most importantly, (3) What do we do for transportation?

A couple of days later, Rick got back to us with good news. Lou had the same cabin, number 5, open for the third week of May if we wanted it. However, before we could commit, we needed to solve our transportation issue. Both Doug and Rick had cars, but none of us were keen on the idea of making another trip up north packed into a single car. It would need to be either two cars or something bigger, such as a pickup. Rick came to the rescue once again. I swear, if it were not for Rick, this whole thing would have fallen apart. We all owe Rick a great deal of gratitude for taking charge and finding out ways in which we could pull this off once again.

Another meeting was called. Rick must have had some private conversations with his dad. It seemed our transportation situation might be solved. Rick's dad was willing to let us use his own pickup if we could make that work in some way. Since most pickups in those days didn't have camper shells, some thought about how we would tote our gear and five guys five hundred miles north in a pickup with no shell took up most of the evening.

With five guys, there was only one solution: three in the cab and two in the back of truck bed. I thought about Leo's car last year and straddling the precious cargo and how uncomfortable that was. Right now, riding in the bed of a pickup for five hundred miles seemed much more attractive than being crammed into another car.

If two guys were going to ride in the truck bed, we needed some way to protect them. Jim and Rick suggested building a homemade canopy or shell using the slots in the pickup bed. Two-by-fours could be used, and with some crafty engineering, we could put together a frame. Then we could drape a canvas over it and attach it by some means yet to be considered. We could complete the work a few days before the trip. Jim thought Leonard, his dad, might have an old canvas tarp lying around we could use for the canopy. The plan seemed sound enough; otherwise, it was five hundred miles in an open pickup bed, exposed to all the elements. Rick called Lou and booked five of us for the third week in May 1968.

Around the last part of April, Rick got back to us with confirmation for a May 18, 1968, arrival. The price had not changed. This year we decided to rent two boats and two motors. It was a colossal mistake last year that was not to be made again. Some added expense needed to be considered. There were no issues from any of us with May 18. We could all make it.

I cannot stress enough how excited we were that Michael would be able to join us. We had all felt a void the year prior because of the absence of Michael. I was excited to be going fishing again back north with four of my all-time best friends. I could not wait to finish my first year at the university, which was a complete farce. The realization of another trip up north was a bright ending to a dismal school year.

We all decided that our departure would come early Saturday morning instead of Friday morning. First and foremost was the task of getting to Milbank for more precious cargo. Realizing that we didn't have Leo's heavy foot and Rick would be watching his speed closely, our departure time was based upon making it to Milbank by nine in the morning. Would the bars be open?

Discretion upon entering Minnesota was on Rick's mind the whole trip. It was a great responsibility he was taking on in driving his Father's pickup, with all of us being underage in Minnesota, and toting the cargo that would get us all busted. We were pushing Murphy's law. However, as a group, we didn't dwell on consequences. We could deal with whatever God threw at us if we could only keep our health and keep ourselves safe. We were to meet at Leonard's farm at 5:00 a.m. sharp on Saturday, May 18, 1968.

CHAPTER 2

Heading North—May 18, 1968

When I arrived at Leonard's farm Saturday morning, the canopy was complete. An old canvas was draped over the top and extended down the left and right sides, secured to a two-by-four frame with lattice boards. It looked like it just might work. Into the bed we loaded all our gear. We made a small accessible area where those in the back could sit. Every conceivable space was used. Looking at all the crap we had in the back of that pickup, we wondered how we'd ever managed in Leo's car. True to form, none of us took a picture of the contraption. Why didn't we take more pictures?

Michael and I drew short straws for our first rotation. Doug and Jim rode up front with Rick. Springtime in Nebraska can have chilly mornings. Michael and I bundled up in our heavy coats and stocking caps and climbed aboard. We were ready to go. It is a good thing I brought my heavy coat. The guys used to call me Nanook of the North in that thing. It was old, heavy, and had a fur-lined hood. I hated to be cold. My limitations regarding my endurance of chilly weather often fueled a good ribbing. The time had come to face another great adventure.

Riding in the back of the bed was noisy, dusty, bumpy, and cold. The canopy did keep out a considerable amount of wind, but for the first five miles of gravel road, a draft of dust blew through the opening at the rear. I remember telling myself, "Could this get any worse?" I was about to find out.

Fremont was about thirty miles from Leonard's farm, and the canopy lasted thirty miles. As Rick picked up speed down the highway, Mike and I noticed the canvas whipping about, making a loud flapping noise that got worse with every mile. Soon we noticed a small tear develop on one of the sides. That allowed a stream of wind to get in and compromise the integrity of the whole unit. That small tear started ripping down the length of the canvas, and before long one whole side was flapping in the wind. Then the top came loose, and Rick had to stop. We were thirty miles out, just north of Fremont. Jim and Rick's first engineering project was a bust! *Those two will make great engineers!* I thought.

It took us a good hour to remove the tarp and disassemble the frame. Into the bed the wood went, along with what remained of the tarp. We decided that if it did rain or got too windy, we could use the tarp for some protective covering. Michael and I crawled back into our space. With our backs up against the cab, we prepared ourselves for the long trip ahead.

There is nothing like watching the world whiz by backward. If I concentrated on it too much, I got dizzy from the sensation of staring directly ahead from where we sat and seeing everything whizzing by in the wrong direction. It was a nauseating sensation that caused a little uneasiness in my stomach. Periodically I had to either take my eyes off the retreating road or look down at something relative to stop the dizziness. I was experiencing motion sickness from being disoriented most of the time. Eventually I got used to the retreating world around me and the ride became more tolerable. None of us ever complained about being dizzy and just learned to live with it.

The best entertainment for us was the cars that approached the truck from behind, wanting to pass. It was not unusual to get smiles or waves from the occupants as we stared back at them. Rick was not pushing it hard. He had too much at stake to get throttle-happy. Leo would never have survived. Eventually we made it to Sioux City. From there it was north to Milbank in search of the precious cargo.

We wondered how the boys in the cab were making out. Lucky guys! Our rotation had to be approaching. We needed to fill up every 150 miles or so. Sure enough, Rick pulled over at a gas station north of Sioux City, Iowa. It was good to get out and stretch and take a piss. A check with the clock indicated we were making horrible time. It was already 9:00 a.m., our estimated time for arrival at Milbank. We still had another two hundred miles to go. It would take us another three hours to get to Milbank.

Not much had changed in the landscape. The trip from Sioux City to Milbank was as boring as it had been the year before. We saw nothing but the flat, gentle rolling hills of farm fields, void of trees. Around noon we pulled into Milbank, South Dakota. We were a good three hours behind schedule.

After we filled up with gas, the next order of business was to find a bar. As it turned out, it was the same bar that Rick and Leo had used last year. Three cases of beer ended up in the back of the pickup, wrapped in our tarp. There went our security blanket if the weather turned nasty. At least I didn't have to cradle it like the year prior.

The day was overcast. I found myself watching the sky and wondering whether at any minute the heavens would open and drench us, but we were lucky—no rain! It was cold in the back of the pickup, and I was glad to be wearing my heavy Nanook coat. We were heading north and having a memorable time. Over the years, getting to our destination was an adventure, and this trip was no exception.

Before long, we were in Wadena, where Rick stopped to fill up. We were just forty miles from Park Rapids. Michael and I rotated into the cab all the way to the resort, which was another twenty miles north of Park Rapids. We pulled into Home Bay around 5:00 p.m. Lou and Betty met us almost immediately with big grins and a big welcome back. They didn't realize all five of us were coming in a pickup. We had some good laughs while explaining our trip. We introduced them to Uncle Mike and then made our way to cabin 5. Lou took us out to the two boats we had rented and made sure the motors would run. One pull and they fired right up. Both were 5.5-horsepower Johnsons. No more green boats. This year Lou gave us fourteen-foot aluminum boats painted in traditional Lund detail.

I looked out over the water of beautiful Lower Bottle Lake. I am not sure how many flashback memories I experienced in just that one moment, most notably that of the five of us in one boat on the first night during the previous year. The lake had taken on a distinctive look. I could not put a finger on it just yet as to why, but it looked different. We were all excited to get unpacked and get settled in.

CHAPTER 3

Fishing the Bottle Lakes in the Spring

W̲e had learned a lot about fishing the Bottle Lakes the previous summer. We were no experts, but we did manage to retain some knowledge about the lake. We had our favorite spots that had provided us with some degree of success. We knew how to fish the weeds and how we could check our depth. We didn't forget about the northern harness's that would sentence an unfortunate chub to certain death. We knew about the shallow peninsula that guarded Home Bay. We were anxious to fish this beautiful lake once again. The year prior it took us until Thursday to land our first northern. We were hopeful it would not take that long this year.

By the spring of 1968, I had finally learned how to swim. It was the only significant accomplishment I had achieved during my first year at UNL. Consequently, getting into a boat was not as intimidating for me as it used to be. By the time we all got settled, we had just a couple of hours of daylight left. We decided to get on the water and wet the lines.

The very first thing we noticed different from last year was the lack of weeds. While leaving the dock, we could see weeds, but they were not as prominent as I remembered; in some places, they were almost nonexistent. We had learned to depend on the weeds for our depth control. I now wondered how this would affect our fishing. We took to the lake that evening with the only thing we knew how to do. We all pulled out our northern rigs. We were confident we could get some hits using those infernal gadgets. Lou provided us with a dozen chubs, and we split them between the two boats. It was nice having two boats; that meant no lottery or dividing up boat time. I wished we had done that the year before.

It was cold out on the water, but it felt wonderful to be back fishing the Bottle Lakes. The trees lacked late summer color. They were in full green foliage, mixed in among the tall pines. We trolled back and forth in front of Home Bay with minimal effort. We didn't experience any trouble tacking in and out to maintain our depth. We quickly realized that the lack of weeds was the reason. Last summer the weeds were so thick we could not help getting mixed up in them.

We trolled back and forth until the lack of sleep took control of us all. Back to the cabins we went for a much-needed night of rest. Doug and I drew the same straw. Rick was on the couch. Mike and Jim took the other bed. We all slept well that night. The day's time on the road had taken a toll on us.

I thought surely we might sleep in. How silly a thought that was! No sleep in the mornings was to be had for me; the Musilek clan made sure of that. Now another cousin had joined us. Michael was just as bad as all the rest of them. The whole bunch simply didn't sleep. I was starting to wonder if Doug had some Musilek blood in him. He, too, was up at the first stir of the clan. It was a big mistake putting Rick on the couch. He was like an early alarm clock set on automatic.

Excitement was running rampant that first morning. Our number-one priority was running into Park Rapids for groceries. Three of the guys went into town. I just remember I was not one of them. We didn't change much from the previous year regarding meals. Breakfast and some sort of weight-loss dinner would work out fine.

The weather during that spring was unpredictable. Sunday was a beautiful, calm day full of sun, but that was to change as the week went on. We experienced all sorts of different weather conditions that week. Storms, cold temperatures, some warm days and some windy days were all mixed in with periodic times of agreeable pleasantness. The weather followed no pattern and remained unsettled.

Our first outing on Sunday was to destination Pork Barrel. While riding out to the Pork Barrel, I finally realized why the lake looked so different to me. There was a noticeable deficiency of reeds. The only reeds visible were those that had managed to make it through the winter without being compressed down into the water by the ice. The new growth had not yet peeked above the water. The whole south shore lacked thick reed lines. The lack of reeds had changed the whole dynamic of the lake.

As we approached the Pork Barrel, I could see something was amiss. There were warning signs all around the area. It was closed to fishing. The Pork Barrel had been designated a bass spawning area. We were not allowed to get into the area. There went one of our best spots. That was a blow to us. We had all looked forward to fishing the Pork Barrel once again. We decided to try the spot where Jim had landed his large northern the year before. Both boats decided to stick together, at least for now.

Nothing had changed in our trolling technique except that we made sure we were going slow and trolling backward. Our first day out resembled our first day out the year before. We caught nothing. The year before, we had absolutely no idea what we were doing. What could possibly be our excuse this year?

Over the course of the week, the northern fishing never did pick up. We caught nothing big. We picked up one here and one there, but nothing that resembled the feeding frenzy we had experienced the previous year on the last two days of our trip.

The lack of northern activity certainly was not the case with walleyes. The walleye bite was on and was sustainable throughout the week. Maybe spring was the season for walleyes and late summer was the season for northerns. We fished the Narrows often, throwing out the jigs Lou had sold us the year prior tipped with a minnow. We had a lot of fun catching walleyes in that manner. We noticed right away the absence of the crawdads that had plagued us the year before—another noticeable difference between the two seasons.

CHAPTER 4

The Lindy Spinning Rig

Early in the week, Lou approached us about using a different kind of rig for walleyes. It was called a Lindy–Little Joe spinning rig. The packet included a number-two long-shanked hook connected to a very heavy thirty-pound-test leader that was about thirty-six inches long. Just above the hook ran about six red beads. Above the beads ran a gold spinner blade. Also included in the packet was a half-ounce Lindy slip weight that was designed to run on the bottom. A snap and swivel were needed to connect the fisherman's line with the loop on the end of the spinning rig. The fisherman's line was first threaded through the hole in the slip sinker, then the snap and swivel, and finally the rig itself.

The rig was set up for slow trolling like the northern harness but without the sadistic wire. The idea behind this rig was to hook a minnow in the lips and lower the whole thing into the water so that the weight would ride on the bottom of the lake. The minnow and spinning blade would ride only a few inches above the bottom. This type of rig cannot be used with a weedy bottom, as just a small blade of grass or weed will hamper the spinning of the blade. The slip weight should bounce along the bottom. They were perfect for fishing gradually sloped bars.

Lou told us of such a bar just between the shallow peninsula and Home Bay camp. He said we should fish that during the middle of the day. We were game to try anything and to learn some new techniques. It is interesting that we didn't know about the bar from the previous year.

Through trial and error, we set up some reference points using boat docks and land waypoints that helped us outline the bar. Eventually the shape of the bar revealed itself.

It was fun to try something different: throw the line out, let it settle to the bottom, start a slow troll, let out enough line to keep the weight riding on the bottom, and hold on. The hit was hard and would yank the rod out of our hands if we were not careful. The action was continuous at times. We missed plenty of hits simply because we were not ready for them or the hit was short. Back and forth we trolled, up and down the bar. At the time, we were not sure how deep we were fishing. If I had to make a guess, it was between five and fifteen feet. We had no depth finder and relied primarily on our reference points, how much line we let out, and the angle the line made with the water.

I caught my first large walleye off that bar one afternoon. I was using the Little Joe tipped with a shiner minnow. Doug was running the boat. I was using my new Johnson Century reel I had bought from Lou last year. Suddenly I felt a hard tap and then a subsequent weight pulling on my rod. I let the rod tip move forward as far as I could and reared back to set the hook. There was no give in the line, and it felt as if I set the hook into a tree stump. "Fish on!" I yelled. This fish fought like a large carp; all I could feel was a steady pull and some strong slow and deep runs. I could feel his strong tail thrashing below. Once he saw the boat and the net, down he went for another run. When I got my first glimpse of him, he looked impressive in the water. When his eyes met the sunlight, they turned into a couple of glittering diamonds. Eventually he tired out and we managed to get him into the net and on board the boat. This was my first ever large walleye. Back at Home Bay, Lou weighed him at just over five pounds and just over twenty-five inches. During that week, we caught plenty of walleyes using the Little Joes. They seemed to run bigger than the ones we were getting in the Narrows. It was exciting for us to finally boat some decent-sized walleyes.

CHAPTER 5

A Brush with Disaster

Most people have a brush with disaster or experience some near-miss situation in their lifetime. Sometimes events like those turn tragic and the people involved do not survive. Those that do survive walk away incredibly lucky. Most dangerous situations develop suddenly and without notice, such as a car pulling out in front of you or a deer suddenly running across the road. We cannot control the outcome. We either survive it or we do not. Mother Nature can throw us into some of the most hair-raising experiences. Sometimes Mother Nature will give us some notice or visual alarm that a dangerous situation could develop. It is up to us to interpret her subtle warning.

One afternoon in 1968, the weather around the Bottle Lakes was unsettled. The morning was sunny and then turned partly cloudy at early noon. Big, puffy clouds started filling the sky; these were what I would call "Minnesota clouds." To this day, I believe this area of the country can display the most beautiful clouds. The clouds that afternoon were every bit Minnesota clouds. The wind was breezy coming out of the west. However, since Home Bay Resort sits on the western side of the lake, the water remained calm in the bay area.

The afternoon started off promising. It appeared we were in for an enjoyable day. Mother Nature was having none of it and decided to play some games with her unsuspecting victims. The recipients of her shenanigans that day were none other than Mike, Doug, and Jim, who were innocent bystanders that got wrapped up in her reckless and malicious behavior.

Jim, Michael, and Doug decided to head out to one of our favorite northern trolling areas just outside the Pork Barrel. The problem with that area was that it took forever to get there using the 5.5-horsepower motors. Rick and I stayed back for whatever reason.

A couple of hours later, the wind kicked up—a gentle reminder of the unsettled weather pattern we were in. Initially it was just a small blowing, but it was strong enough to get our attention. Suddenly we noticed the wind had shifted to the east and was getting stronger. The waves started pounding Home Bay's shoreline. The sky had clouded up but was void of any serious storm clouds. Soon the lake had turned into a raging mass of white-capped waves. This was a scary sight for us, as it was the first time we had seen the Bottle Lakes turn dangerous.

Our thoughts right away were with the guys out on the lake. We walked out onto the beach and set our sights east, hoping for some sign of where they might be. It didn't take long before Lou was right next to us with his binoculars, wondering where they were. As a resort owner, a storm like that was one of Lou's worst nightmares. Lou told us those small boats would not survive lake waves of the kind that were crashing into the beach. He was hoping the others would just stay put and wait out the storm for whatever the length of time that would be. The waves were relentless, pounding up against the shore and rocking the docked boats to the point of snapping their mooring lines.

The straight-line winds continued. Lou continued to scan the lake, looking noticeably concerned. Rick and I were discussing their situation and, like Lou, were hoping they would just wait it out and not even consider trying to make it in. But we were wrong. They did try! Lou spotted them just on the other side of the peninsula, engulfed in the waves. Lou said they were going to try to crash through what reeds there were that covered much of the shallow peninsula. The reeds would act like a buffer for the waves. It would be a smart decision if they could make it into the reeds before they capsized. They would have never made it around the peninsula, where the waves were a good four to five feet high. There they would have capsized for sure.

Lou watched them claw their way through the reeds using the oars in the boat. Eventually we saw them appear from the Home Bay side of the reeds. Once clear, they hugged the shallow shore that led right to Home Bay's beach. They were safe. If ever a sigh of relief engrossed a person's face, it did so with Lou's that day the minute the boat touched the beach. Once we had secured the boat on the beach, we retreated into the privacy of the cabin, where Rick and I wanted to know the rest of the story.

Inside the cabin, we all sat down with a beer in hand. Rick and I listened to their story. Michael started out: "When we left the dock, we headed straight for the Pork Barrel. When we arrived, the weather was good. Suddenly the temperature fell just enough to notice. We realized the breeze was getting stronger." This was their chance to get out of Dodge, but they stayed for one more troll. That last troll cost them about twenty precious minutes—about the same amount of time necessary to get back across the lake and safely back to Home Bay.

By the time they got done with that troll, the wind had reached gale force and the waves on the western end of the lake were white capped and growing. Michael continued: "We realized very quickly that we screwed up. We never thought about staying on the east end and waiting it out." Tucking themselves back into the Pork Barrel would have protected them from the easterly winds, which by now were straight-line winds blowing toward the west.

Doug was manning the motor, which was not much of a motor to help deal with whitecaps. Jim was at the bow and described his ride by saying he saw land and then suddenly saw only the top of the wave in front of him. The only thing that saved them was the wind direction. It was blowing straight into Home Bay, which was directly west of their location. Anything broadside would have capsized their little boat.

The decision that saved their lives was going for the reeds. Michael described the exact moment: "We were riding the waves as best we could. I could see that we were heading straight for the thicker reeds on the northeast side of the peninsula. Doug asked me what we should do, as he also noticed the reeds fast approaching. Doug shouted, 'Should we try to make it across to the south?' I told him, 'Steer as best you can right into the reeds. There is no way we are going to make it around the peninsula or across the shallow bar.'" Michael was right. Trying to steer to the south and make it around would have been suicide. They didn't realize the waves across that bar were every bit of four to five feet. Rick and I could see the immense waves from the beach back at Home Bay. They would not have lasted ten seconds on the bar.

Jim said that as they approached the reeds, he could see the waves getting buffered or cushioned. The danger they faced was hitting the reeds and coming to a complete standstill. If that had been the outcome, the waves would have drenched them from behind. Doug realized the danger of coming to a complete stop. He said, "I pointed the bow into a small opening in the reeds and tried to keep the boat moving forward until we were well inside the confines of the reed beds." Jim continued: "Once inside the reeds, the waves were still a threat. We could not allow ourselves to get broadsided. Otherwise we risked getting overcome with water." Jim and Mike were manning the oars. Doug had his hands full dealing with the motor. He told us, "Slowly we made our way through the reeds. I had to lift the motor up and keep it tilted and latched just to get us moving forward in the shallow water." The shallow draft of the boat would have caused them to capsize on the bar. Now it allowed them to maneuver through the reeds.

The deeper they got into the reeds, the calmer the situation was. Jim, manning one of the oars and still trying to keep his balance at the front of the boat, could see the other side of the reeds. He told us, "There were still plenty of waves to deal with." Once through the reeds, Michael told Doug, "Run us onto the beach!" And that is exactly what Doug did. Trying to dock in that wind would have been extremely dangerous.

Rick and I ran out to meet them and help them with the boat. We pulled the boat up onto the beach far enough to escape the pounding waves, which were still crashing onto shore. Jim, Doug, and Mike stared out toward the shallow bar on the peninsula and realized right then that they had made the right decision. The waves were still moving over the bar with great speed and intensity.

We all still talk about that day, remembering it fifty years later. Michael still regrets their decision to stay for one more troll. Doug still shakes his head. Spitting into Mother Nature's face can have dire consequences. Mother Nature had a sense of humor that day. Luckily they survived to tell the story. Since we began coming to the Bottle Lakes fishing, I do not recall another time when we experienced winds that strong. They were all incredibly lucky.

CHAPTER 6

Lake Emma

Now that we were old veterans fishing Lower Bottle Lake, Rick, Jim, and I decided to go out exploring other areas of the lake that we had only glanced at. One such area was located on the south shore. There is a large water drainage system in the upper central part of Minnesota called the Mantrap Valley Watershed. One drainage area of this watershed forms the Mantrap chain of lakes. It is a continuous flow of water from one lake to another via a small river system called the Mantrap River. The first lake in the chain is called Big Mantrap; many inlets feed into the large lake. The water coming into Upper Bottle and then into Lower Bottle Lake flows out of Big Mantrap Lake via the Mantrap River. Since the water coming into the lake was constant, it stood to reason it had to be leaving the lake somewhere. That location was in Lower Bottle Lake, on the south shore.

The south shore of Lower Bottle Lake is a vast shallow bar filled with reeds. Just to the north of the south shore exists the deepest depths of the Bottle Lakes. Years into the future, when we started using depth finders, we found an area not far from the reeds on the south shore that was 110 feet deep. In the late summer and into fall, the south shore is almost impenetrable because of dense reed lines. However, in the spring, most of the reeds were matted down by winter ice and snow, revealing a small passage through which a small boat could navigate. We could not resist the temptation to try to see what was on the other end of this vast shallow watery area.

We entered the small passage and followed it onto a shallow bar. At times, the water depth forced Rick to raise the motor. Jim and I also had the oars out just in case. We found out that if Rick stayed within the confines of the narrow passage, our small boat had a chance of getting through.

Slowly we made our way through the passage. Deep into the shallow bay, we came across a large area that resembled a small lake. As we made our way through this part of the bar, we could see the bottom full of weed beds and shallow reeds. We could see baitfish of all sizes darting in and out of the protection of the weeds. Occasionally we could see small perch swimming close to the beds. I suspected that by the fall these weed beds would be formidable obstacles to navigate.

As we circled the small body of open water, we came across what had to be an exit stream of water from the bar. Rick guided the boat into this small stream, which picked up speed as we navigated farther out of the confines of the small lake. Soon we were negotiating the boat down another narrow corridor where we didn't need the motor to move forward.

We had entered the Mantrap River, which connects Lower Bottle with the next lake in the chain. The small stream was running just fast enough to carry us down through a narrow winding passage filled with reeds and dead timber on the banks. Rick used the rudder of the motor to keep us straight as best he could. Jim and I used the oars to prevent the bow of the boat from running into the bank. Onward we went, not knowing what was ahead. Would we run into another lake? Most importantly, how far would we have to go before we would get to another lake?

The landscape was full of young and old trees that were overgrown in dense bushes and surrounded by the foliage of vines and tangled vegetation. It would have been impossible to walk through any part of this mangled array of obstacles. It was beautiful to look at, but that was it. I was glad to be in the boat.

Eventually the speed of the water diminished to such a degree that Rick needed to start up the motor. The passage got wider, and around the next bend we entered another lake system. The bottom structure disappeared into clear, deep water as we moved away from the lake shore and the confines of the Mantrap River channel. What a neat little lake! We could see the shoreline all around. It was not a large lake—no more than one hundred acres. We decided to take a slow tour around the perimeter.

The shore was filled with reeds and weed beds. The lake resembled a bowl with large hills on the north and east shorelines. There were large beds of water lilies along the north shore that were already in bloom. Other than one old cabin set back into the landscape on the western shore, there was not a house to be seen. I wished we had brought our fishing tackle.

As we slowly made our way along the south shore, we came across a large culvert with an opening just large enough to let through a small boat. Water from the small lake was running through the culvert and out the other side, where we could see another lake. We decided to try to navigate through the culvert. Again Rick had to tilt the motor. Jim and I used the oars to push us along. Once we came out the other side, a large lake came into view. This lake was impressive. It was much larger than the Bottle Lakes, as we could not make out the shoreline on the opposite end.

We decided this lake was not to be challenged with small boats, so we decided to head back to the confines of the smaller lake. It was not an easy task. The small stream had some power behind it. Using the oars, Jim and I struggled to make headway against the current. Eventually we made it through the culvert to where Rick could finally put the motor down.

It was time to head back to the Bottle Lakes. There was some question in our minds as to whether getting back was even possible. If the current going back to the Bottle Lakes was as strong as it was going through the culvert, we had a strenuous adventure ahead of us. We began to think this was not such a clever idea after all.

We continued our perimeter cruise around the lake until we found the entrance to the river channel back to the Bottle Lakes. While coming downstream, we had not paid attention to the speed of the channel except to note that the going was easy. Now, heading upstream, we were facing a small, fast-moving current meandering its way among the reeds, bushes, and small birch trees.

Rick pointed the bow into the narrow passage. Jim and I had the oars out, ready for duty. Right away Rick had to tilt the motor just to make it over some of the shallow parts. It was not easy for him to keep the boat straight, especially with the motor tilted. When we got too close to the shore, either Jim or I would give a push with the oar to keep us in the middle of the channel. None of us could let our guard down. One ill-advised maneuver and we would end up broadside to the stream, which could lend itself to upending the boat.

It didn't take long to get the hang of things. Up the stream we went, maneuvering ourselves ever closer to the small, shallow lake and bar that would lead us back into Lower Bottle Lake. It felt like a home coming after a trip from a great adventure. Once we escaped the confines of the shallow bar, Rick dropped the motor, and it was full throttle back to Home Bay camp.

Back at Home Bay, we went to see Lou's large map of Hubbard County hanging in his office. It had all the lakes on it. The small lake was called Lake Emma. The large lake was called Big Sand Lake. Some years later, we found out Big Sand was the main fishery for walleyes in the Mantrap chain. In fact, every spring the DNR traps large females in Big Sand to harvest their eggs. Some of the big females try to run up the Mantrap River and enter the Bottle Lakes to spawn, contributing to the natural reproduction of walleyes. Our Lake Emma adventure was over, but we vowed to revisit that area once again if ever we returned for another trip up north.

CHAPTER 7

Reflections on Spring Fishing on Bottle Lakes

As the week went by, I had the feeling that Lou was more comfortable with us. I never felt that he was watching us the way I know he had the previous year. Apart from the scare we put into him during the windstorm, we really didn't have much interaction with Lou during this trip. We still had to check in all our fish, and he continued to keep a log of everything we caught. He continued to call us "Uncle," and his charisma made all of us feel quite at home. He always carried a smile and was always willing to help us out.

Lou still managed to head out to the Narrows for some evening walleye fishing. We never saw him fish for northerns. Even though Lou loved northerns, he would fish for walleyes. I suspect he enjoyed eating walleye better than northern. However, his love for the great northern pike was reflected in his rearing pond. He was committed to supporting the northern pike in the Bottle Lakes system because he knew people would come back after experiencing the fight of this great fish. The rearing pond was Lou's contribution to the great northern pike fishery associated with the Mantrap chain of lakes.

Bullheads were nonexistent in the spring. We tried beaching the boats as we did the year prior but experienced not one hit. It was a disappointment. The same was true with the perch in the weed beds. We had to work for all we got.

Not being able to fish the Pork Barrel was most disappointing. It had been our go-to spot. There were plenty of other areas to fish, but this location had been productive for us in the past, and we simply didn't have the time to explore new locations.

Our meals were limited once again. Normally for breakfast we would have toast or cereal with coffee or milk. Usually we ate no lunch. Evening supper was either SpaghettiOs, hot dogs, soup, or pork and beans, and a beer. We did eat fish one night, which was the highlight of our meals. My weight dropped another ten pounds.

In the spring of 1968, we left Home Bay camp early Saturday morning. Our rotation for the back of the truck bed had not changed. Michael and I once again drew the short straws. Early Saturday morning, Lou and Betty were out to see us leave and wished us safe passage. We didn't have the abundant packages of fish this year like we had the previous year. A small package of dry ice was enough.

Our trip home was uneventful. Once again, we took no pictures, so we have only faint memories. We all embarked on our own ways when we arrived back at Leonard's farm. I would see Doug and Jim often during the summer of 1968, as we all landed summer jobs in a trailer house factory close to our home in Prague. I continued to stay in contact with Rick and Mike over the weekends.

I left Park Rapids with a heavy heart. I didn't know if we would be coming back. For many of the upcoming unsettled years, planning for the next year's fishing trip did not take place. When the time came, we simply decided to go or not to go depending on our own personal situations.

CHAPTER 8

Week of August 17, 1969, at the Bottle Lakes

During the fall and winter of 1968, I found myself spending more weekends on campus. Rick and Jim lived in the same dorm, so I got to see them often. However, I saw little of Michael and Doug. This school thing hung over my head, and I hated it. I found myself struggling with my justification for changing my major to music. I didn't realize the mistake I had made until much later, when it became too late to back out, but I gave it my best at the time.

Sometime during the summer of 1969, fishing in Minnesota suddenly became a hot topic. Rick had a car that he was willing to take, so we had no issue with transportation. It was just a matter of deciding who could go on short notice. Michael could not. He had already moved past spring and was entering his junior year playing football; his team at Doane College would continue to rack up win after win. Jim was in, and so was Doug. As for me, I was anxious to get back for another week's fishing. Rick had called Home Bay and reserved us a one-week stay.

We departed Prague the third week of August. We were down to four: Rick, Doug, Jim, and me. We decided to rent two boats again that year. Two boats just seemed to work better. The last two years had taught us a great deal about fishing Bottle Lake. We were anxious to get back in the late summer once again, when the weed beds were abundant; we knew how to fish them.

The momentous change that year regarded our precious cargo. Rick was now twenty-one and could buy what we wanted in Park Rapids. This was a refreshing alteration from the last two years. We didn't have to travel out of our way to Milbank, South Dakota, just because we were underage. We could now go through Sioux City and head directly into Minnesota without fear of the law. That knocked a good two hours off of our travel time. The drive through Minnesota and northwest Iowa was pleasant. The scenery was much more interesting than the boring landscape of South Dakota. We arrived in Park Rapids midafternoon, took care of cargo business, and headed for the resort.

It is hard to describe in words the emotional sensation I got as we approached the entrance to Home Bay Resort. I knew that for one week my little world would transform itself into something magical. Seeing the beautiful Bottle Lakes once again made me wish I were living there permanently, but those thoughts were only fleeting, as the real world back home awaited us soon enough.

It did make me wonder just how much those who did live in this region really appreciated it. It was truly a gift of God to be there. How fortunate we all were to take part in an activity that would bring us together once again and to enjoy something we were all fond of. This week I could dream all I wanted and, for a brief period, live in paradise with my friends with only the weather to dictate our daily activity.

Lou and Betty were once again there to greet us. Lou popped out of his office smoothly and confidently. Betty was wearing a big smile, as always, from ear to ear. Lou's and Betty's demeanors would make anyone welcome. The resort was bustling, as all the cabins were rented out. The docks were lined with boats. Once again Lou had placed us into cabin number 5. Nobody needed to sleep on the couch. Lou always mentioned his rearing pond. He told us the northerns that year were as ferocious a bunch as he'd ever had. He was so proud of his relationship with the DNR and his rearing pond.

Lou gave us a little fishing report. There were jumbo perch in the deep weed beds, there were walleyes in the Narrows as always, and northern pike were hitting chubs or spinners. He also mentioned bass, which was the first time we'd heard anything about them. One old timer in the resort went after only bass. He would fish with a bobber and use frogs for bait right up against the reeds. He fished only early in the morning or late in the evening. He would approach the reeds quietly to within casting distance and then pitch a small green frog that was hooked shallow through one of the back legs. He would slowly move himself along the reed line using his oars. Fishing like that required the lake to be flat and still. If there was wind, the old timer just sat in his cabin and waited for a change. Lou thought we should have a go at some bass.

CHAPTER 9

Hornets

We didn't change our fishing methods at all during 1969. We still-fished the weed beds, and we trolled with the wire harnesses for northerns. The Pork Barrel was open to us in the late summer, so we took full advantage of that. It was good to get back into the Pork Barrel once again since it had been closed to fishing the previous spring. Fishing the Little Joe spinners was troublesome for us in the fall. The weed beds were in full growth, and just a sliver of vegetation on the spinner would render it useless. In 1969, our walleye fishing was reserved for the Narrows.

Our fishing techniques were improving. We were getting better at hook sets and gauging our water depth. We were getting better at trolling and reading the wind as well. We got to know the lake and not just go blindly into an area and start fishing. We were targeting locations that always produced fish and locations where we had gotten at least a hit or two in the past years. In that manner, we had no trouble catching our share of northerns and panfish. Lou's motors always ran well for us. That is one favorable judgment I had about Lou's resort: everything seemed to work for us.

One afternoon we decided to take both boats to the east shore and fish the Pork Barrel. This little gem of a lake was full of cabbage weed, underwater weed beds, and water lilies. Fish were plentiful, and we managed to catch our share of northerns out of that area. While we were making one of our trolling passes down the middle of the Pork Barrel, I noticed a For Sale sign nailed to one of the trees at water's edge. I thought nothing of it until I saw another and another. There were four or five For Sale signs nailed to trees all along the eastern shoreline of the Pork Barrel.

I yelled out at the other guys to notice the signs. This was the first indication we had seen that the lake was moving toward lakeshore development. We decided to dock the boats on the east shoreline and do some exploring. The last time we did this, we got into trouble with the bat. This time all we wanted to do was stretch our legs and check the area out.

The east shore of the Pork Barrel is hilly. We had to climb upward for some time before the land leveled out. Up on a little knoll, we turned around toward Lower Bottle Lake and witnessed the most beautiful picture. (See figure 6.) Nestled between birch and pine trees was the outline of the Pork Barrel and, beyond, Lower Bottle Lake. I remember having a brief thought of a cabin built right where we stood. That beautiful thought quickly left me when I heard Jim start yelling. He was pointing up into one of the nearby birch trees.

We all looked up toward where Jim was pointing, and we noticed a large mass of something, shaped like a pineapple, hanging from one of the stronger limbs of the tree. Jim knew right away what it was—a hornet's nest. It was at least the size of a five-gallon bucket, and by all indications, it appeared to be occupied. There was activity leading into and out of the lower part of the nest. Mischievous as we were, and before any one of us thought about the consequences, we each gathered a couple of rocks, which were abundant all along the hillside, and tried to hit the nest with them. Out of a dozen or so that we threw toward the nest, one of us finally hit it. That was a major mistake. In seconds the whole nest was swarming with hundreds of pissed-off hornets. Someone yelled, "Let's get the hell out of here!" As fast as we could, we ran down that hill back to our boats. Luckily they didn't follow us. It was a narrow escape for sure. We vowed not to tell Lou.

CHAPTER 10

Back to Lake Emma

During our weeklong stay, we decided to reserve one day for another adventure back to Lake Emma. In the spring of 1968, we had managed to find the fast-moving stream of the Mantrap River within the confines of the south shore bar. This time we brought our fishing gear, plenty of bait, a small lunch, and some drinks. Both boats made the trip to where we planned to make a day of it fishing Lake Emma.

I am not sure Lou would have approved of our little plan, but we headed out of Home Bay anxious for an exciting adventure. We set our course for the large, shallow bar on the south shore, where the waters of the Bottle Lakes retreat into the small river channel that empties into Lake Emma.

When we approached the entrance to the bar, we could not make out any definite path through the reeds. The reeds had engulfed the whole area except for one very narrow passage. This had to be our entrance.

Slowly, Rick and Jim, who were in the first boat, tried to navigate through a small opening where the reeds were thinned out. A guy could get lost in this maze of reeds and wild rice. Doug and I followed suit. Rick had to lift the motor just to keep the boat moving forward. I could see their small prop cutting through the reeds as it churned up soil and weeds just below the water line. Doug had to do the same thing. Sometimes we could hear the prop hitting small rocks and stones as we bulldozed our way through the small opening. We never once busted a prop, which would have led to multiple questions from Lou.

On we went. The Bottle Lakes disappeared behind us as we ventured farther along the small passage that led us into the maze of tall reeds. Rick was doing an excellent job of navigating a route without getting hung up. Doug and I followed right behind. Eventually we broke through into the small lake we had found back in the spring of 1968, where the water was deeper and protected by large patches of wild rice, reeds, and lily pads. What a change the summer growing season can make on these lakes. The shallow bays get transformed from matted-down weed beds to a gauntlet of reeds so thick one can walk on them.

We knew the general area where the water from the bay fed into the small Mantrap River. We maneuvered toward the southeast part of the small lake and found the entrance we were looking for. Rick and Jim pointed the bow of their boat into the small opening, sending them downstream. They quickly disappeared into the winding labyrinth of the Mantrap River. Doug and I followed and quickly realized we didn't need the motor but only had to use the rudder and let the fast-moving stream carry us onward.

The land area was amassed in dead timber and the tangled foliage of vines and bushes of all sizes. Only by using the waterway could a human being make passage through this vegetation. All Doug and I could see of Rick and Jim ahead were the upper parts of their bodies as they meandered down the stream. This was great fun for us, as we were headed into another great adventure and really were in no danger. The only threat we could face was getting in trouble by Lou.

Soon we were at the entrance to Lake Emma. The reeds and lily pads lined the shore in abundance. We could see the entrance to the big culvert that led to Big Sand Lake just on the other end. We put the minnows in the water, pulled out the wire harnesses, and started trolling for northerns.

The lake was shaped just like a big bowl. We found it easiest to follow each other around the bowl in one direction. We followed the same procedure regarding our depth control, keeping a lookout for weeds and adjusting our depth accordingly. After a few passes around the lake, we decided to check out the panfish. There were a few spots we took notice of, and we decided to anchor. We caught some nice bluegills, but the perch were about the same as we had been catching in the Bottle Lakes. There were some nice ones mixed in with many small ones that ended up as seagull food. Just as with the Bottle Lakes, the larger bluegills we caught were caught on small minnows. We managed to pick up a couple of northerns, but nothing big. And we found no crappies. Where were the damn crappies? We suspected they were deeper but had no way to find that depth. There had to be crappies in there, as it appeared to be a perfect little lake for them. Being unable to find crappies anywhere in the Bottle Lakes and now in Lake Emma was frustrating to us.

The day wore on, and we were ready to get back to Home Bay for supper and then head out to the Narrows for some walleye fishing. The trip back up the Mantrap River was exciting. I had the oar out, trying to keep us in the middle of the channel, as Doug had control of the motor. So far we had been lucky in this prop business, since explaining a busted prop to Lou could be challenging. In all the years we used Lou's boats, we never busted a prop or damaged a boat in any way. I guess we were lucky in that regard. Chugging along, we finally escaped the river channel and made our way back into the Bottle Lakes.

Our adventure to Lake Emma was over. For us it was the thrill of getting there and trying to make it back without incident that made it all worthwhile. Fishing Lake Emma was nothing special except that it was a different lake. We caught nothing big, and the action there was about the same as on the Bottle Lakes. The lake simply attracted our inquisitive nature. However, if we had found crappies in that lake, I suspect we would have made the trip daily.

The minute we made the turn into the entrance to Home Bay Resort on the previous Saturday, all my cares disappeared, and my thoughts and feelings were thrown into another world full of beauty and expectation. There were times when I wished I could exist forever in the world of Lou and Betty's resort life.

When Saturday arrived and we said our goodbyes to Lou and Betty, I always felt just a little sentimental. Just as the case had been during the previous two years, the feeling that this might be my last trip to this paradise was ever present. The quarter-mile drive to the exit of Home Bay was melancholy. Harsh reality awaited us all.

When we arrived back home, we divvied up the packaged fish and again went our own ways. I remember feeling a strange uneasiness after that trip—a feeling of separation. Rick was going into his senior year. Doug, I felt, was going to make some decision to move his life forward. Michael was going into his junior year at Doane playing football. Jim was going into his third year at UNL majoring in civil engineering. I also was entering my third year, but with no motivation. Why was I not motivated? I can only explain it as not understanding the reality of what I was trying to accomplish. I was having doubts about a music career. Was that really what I wanted to do for the rest of my life? I was getting mixed up. I tried my hardest that third year, not realizing that all along I was slowly falling into an out-of-control spiral for which there was no correction simply because I could not face the truth. The reality was that I had no business trying to be a music teacher.

CHAPTER 11

That Dreadful Winter of 1969

The escalation of the Vietnam War during 1968 and 1969 forced the realization that an all-volunteer armed forces, along with the inequities of the current draft system, could not bring the number of military personnel to the levels that were needed for the Vietnam War. The awful truth associated with the events that took place in the fall of 1969 is that Nixon, ten months before November 1969, promised to start the withdrawal of troops from Vietnam. By November of 1969, President Nixon had yet to start upholding his promise.

The unpopular war saw the number of young men willing to volunteer for the armed forces drop to alarming numbers. Many young men just out of high school sought the 2-S deferment. Thousands burned their draft cards illegally. Others sought legal sanctions, such as imprisonment. Others simply left the country, moving to Canada.

The Selective Service Act of 1967 prevented the president from altering or modifying the selection procedure for military service. College students were entitled to a 2-S status deferment but were subject to the draft if they dropped out or graduated. Consequently, colleges and universities all over the country were getting flooded with students wishing to enroll.

Congress and the president knew they needed to change something. On November 26, Congress abolished the provision that prevented the president from changing the selection procedure for military service, and immediately Nixon issued an executive order prescribing a process of random selection. The dreaded draft lottery would take place December 1, 1969.

In the fall of 1969, Jim, Rick, and I decided to rent a house together and share expenses. During the past two years, we had all been staying in dorms on campus. The price to stay in the dorms was going up, so we decided that sharing expenses would be cheaper. This was a suitable idea for Rick, as he had only one more year at UNL. However, the decision to stay in a house was not the right one for me. I was struggling with my own direction at the time and did not need the added distraction of the inevitable. Countless parties, meeting new people, and beguilement for attending classes ran my life. That is to say, this was the beginning of the end at UNL.

Everyone was talking about the lottery. Lottery parties were held everywhere. I can only imagine what was going on in the dorms. Such was the case in our own little rented house, where we planned a lottery party. The house was full of people. Friends and friends of friends were invited. As I thought about the lottery and what I would do if I received a low number, I made the decision I would enlist if the outcome was not favorable. At least then the decision would be made for me, since staying in school was no longer something I desired.

My number came up at 234. Michael's number was low. Rick's number was also low. Jim's number was high. Doug decided to enlist in the navy before the lottery was held.

Rick was distraught after his number came up. He knew at once that after he graduated the following spring, he would have to enlist to avoid getting drafted. When the summer of 1970 arrived, Rick enlisted in the army. Michael, after he graduated from Doane, got a medical deferment.

Jim's and my futures regarding military service were clear after December 1. With high numbers, if we maintained an undergraduate status in good standing, we had nothing to worry about. Even after graduation, the high numbers would keep us from getting drafted. The same would hold true if either one of us decided to quit school. Moving forward was easier, but my stay at the university was slowly coming to an end.

CHAPTER 12

Wayne and the Spring of 1970

My attitude toward continuation at UNL had tumbled to an all-time low. My grades in the School of Music were good—much better than I deserved because of my extremely poor attendance and practice habits. Practicing didn't occur for me, because I hated to practice. However, I still cranked out good grades. Music theory and ear training came extremely easy for me. What was becoming a noticeable barrier was individual performance. A constant awareness that I had major stage fright was seeping into my ability to perform. Nobody graduates from the School of Music without going through something called "individual senior recitals." They are mandatory, with no exception. The performance takes place in front of the whole student body enrolled in the School of Music. I simply had a tough time pushing forward while knowing that senior recitals were looming over my head, threatening my future.

In the spring of 1970, I met Wayne Urbanec. Wayne had become good friends with Jim through a lengthy list of friends Jim had from his high school days at Bishop Neumann High School in Wahoo. Wayne had attended many of our get-together house parties that winter, and I at first thought I had him pegged as a rowdy, happy-go-lucky type of guy. One thing was for sure, Wayne loved to party; and since that was a common occurrence for us during the first part of 1970, I saw him often and soon found out that he loved to fish.

Wayne always had a smile on, especially when he was shitfaced. He had a way about him that seemed to liven up a potentially dead party. Not only was he a happy partier, but he also had a sarcastic side to him that stirred the crowd into the next level, whatever that might be. One might say that at times, he was the life of the party.

Wayne had already bought a house in Raymond, Nebraska, where Wayne's family had their roots. This small town was located not ten miles north of Lincoln. Wayne had a dog he promptly named "Dog," an exceptionally beautiful and exceptionally large Great Dane. Wayne loved motorcycles. He always owned a Harley. Even when the Harley Davidson brand was on the way out, he still managed to own one.

Wayne was two years younger than Jim. The lottery of December 1, 1969, did not affect him. Only those born from January 1944 to December 1950 were exploited by the lottery. Wayne was safe from getting drafted that spring, and the thought of Minnesota fishing started to creep into our conversations with him.

In the spring of 1970, only Jim and I could expect to leave on another fishing trip. Michael, Rick, and Doug were all moving forward with their lives, so Jim and I recruited Wayne. It didn't take much talking for him to agree to come with us. He was in a position where he could make a spur-of- the-moment decision and not have anything holding him back. Jim contacted Lou in the spring of 1970, and the three of us booked a single-room cabin with one bed and one couch. It would be good enough.

None of us were looking at a yearly fishing trip to Minnesota as a tradition just yet. Our lives were still unpredictable, and our paths could change overnight. We were down to two. My future was soon to be up shit creek; however, at the time, I didn't realize it. I believe each one of us certainly was starting to carve out the idea of a tradition.

Our old nemesis came back to haunt us—transportation! Pathetically, I still didn't have a car. Wayne had nothing except his motorcycle. That left Jim. Jim's parents decided to let us have one of their cars. Our transportation problem was solved.

I was not that keen on going again in the spring, but we went when the chance presented itself, and this year it was the spring. We were heading north once again, and I was full of eagerness and enthusiasm. This year would be different in some notable ways. We had a different cabin, there would be only three of us, and we had only one boat. We also had a rookie with us who was eager to fish. Wayne fit right in.

Jim, Wayne, and I met around midnight in Prague. We drove all night and took a chance we could get into the resort early. For some reason, Lou obliged us, and Saturday morning we took residence in a one-room cabin that was tucked back into the trees for a one-week stay.

None of us minded the cramped quarters that were fit for one person or, at most, two. We ate the same food as on the previous trips. The view to the lake was disturbed by clump birch and pines, which was a little disappointing. We were given a nice fourteen-foot aluminum Lund fishing boat with the same 5.5-horsepower engine. Lou's rules didn't change. He logged everything and froze the fillets for us.

CHAPTER 13

Too Big to Imagine

O ne of my fondest memories of all my fishing trips to the Bottle Lakes happened in 1970 with Wayne and Jim. It seemed as though it happened yesterday simply because it made such a vivid impact on my imagination.

One evening, we were fishing for walleyes in the Narrows between Lower Bottle Lake and Upper Bottle Lake. The boat was anchored in shallow water—about four to five feet deep—but we had to cast only a short distance to be in deep water. We were using minnows on a bare hook with a weight. Once the bait hit the bottom, we would make a slow retrieve back to the boat. The walleyes were hitting on almost every cast, but they were small; "ten-to-twelve-inch cigars" was the general term. Sometimes we would land a larger walleye fit for the table, but for the most part they were small. We gave them each a scolding for trying to commit suicide and then released them back into the water to grow up. All three of us were catching small walleyes. It was fun, but we were looking for larger walleyes.

I felt a tug on my line that was reminiscent of many before that. Sure enough, I could feel the thrashing about of the small walleye on the end of my line. I said to Jim and Wayne, "Just another small one." About halfway to the boat, suddenly, without any notice, everything went solid. No more could I bring any line in. I thought to myself, *Did I get snagged?* I thought my reel had crapped out.

I pulled back on the rod, but it felt as if I were hooked to a tree. I'd had enough experience fishing in the river to know when I was snagged. This felt to be the issue for sure. However, slowly but surely, the bend in the rod took on a drastic change. I said, "Hey guys, check this out!" Whatever was on the end of my line was moving away. "I cannot stop it!" I yelled. Jim and Wayne stared at the unfolding scene. I had to constantly give out line; otherwise I risked it snapping. There was no fight, no sensation of any pissed-off fish, only a slow, steady pull away from the Narrows. This was no small walleye. This was no small fish.

My line was nearing its end. My Johnson Century reel didn't have much line capacity. We all quickly discussed my options, as we had never experienced anything like this before. Jim and Wayne decided we should up anchor and follow this guy and see what would happen. I was all for that, as my line capacity was all but out. Before we could get one anchor up, my line broke free. I didn't know if it had snapped or what had happened until I reeled in all my line only to find half of a walleye hooked to the end—one half of about a twelve-inch walleye! To this day I remember seeing only the head, which had been severed just behind the gill. *My God, what could have done that?* Lou often told us that if we wanted large northerns, we should fish in the Narrows with big bobbers and large chubs. We never did that. We didn't need to. All we needed were small thrashing walleyes. That fish got only part of its meal.

It could not have been fifteen minutes later when Jim yelled out that he was snagged. The same thing was happening to him. He needed to give out line or it would snap. Was it possible there were more than one of those monsters on the prowl, or had that same fish come back to get more? This time I could sit back and watch someone else experience the unimaginable. Jim was using his open-face reel. This reel had much more line capacity than my Johnson Century. The same scenario unfolded. There was no question about it; he was hooked into something noticeably big, just as I had been. The large fish had latched onto another small walleye that Jim was slowly bringing to the boat and then decided to head for the depths.

For some reason, during the fifteen minutes between the two hits, we decided that if this ever happened again, we would let the fish take some line out and then set the hook instead of pulling in the anchors to follow him. Jim had out a lot of line. He yelled that he was going to try to set the hook. Before he was able to get himself set, the line snapped. Back into the reel came the loose line with nothing on the end of it. Could that fish have been so big that it inhaled the whole walleye? We all believed it was.

We fished the Narrows often that week but never experienced another encounter with a fish at the top of the food chain. It would be decades before something like that happened to us again. Ironically, it would be Wayne's turn, during one afternoon of bluegill fishing, to come face-to-face with a fish too big to imagine.

When we got back to the resort, we told Lou about our experience. Lou told us those were "twenty-five to thirty-pound northerns." He continued, "No way to land them unless you have the equipment for it." Although I would have loved to see just a shadow of one of those two fish, it was left to my imagination what they must have looked like. It is scary to know such fish exist.

CHAPTER 14

The Little Varmints

One day during that week, we decided to plan another trip to Lake Emma. We had made the trip twice before, and it was always an exciting adventure for us. We packed a lunch and got plenty of bait from Lou: minnows, chubs, night crawlers, and some small leeches.

We had finally broken down and bought one of Lou's trolling-style minnow buckets. Since it would float, we could secure it to the side of the boat with a stringer or a length of dock line. We found out that the worst situation regarding this type of bucket was forgetting to pull it back into the boat before we went full-throttle ahead. Many times, we would be cruising wide open only to notice the minnow bucket bouncing along outside the boat, causing us to stop abruptly and pull the damn thing back in. Other than that, it was a wonderful addition to our equipment.

When we found the entrance to the small stream which was the Mantrap River, we embarked confidently. We knew what to expect from our other adventures down this small channel. Suddenly, halfway down the stream, in the middle of nowhere, we ran into a beaver dam. *Where did this thing come from? Last summer it was not here.* Those clever little varmints had managed to build a very impressive dam in just a few months. If we wanted to get to Lake Emma, we would have to find a way around this obstruction.

Before we slammed into the obstacle, we managed to secure ourselves up against the bank. The stream was moving at a good clip, and it took a bit of doing just to exit the boat. There we stood on the bank, which by our understanding was the only place the clever guys could have built this dam without letting the water spill out into the surrounding flatlands. For now we stood on solid ground. We secured the boat with a tow line and proceeded to investigate our situation.

The dam itself was no more than three feet from top to bottom, but that was enough to prevent us from going over it with the boat. We needed to clear away some debris to allow us to maneuver the boat over the dam without us in it. Portage would be impossible with the motor on the boat. We started to tear away at the confounded thing, removing sticks and logs as best we could until we were satisfied that we had removed enough material to allow us to guide the boat across without wrecking it. I don't believe we thought about the return trip. As for now, the beavers were tapping into our fishing time, and all we wanted to do was get into Lake Emma. If Lou had seen us, he would have kicked us out of the resort for sure.

Back to the boat we went to lift the motor and lock it in place. Then we let the stream take the small fourteen-foot Lund and send it over bow first. We placed ourselves standing on the banks to either side of the dam to help guide the boat. After a few bumps and some persuasive tugging, the bow hit the lower stream bed, and the stern followed without mishap. We climbed back into the boat and we were again on our way, navigating the fast-moving river until it emptied into Lake Emma. We spent the full day fishing that neat little lake.

Without any records, and being unable to remember an account of our luck that day, I can only assume the trip was not wasted because of a lack of fishing time on the water. We always fished long and hard no matter where we were fishing, and those manning the motor really did put in a long and tiring day, but the sheer beauty of these lakes can make the duty enjoyable, regardless of fishing success or lack of it.

In late afternoon, we decided to try and make it back to the Bottle Lakes. We entered the mouth of the Mantrap River and proceeded to motor our way up stream. It is amazing how much the stream can affect the directional control of the boat, especially when the motor is tilted upward just enough to allow the prop to propel us forward. Jim and I were on either side of the boat with oars in hand, trying to keep us in the center of the stream.

It was not long before we were facing the beaver dam. Wayne maneuvered the boat to the bank, where we all got out. He took control of the bow line and positioned himself on top of the dam while Jim and I stood on either side to help lift and guide the boat up the small waterslide that had developed over the course of the day by the fast-moving stream of water. It was not that bad. With some "heave-ho" by Wayne and some guidance and lifting from Jim and me, we managed to get the boat above the dam without much issue.

I can only imagine the little varmints staring from a distance, hidden in the dense bog wasteland, all pissed off at us for invading their property. But I suspect that by next morning's sunrise, the minor damage we did to the dam was all repaired by these engineering masters. We climbed into the boat, Wayne cranked up the engine, and we were off.

Before we knew it, we were in the center of the southern bay of the Bottle Lakes and were headed back to Home Bay. As an interesting side note to our stay that week, there was a noticeable lack of anyone meeting us at the dock. There were no dock stories to share with anyone. In past years, there had been at least a couple other guys that would meet us at the dock to share stories. That may seem a little nostalgic, but walking down the dock and having nobody to share your adventures with was not the same and seemed a bit melancholy.

That Friday, at the end of our stay, we decided to leave late in the evening. Lou checked the gas we had used, and we settled our bill. It was a cheap trip that year. The cabin was priced low, and we could split everything three ways. In the future, year after year, riding back and forth to Park Rapids at night became the norm. Those that made the trip would experience sleep deprivation, vehicle breakdowns, and, a few times, getting lost. The trip I took in 1970 with Wayne and Jim would be the last time I would fish the Bottle Lakes for many years to come.

CHAPTER 15

The Seventies

Regardless of my reasons for not making any more trips back to the Bottle Lakes in the seventies, it had absolutely nothing to do with personal feelings toward any of my friends. Looking back at my situation that I got myself into after 1970, it was all my doing, and accountability must rest with me. I simply had to straighten my life out, and by the end of 1971 I had quit UNL and was struggling to find myself. I went from job to job without direction. Finally, in 1972, I went back to UNL and talked to an advisor in the teacher's college to try to find out what I could get into that would take advantage of all the credit hours I had amassed during my years at UNL. We had put together a plan, but the road ahead would be long and all-encompassing. It would require long hours in the classroom and some sacrifices. I could no longer afford to be distracted even for a one-week fishing trip. From 1972 to May of 1978, all my efforts went to that end.

Sometimes a little luck doesn't hurt. I needed a little luck, and it came to me in the form of one individual who was just starting an industrial education course of study in drafting technology for the newly upstarted Lincoln Community College in Lincoln, Nebraska. The applicant would receive an associate degree in drafting technology from LCC and then transfer to UNL to finish the required hours for a BS degree. More luck: credit hours could be transferred to LCC from UNL to cover all the elective courses LCC needed. All I had to do was take drafting courses. Lots of them. I started at once.

I simply could not look back. As depressing as it was to me, I was eager to put my whole self into achieving some measure of accomplishment for my future and finally move my life forward. Thus began my quest to become a draftsman and, I hoped, a teacher of this discipline in the upcoming years.

During those trying years, Jim continued to go fishing up north on the Bottle Lakes, taking along whomever wanted to go. He didn't let anything hinder his determination to set aside at least one week per year to visit Lou and Betty at Home Bay. It was this firmness of purpose that gave birth to our ritual that continues to this day.

Jim abandoned any method of planning his yearly trips to Home Bay. Apart from making reservations, normally late in the season, most of the preparation occurred on the night of departure. He simply called everyone up and asked whether they wanted to go. Those that did would meet Friday night at the local bar in Prague, where transportation was canvassed for, and last-minute preparations were made for a midnight departure to Park Rapids. The most disheartening phone calls I ever received were from Jim, asking if I wanted to go fishing that year. Saying no year after year depressed me to the point at which I was embarrassed. Not being able to fish once again with my friends and experience all the camaraderie that went along with it was hard to face.

Eventually the phone calls stopped. We all had gone our own way to find ourselves. I succeeded in getting my BS degree in 1978 and landed a job with the Goodyear Tire and Rubber company, where I still work to this day. Jim started his own civil engineering business. Doug became a PA. Michael was working for the State of Nebraska. Wayne worked for the Burlington Northern Railroad. Rick was in Colorado, carving out a lucrative career as a software engineer. Jim, Mike, and Rick were all family-related, so they continued to stay connected. Mike stayed in contact with Doug through a mutual love of hunting. Wayne continued to go with Jim year after year, keeping the tradition alive. If it hadn't been for Jim and Wayne finding ways to continue our tradition, this story would have ended. Jim told me one time that he missed only one year out of the fifty. He could not remember which year that was. Wayne had missed only five.

On the year Jim missed, Wayne was able to put together a trip with a few of his friends, continuing the tradition.

The ritual Jim and Wayne started in 1970 continued every year since. On one special fall Friday evening, a few of Jim's and Wayne's friends would gather in Prague for the start of another grand adventure. The midnight strike of the clock called for their departure, which sent them once again heading north to Park Rapids and our beloved Bottle Lakes.

CHAPTER 16

The Grandest of All Phone Calls

I told myself when I started writing about our adventures on the Bottle Lakes that I would not bring into the story line any personal matters. I wanted to stay away from private lives and not introduce personal tragedy, personal accomplishments, or personal failures into the dialogue. We all had them, and nobody wanted to know about them. Some of us had gotten married and started families. Some of us had gotten into relationships destined to be lost. We all had our druthers. We all made sacrifices. We all became successful in our own ways. We all managed to be unscathed in health. And the best part of all is that we all managed to come back together once again in the latter part of the 1980s.

As for me, it was not until 1984 that I received the phone call of all phone calls. When I answered it, I swear my heart skipped a beat. It was Jim. My dear friend Jim had called me about a fishing trip in the upcoming fall. Jim's almost exact words were, "You need to come. It has been too long."

I screamed into the phone, "Yes, I'm coming!" I was so excited I could hardly control my emotions.

Jim told me he was planning a trip for two weeks in the coming fall. Wayne and some other friends were coming up for only the second week. I decided to join Jim the first week so he would not have to be there alone. It seemed we had talked forever before we ended the call. I agreed to drive, since Jim would be coming back with Wayne's crew the second week.

It was settled. I would meet Jim at Leonard's farm in Prague on Friday, September 19, 1984, around 11:00 p.m.

Friday, September 19, crept up on me quickly. I decided to take that day off to pack. That morning, I pulled out my fishing reels and got them in order. I changed line and made sure all two of them had no issues. I still had my Johnson Century that I had bought from Lou years ago, along with a casting rod and reel for bass. I had not fished out of a boat since my last trip to Home Bay in 1970. To say I was nervous, excited, and anxious would be an understatement.

Jim had told me to pack for chilly weather: insulated underwear, warm socks, heavy coat, and coveralls. I didn't have rain gear. I tore through my tackle box, trying to arrange everything in some meaningful order. In so doing, I managed to come across one of my old northern harnesses. A few memories started to fill my head as I ran my hands across the old wire and felt the rusted hook. I was sure things had changed over the years, and I hoped the use of those harnesses was one of them. I hated those rigs. I had paid a visit to Mom and Dad earlier that day to try to get some rest before it came time to head out to Leonard's farm that evening. I think I slept.

CHAPTER 17

Heading North Once Again

It was close to 11:00 p.m. when I drove down the long lane that led to Leonard's farm. I could see a couple of yard lights glowing in the dark. It had been a long time since I had been on this farmstead. Years ago, we had used to fish Leonard's dam, which was loaded with bass and crappies. We used Leonard's farm as a staging area when we hunted pheasants back in the sixties. I can remember riding my first horse on this farm. It bit me! I've hated horses ever since, but that was a long time ago.

As I rounded the final bend of the driveway, the farm came into full view. I always loved Leonard's farm. There were lots of well-maintained buildings, a large barn, and a working windmill. One of the yard lights lit up the house. There was nothing fancy about the farmers' homes around Saunders County Nebraska, but they were well built. I stopped in front of the house, and before I could shut the engine off, Jim walked out to greet me. Leonard followed.

After a couple of hugs and a shake of hands, we went back inside, where we sat and talked for a good while. Jim was in no hurry to leave. I found out that Leonard was going to come up during the second week for a few days with Wayne's crew. I still considered Leonard to be Jim's dad. In future years, Leonard became one of my best friends. Even though he was a generation older, I never looked at him as a fatherly figure but rather as just part of the gang. He loved to fish and never complained about anything.

Before we knew it, midnight had come and gone. It was time to get going. The bed in my 1984 Ford Ranger was wide open. After Jim loaded all his stuff, Leonard came out with a large canvas cover that we secured over our belongings. We had a long drive ahead of us under clear skies. We had a lot to talk about.

Our trip north to Park Rapids would take us through Sioux City, Iowa, and then up I-29 to Fargo, where we would catch Minnesota Highway 10, which led into Park Rapids from the west. I had never traveled I-29 before this trip, so I didn't know how desolate that part of the interstate was. I topped off in Fremont, Nebraska, and away we went, not realizing the lack of gas stations between Sioux Falls and our first designated stop—Brookings, South Dakota.

A couple of hours into our trip, I started staring at the gas gauge. We were well past Sioux Falls, and my little Ranger had just an eighteen-gallon tank. There was no emergency reserve like the ones vehicles have now. Empty meant *empty*, and the needle was getting close to empty. I asked Jim just how much farther Brookings would be. The perennial optimist Jim said, "We should be okay." When the needle was touching empty, our conversations started to center around my gas gauge, as if we could magically manufacture more gas into the tank.

To say this was a desolate road was an understatement. Not only was it desolate, but there were hardly any distance signs for upcoming towns. I really needed to know how much farther we had to go. Finally, we noticed a sign ahead: "Brookings 20 miles." Did I have twenty miles of gas left in this truck? I slowed down to conserve fuel. My foot wanted to get going and close the distance faster. I knew that would be a mistake. We were both anxious as we discussed gas consumption—not the topic I was wanting to talk about.

Lights appeared on the horizon! Brookings was straight ahead. I was waiting for the sputter of the engine at any time. There was only one exit into Brookings, which was a blessing, as I doubted we could have gotten much farther. A gas station located just off the exit ramp was lit up like a lightbulb. Jim and I breathed a sigh of relief. I quickly parked the truck and filled it up. 17.7 gallons went into the 18-gallon tank. I will never forget it. A couple more miles and we would have been coasting.

CHAPTER 18

Wambolt's Resort

W e felt refreshed after our pit stop. We were back on the road for another two hundred miles to Fargo. During our drive north, Jim told me some interesting stories—most notably one about Lou and Betty selling off Home Bay Resort. According to Jim, the new owner had turned the place into a family-oriented resort that included the addition of a swimming pool. Fishermen do not need swimming pools. They also got rid of the rearing pond. They demanded a deposit for any weekly stay, which had to be turned in before the season started. As Jim talked about all the changes, I knew right away that would not sit right with him. Jim told me, "It is not the fishing resort it used to be."

So that was the end of Home Bay Resort. Jim had been going to another resort located on Upper Bottle Lake called Wambolt's Resort since 1980. Jim said, "Wambolt's is the perfect fishing resort. Each cabin has a screened-in porch and is built of pine logs." Jim described the cabins as "cozy and outdated." I was anxious to see it and to fish Upper Bottle Lake.

Wambolt's Resort had a lot of history associated with the Bottle Lakes and the area. It was the oldest resort on Upper Bottle Lake and had the oldest buildings on the lake. It had been built to house loggers during the 1920s. In the 1930s, it was turned into a resort for fishermen. Fishermen would arrive into Dorset or into Park Rapids by train. The resort owners had horse-drawn carriages they would use to pick up the fishing parties and bring them into the resort for their stay and then return them to their departure station at the end of their stay. The resort would provide lodging, boats, and all the meals for the guests. It must have been a wonderful time and great adventure for the fishing parties, as the location of the Bottle Lakes was truly remote.

We would be fishing at night a few times if the weather allowed. Jim knew where the crappies were and knew how to fish for them at night. That aroused my interest right away and explained the reason for the small flashlight Jim had told me to bring. He'd said I would need it.

Jim told me, "No more harnesses for northerns." Lately he had been using medium sucker minnows trolled slowly behind the boat using either a Lindy rig with a spinner or by themselves on a hook. He told me, "Wayne started using just a jig with a minnow and was having remarkable success. He never knew what he was going to catch using the jig. It could be a northern, a walleye, a smallmouth bass, or even a largemouth bass. Sometimes we just anchor and sit with a bobber and a minnow." That sounded like great fun! I had missed a lot.

About 10:00 a.m., we pulled into Park Rapids. My eyes were heavy and starting to burn. Nothing had changed in me over the years regarding the need for sleep. I could get physically sick if I restricted my sleep—something the Musilek clan knew nothing about, and I suspect that has not changed much over the years.

Park Rapids was a bustle of activity. There was a lot of construction on Highway 10, as they were expanding the road through the town. There was single-lane traffic everywhere and what a mess! People and cars were everywhere. We stopped to get some groceries and then to get our fishing license at Reed's Sporting Center on Main Street. Then it was off to beautiful Upper Bottle Lake. I was so excited I didn't notice how exhausted I was from driving all night.

The road to Wambolt's took us down the same highway north out of Park Rapids along St. George Road. We went past Deer Lane, where Jim had weighed in his northern our first year. A new highway had been built that bypassed the small community, and we continued north until we reached Emmaville, which was another two miles. Emmaville was somewhat of a roadside diner. They had a bar, gas, groceries, and a small café. Emmaville boasted of being the smallest town in the United States simply because it had a functioning post office. From Emmaville we turned east and headed down a two-lane highway to another side road that led to Wambolt's driveway. The property was positioned on the northwestern side of Upper Bottle Lake.

The driveway was ragged and irregular. It led down into a large grove of trees which opened to a large expanse of property with many old buildings. A row of cabins dotted the shoreline. The cabins were of varied sizes but were all the same shape and style. We stopped next to Daryl's and Rosemary's residence, which was tucked back into the property. Scanning the property, I counted at least seven or eight broken-down outbuildings scattered across the property. One small building tucked up against the trees had a sign on it that read, "FISH CLEANING HOUSE." This truly was a resort for fishermen.

Jim had told me about Daryl and Rosemary. They had bought the property in 1963. Daryl was a piece of work. Upon meeting him and his wife, I decided that rules and regulations could be thrown out the window and, to an extent, Daryl would not care. He still had to abide by rules, but I quickly decided he was not associated with the DNR like Lou had been and that keeping a log of the fish we caught was about as far from his mind as anything. I could see right away why Jim would fall in love with this resort. Daryl was a man after his own heart.

Rosemary came out to greet us. Rosemary was a larger woman that walked with a small side-to-side sway, I suspect from bad hips. Daryl was a smaller-framed man that had a weathered, rough look about him. They were both as nice a couple as you could meet. Daryl never showed much emotion, but we knew he was happy to have us.

We followed them into their office, which was attached to the main living quarters. Daryl talked with a high-pitched voice that sounded scratchy. He was a chain smoker. I doubt I ever saw him without a cigarette in his hands the whole week. Rosemary took our registration, which was all very informal. The check-in process was nothing like Lou's methodical attention to every detail possible. There was no logbook to sign, only a tab they started for our cabin that would show us our purchases of gas, bait, and miscellaneous items. The informal process was refreshing. I suspect that was another reason Jim loved it here at Wambolt's. We had a freedom from constraint. Daryl left us alone. All we had to worry about was catching some fish.

Jim asked about the fishing. Daryl said, "You should catch something," which is about all one will ever get out of Daryl. He said, "A few walleye at night." He warned us about the weather for the week. A cold front was heading down through Canada. It was going to be a cold week for sure. I'd brought chilly-weather gear, but I had no rain suit. It was mid-September, and I had never been here that late.

From Daryl's and Rosemary's house, it was difficult to see the lake, as it was obscured by the guest cabins that lined the lakefront. The whole property was basically level, but the elevation was higher in relationship to the lake than Home Bay's property was. The cabins sat about six to eight feet higher than the shoreline. I'd thought Home Bay's view was something. The view we would get from these cabins would be spectacular.

Daryl had ten rustic cabins facing the lake (See figure 7.) All the cabins were in various stages of degradation, needing some work either on the interior or the exterior. Some of them were broken down to an unrentable condition. Daryl told us he had eight cabins that were fit for rent. Cabin 10, toward the east end, looked as if it could topple into the lake at any time. There was one large three-bedroom community cabin situated in the middle of the line. That is the one the guys next week would occupy, along with another two-bedroom cabin just next door. Our cabin for the upcoming week was cabin 1, which was tucked up against the pines at the west end of the resort.

The property was kept up nicely except for a few of the outbuildings. There were no high weeds, and the whole yard was mowed and well kept. The resort had a homey, relaxing atmosphere about it. I could only imagine the wonderful fishing experiences the guests must have had decades ago when this resort first opened. Wambolt's was a true fisherman's resort and was well-suited to Jim's liking.

After we got registered, we got into the truck and made our way to cabin 1. It was a two-bedroom cabin with a kitchen. We would have to use a community bath, which Jim said was well maintained and had good shower stalls. A wonderful add-on to all of Daryl's cabins were the screened-in porches. We could put all our gear on the porch, where it would be out of the elements. Just sitting out on the porch and gazing out over the beautiful lake sometimes passed my time.

Our boat was already docked and ready to go. Daryl used nine-horsepower motors on his boats. They were all fourteen-foot aluminum Lunds, much like the ones Lou used for his guests, except for the motor size. Daryl's docks were of all-wood construction and had to be taken out, section by section, for the winter. The last section was anchored in the lake by two long two-by sixes set deep into the lake's bottom. The rest of the dock was primarily made from two-by-fours, with each section itself anchored to the bottom. Keeping in stride with the condition of the resort, the docks were weathered, and when one walked on them, they swayed back and forth. I always had a conscious realization that at any moment the whole dock might collapse into the lake with all involved. Daryl had four docks spaced across his shoreline. The dock we had stretched out into the lake an appreciable distance farther than the other docks, owing to the depth of the lake at that location.

It is hard to describe the absolute beauty of Upper Bottle Lake, which I experienced when I first walked out onto the dock and stared out over the water. The fall season arrives early in northern Minnesota. In late September, the deciduous maples and clump birch varieties were already starting to show their fall colors of various shades of yellow and orange. The sumac foliage had already turned to its fiery crimson appearance. Add to this the deep green of pines and other evergreen trees. One could not paint the visual effect as well as Mother Nature does. Everywhere I looked, I could see golden shoots of reeds and wild rice beds covering the shorelines. It was truly breathtaking scenery. I could not wait to see the shoreline from a boat.

CHAPTER 19

A Tour of Upper Bottle Lake

Wambolt's Resort was set on the northwestern shoreline of Upper Bottle Lake. Wambolt's property amounted to around 107 acres. About 20 of those acres were the actual resort. The rest of the property was virgin landscape untouched for centuries. The resort shoreline was shaped like half of a bowl. Consequently, a natural bay existed in front of the resort. Wambolt's Bay was a popular destination for fishermen that had experience fishing on Upper Bottle Lake. In part of Wambolt's Bay to the west, and extending out to the east, there existed a gradually descending bar. That bar, in future years, provided us with as much fishing action as anywhere on the lake, including Lower Bottle Lake.

Daryl did sell bait on his resort, so he asked us what kind of bait we would like. I left that all up to Jim. Before we knew it, Daryl was off in his old pickup after the bait Jim had requested. It could not have been half an hour later when Daryl came back with northern sucker minnows, walleye minnows, crappie minnows, night crawlers, and leeches. His ability to get bait so fast seemed puzzling to us, but we never gave it a second thought. At least Daryl always had a plentiful supply for us. I wondered if Daryl counted out the minnows like Lou used to do. Jim thought Daryl was a little less tight on dishing out his minnows and chubs. That was a refreshing thought.

We stayed in Saturday evening, as we were exhausted from the drive. The next morning, after a good night's sleep, I felt refreshed and was anxious to get out on the lake. Breakfast included some eggs and bacon with toast and coffee. Man, that hit the spot! Jim did most of the cooking during the week, and I realized right away that it was possible I would not lose weight but would, in fact, gain a couple of pounds.

We needed to find Daryl for some bait. After some scrounging around, we found him treating the base of one of the cabins with creosote. It smelled God awful and he was all dressed up in the same blue denim jacket and shirt he'd been wearing yesterday. He was wearing a mask filter over his mouth and nose. He told us to get with Rosemary, as he could not stop once he started. Most of the time, over the course of the week, it was Rosemary that fetched our bait.

Daryl was always doing something somewhere. When we did catch him for a chat, listening to him talk was like listening to a scratchy record. Daryl never said much but always wanted to know how we were doing fishing. "Did you catch anything?" he would ask. "How did you do yesterday?" he might say, or "How did you do last night?" That is about the extent of a conversation we could expect to get out of him.

Daryl loved to fish. Jim knew he liked to go out at night trolling Rapalas or just pulling a minnow behind the boat. One perk about owning a resort was that Daryl could pick and choose his nights to go fishing. Jim said he always went out late, after dark.

After we got our bait, everything was ready to go. Our tackle was in, and Jim cranked up the motor. With the first pull, it fired. I untied us from the dock and climbed aboard. This would be my first time out on Upper Bottle Lake. These boats were much like Lou's boats, so I took up residence in the bow, where I could lean back and stretch my legs if I wanted to. It was Rick's sacred throne that now would be mine for the week.

I was extremely excited, and memories from Home Bay rushed through my mind. Jim thought a small cruise of Upper Bottle Lake was in order. I could not have agreed more. As Jim pulled away from Wambolt's Bay, I sat back and stared out at the receding shoreline as more and more of the lake came into view. Jim headed east down the north shore, which was lined with reeds. Another small resort came into view toward the eastern side of the shoreline that appeared to have closed for the season. There were few cabins on that resort, and all were small. I wondered how they could stay in business.

We started heading south along the east shoreline, where more reeds extended out to a shallow point. The whole eastern shoreline was lined with reeds, and the elevation rose quickly to a higher plateau. I could make out a few houses on the plateau that were tucked away among the pines and evergreens. The owners had to build complicated stair steps down to the shoreline just to get to their docks. *I would not want to make that descent every time I wanted to go fishing*, I thought to myself.

The eastern shoreline was the longest shoreline on Upper Bottle Lake. From the east shoreline, Jim pointed out our beloved Narrows, where we'd spent so much time walleye fishing with Lou—the same spot where Jim let loose the crawdads in the bottom of the boat that wanted to eat my ankles. I do believe that at one time I had a nightmare about those damn things severing my Achilles' heel. I hoped Jim had outgrown that practice, but I doubted it.

At the end of the eastern shoreline, we headed west, following the south shoreline. We were heading down the peninsula that runs into the Narrows. This was the same peninsula where we docked the boats late one night back in 1967 and slaughtered the bullheads—the same peninsula where one night we caught a bat that nearly ended our relationship with Lou. It was also the same peninsula that had guided us to the Narrows when we were unfamiliar with Lower Bottle Lake. Only we were now looking at it from the south shore instead of the north shore.

The whole peninsula was loaded with houses and cabins. I can remember the For Sale signs tacked to the trees and spaced out along the shoreline back in 1970. I didn't give it a second thought then. Now, something inside me wished one of us would have had the foresight to snatch one of those properties up and build a cabin on it. In fact, looking out across the lake, I could not believe the amount of development that had taken place. I wondered if Lower Bottle had experienced the same explosion of houses and cabins lining the shoreline. I could not help but feel that I had lost a chance or had missed out on something fine.

We moved slowly across the Narrows, which continued to be a no-wake zone, and then we headed down the west shoreline. Houses and docks lined that shore also. The west shoreline was interrupted by a large expanse of a shallow bar that reached out to the east, almost cutting the lake in half. The bar was filled with thick reeds and wild rice. There was no shortcut through this surface area, so we had to follow the bar around its perimeter to continue our tour of the lake.

Once we moved around the far end of the bar, we headed back to the west shoreline, which eventually led us into Wambolt's Bay. My tour was over. "What a beautiful lake!" I told Jim. I was anxious to get a line into the water and, with Jim's guidance, see how his fishing technique had changed over the years.

The weather was sunny, but there was a definite chill in the air. The wind was brisk from the north, requiring us to wear heavy coveralls and stocking caps just to keep comfortable. Jim wanted to slowly troll Little Joe spinner rigs with large chubs. Jim said the northerns loved this type of presentation. He said, "Hold on to your rod when they hit." At least Jim had stopped using the sadistic harness rigs. I hated those things.

I had my trusty Johnson Century in hand—the same reel I'd bought from Lou back in 1967. It had never failed me. Jim was still using his open-faced reels. For the life of me, I do not know what he saw in those open-faced reels. Jim also brought along a collapsible cane pole, something he had started using years ago in Minnesota that was reminiscent of our days of cane pole fishing when we were kids. I could not wait to see how he worked it here on the Bottle Lakes.

CHAPTER 20

Fishing Upper Bottle Lake

J im brought along his flasher depth finder. It was a portable model with a sonar unit that attached to the rear of the boat below the water line using a suction cup. When set right, Jim could maintain a course at a certain depth by watching the flasher. It was unusual to see Jim at the helm checking the depth finder instead of staring down into the water, looking for weeds. We used to be so dependent on sight to control our depth. Now it was just a matter of watching a display. This was my first time on the Bottle Lakes when we would know our depth. *How neat is that?* I thought to myself. Jim had told me the deepest spot he could find reached fifty feet. There was a spot in Lower Bottle Lake that reached one hundred feet.

The wind howled from the north, which forced us to stay close to the north side of the lake. We started trolling along Wambolt's Bay. Jim told me he wanted to stay in water about ten to fifteen feet deep. Jim was in his element: a flasher depth finder; his open-faced reel; a Little Joe spinner; a good, slow motor; and a place to set his rod down when he wanted to. (See figure 8.)

It looked weird to see a large chub trailing a little spinner. All Jim used was a ⅜-ounce sliding ball weight. He liked to get the bait down to the required depth by letting out a lot of line, and a lot of line he did let out—up to seventy-five yards. This was enough that his partner in the boat needed to fish with a shorter leash. I rigged up with a half-ounce sliding sinker and a split shot. That allowed the bait to get down quickly, and I didn't have to let out so much line. I was hopeful we would not tangle up.

Jim was right. My first northern hit nearly jerked the rod out of my hand; plus they fought like the devil. I noticed right away this rig was far superior to the old harness rigs. We didn't experience as many missed hits or poor hook sets as I remembered happening with the harness.

Every time we went out for northerns that week, we had reasonable success when the weather allowed, but the weather was playing games with us. The wind just kept blowing and blowing. Day after day, the relentless winds kept up. We had to get out when opportunity presented itself. Later in the week, it turned bitterly cold and the fishing came to an abrupt halt.

On Monday, the winds changed to the south. The gale-force winds came up close to noontime and blew all day. Thank God we were not in them. The waters of the lake were lashing about, turning ordinary waves into angry whitecaps. This reminded me of the day Jim, Michael, and Doug got caught in such winds back at Home Bay. They were lucky to get out of that situation alive. Jim and I were very content to sit in our cabin and watch the pine needles ride the wind in a horizontal path past our window. It blew all afternoon.

That evening, the winds subsided enough that we thought about heading out. Jim was anxious to introduce me to night fishing on Upper Bottle Lake. Jim's plan was to find water around ten feet deep, drop anchor, and then fish into fifteen feet of water. We were going to rig for crappies. We got some minnows, and off we went. Our destination was the large bar extending from the west shoreline. The bar itself resembled a triangle. The point of the bar reached well into the middle of the lake and then descended into very deep water quickly. It was the point of that bar we were after.

Jim was looking for one specific area on that point where the depth descended on a more gradual slope. He was looking for a ridgeline. Jim had fished this spot many times at night, and he appeared to know where he was going. I was ready to drop the anchor on his command. We both had our flashlights on, as it was pitch dark by the time we got there.

We had a new moon that week, so we would not have any help from that ghostly body. I was using one of Jim's six-volt flashlights, keeping it trained on the reeds behind us. It was not that easy. We had to make a couple of tries at it. If we drifted too far left or right, we fell off into deep water. Plus, it didn't help that the wind was still blowing. The reeds behind us provided some relief from larger waves, but it was difficult to find the exact spot Jim wanted. Finally, Jim yelled, "Let's drop here!" We both dropped our anchors together and waited to see whether we could hold the boat. There we sat, in the middle of the pitch-black night, on the crest of a ridge. Remarkably, the boat held. There was enough protection from the reeds on the large bar behind us, where waves were not an issue.

The first thing Jim did was bring out his Coleman lantern. He fired it up, which gave us an abundance of light in the boat. Jim told me, "Fish as deep as you can." I was already rigged with a bobber and split shot. I hooked on a minnow, and the whole thing disappeared into the darkness. I pulled out my small flashlight and searched for my bobber. There it sat, a few yards from the boat.

Jim was messing around trying to extend his cane pole. I had never seen a cane pole so long. It was all fiberglass and appeared to be at least sixteen feet long when extended. The cane pole had eyelets spaced down the length of the pole, and Jim mounted an old casting reel to the bottom. He put on a minnow, peeled out some line from the reel, stood up on the seat, and heaved it out. Jim was fishing deeper than I was, since he could raise the bait using the long pole. I figure he was fishing at least ten feet down. Finally, we settled down, all the time wondering whether the boat would hold. Trying to see a small bobber in the dark water was difficult. We resorted to checking the bobber occasionally with our flashlights.

Suddenly Jim's bobber was not there anymore. Jim stuck the hand-held flashlight into his mouth and pulled ever so slightly up with the cane pole. Once he felt some resistance, up went the tip in one long tug. He had a fish on. At first we could not tell what he had, but the way it fought, Jim thought it might be a crappie. I put the dip net in the water, and Jim pulled up one of the biggest crappies I had ever seen. It reminded me of the two we had caught the first year we came to the Bottle Lakes. "Wow!" I said to Jim. "Are they all that big?" It must have been over fifteen inches in length. Jim thought they averaged twelve to thirteen. He said, "This is a big one."

Jim rebaited, and out his line went. Before long he had another one on. This one was not as big, but nonetheless, it was a crappie. Jim thought this was of more average size. We sat for some time without a hit, and then my bobber was gone! *I wish I could see the hit*, I told myself, but that bobber was nowhere to be seen. I stuck the flashlight in my mouth, and Jim grabbed the net. Up came a small walleye of about sixteen inches. "A walleye!" Jim yelled. Well, crap! I wanted a crappie. Before long, my bobber disappeared once again, and up came another walleye that was a twin to the first one. Then for the longest time, we sat and sat. Nothing was happening.

We had sat for a good thirty minutes without a hit when we noticed the wind picking up. I could feel the rat-a-tat-tat of waves splashing against the boat. The south wind had picked up. A quick check of our bobbers revealed a startling scene. They were right next to the boat. We had blown off the ridge and were in danger of drifting over our lines. We quickly pulled up our lines and the anchors. It is bad enough in the middle of the day for this to happen; it is a real mess at night. *Damn the wind!* That was the end of our ridgeline. There was no way we were going to hold a boat in this wind that had suddenly freshened. Jim had another idea to try.

Once everything was secured and the stringer of our four healthy fish came aboard, Jim cranked up the motor and headed back to the reed line. He knew that the reeds could still protect us to a degree if we could cozy up to them and anchor in them. The depth gradient just off the reeds was very steep. One side of the boat could be in three feet of water and the other in ten feet of water. However, it was our only choice. We could try it or give it up and go in, and we were not ready to go in just yet.

We got the boat close to the reeds and heaved the anchors off the back of the boat. We were secure for a while. It took us a few minutes to get oriented, and finally both our rigs were back in the water. Jim hooked into another crappie and lost one. The wind was playing tricks on his cane pole. It is not easy fishing in the wind at night, especially with a cane pole. Then came the inevitable. The wind came up harder, and we could not hold it, even anchored in the reeds. The fish were hitting, and I could tell Jim was getting pissed. "Fucking wind!" he finally roared. In came the anchors, and when we were all situated, it was back to the cabin, grumbling the whole way. The waves pounded into the bay, and it took us some doing to dock the boat. Jim, already an old hand at this, maneuvered the boat flawlessly. We had five nice fish to clean, and I had gotten a taste of night fishing on the Bottle Lakes, which in future years would become the norm for us. We never did go out again at night during the rest of the week. It was just too windy. Daryl, who loved to fish at night, didn't venture out the whole week we were there.

CHAPTER 21

Fun with Bass

J im had told me how much fun bass fishing was in the Bottle Lakes. He was anxious to get me out and try it, but the weather in the mornings didn't cooperate. We were looking for a morning where the wind was almost nonexistent and the water was flat like glass. These are almost essential conditions for bass fishing with plastic worms in shallow water among the reeds, which is the way Jim fished for bass. We were wondering if that type of morning would ever present itself, as it was getting late into the week. One morning the conditions were exactly right.

We headed out just after sunrise to fish the reeds. It was brisk that morning, and the weather report did not sound good. A cold front was racing toward northern Minnesota that was going to put the temperature near or just above freezing. It was the calm before the storm. Since we didn't have a trolling motor, Jim would get within casting distance of the reeds and put the motor in neutral, and we could then make a few casts. We moved down the reed line in that manner.

This was my first time fishing the reeds, and I was not sold on the technique, as they were only a couple of feet deep. What bass in its right mind would be lurking in such shallow water with no protection? When I got my first hit, I was not ready for it, and before I knew it, that bass was gone. That told me what I knew about Minnesota bass fishing—nothing! A few casts later, again I felt a thump, but I didn't react to it. Before I knew what was happening, the line pulled tight and that one was gone.

Jim told me, "As soon as you feel the thump, you must set it; otherwise, it is too late."

Suddenly Jim tied into one. What an explosion! He had a tough time getting him out of the reeds. At times I thought Jim was going to break his line trying to get that bass to turn toward the boat. The tug on the line was pulling the boat sideways. I could not believe it. Finally, Jim was getting the upper hand. I could see the bass in the shallow, clear water darting back and forth. What a thrill to see this unfold! I put the dip net into the water and pulled the bass into the boat with one swipe. What a beautiful fish.

Unlike bass in Nebraska, I quickly realized these bass resembled large footballs. Nebraska's bass, pound for pound, seemed to be a lot longer and not as thick. This guy was so thick in the shoulders I could not get both hands around him. What a beautiful color! Jim put him in the water, and we watched his escape. Now that was something.

We fished the middle reeds and the east shore reeds without another hit. It was getting windy out of the north. I wanted another shot at those bass. Jim had another place to try. Just east of Wambolt's existed a large reed bed that ran down the north shoreline. Inside the reed bed was an accessible area of open water bordered by reeds and lily pads. The north bluffs protected us from the ever-increasing north wind. Once we navigated through a small entrance, Jim shut the motor down right in the middle of the open water that was, at best, two feet deep. From that vantage point, we were in casting distance of lily pads, reeds, and wild rice paddies that existed all around the boat.

After a few casts, I finally tied into a bass. I felt a thump on my line, and this time I reacted in time. I set the hook, and the fight was on. I'm here to say there is nothing quite like it. I was tugging, pulling, and hanging on, trying to keep him from getting hung up in the reeds. This bass had so much strength in him. Suddenly he came crashing out of the water thrashing his gaping mouth, trying to throw the hook. "Did you see that?" I asked Jim. What a ruckus this guy was creating. Eventually I got him close enough that with a gentle net, he was safely in the boat. After discharging the hook, we watched him make his escape back to the protection of the reeds.

I do not recall the length of that bass, but it was my first Minnesota largemouth, and I was hooked ever since on bass fishing in Minnesota. Jim and I both caught a couple more in that small area before we decided to head back and eat some lunch. It was the only time we made it out bass fishing that week. The weather just did not cooperate. In fact, the cold front was about to hit northern Minnesota.

CHAPTER 22

Another Crappie Story

The weather that week was testing our patience. Jim did a fantastic job trying to maneuver the boat in high waves, blowing winds, and cold temperatures. Regarding the weather, there was always something we had to deal with. If the winds were calm, it was very cold outside, requiring us to wear gloves and heavy clothing. A warm stocking cap was a must at times. It never rained on us, so we didn't have to worry about wet conditions. It was the wind and cold temperatures that did us in most of the time.

One evening, just before dark, we were trolling Little Joe rigs for walleyes in Wambolt's Bay. Jim was fishing his normal way; he had lots and lots of line out. I never could figure out how he did that. Every time I tried it, I always got hung up in weeds, forcing me to reel the whole damn works back into the boat and clean off a hanging piece of weed that hitched a ride. We all had our ways of fishing, but Jim always caught his share of fish, and honestly, throughout the years, he always caught bigger fish. He truly is one of the better fishermen I have ever had the pleasure of fishing with.

Jim got a hit. He reared back and set the hook. He could not tell what it was at first. Running a small boat in waves dictates your every move, and at dusk, trying to land a fish is difficult at best. Eventually he was getting most of his line back into the reel. Jim thought the fish to be a walleye, but to our surprise, as Jim guided the fish into the net, up came the biggest crappie I have ever seen. It was every bit of seventeen inches. It was wider than my thumb to little finger outstretched. The length went from my middle finger to my elbow. I thought Jim might have caught some sort of trophy crappie for these parts. We had nothing on the stringer yet, so on went this gigantic crappie. We were going to have Daryl look at it later that evening.

Sometimes fishermen can get caught up in the moment and the thinking process becomes gummed up. The only stringer we had in the boat was a long twelve-foot light cord stringer. We tied on the crappie, ran the needle through the large loop at the end of the stringer, put the crappie in the water, and tied the stringer to the boat. What we didn't do was take up the slack. We had most of the twelve-foot cord and the crappie in the water. Worst of all, we tied the stringer to the back of the boat, near where Jim was sitting. That allowed the crappie about a ten-foot free rein behind the boat. Well, it didn't take long. Jim had the motor in neutral, and it was time to head back up the bar and drift back. As soon as he engaged the forward gear and turned the boat, *Thinggggg!* The sound reverberated through the boat. "What the hell was that?" I yelled at Jim. Well, Jim knew right away what had happened. We'd had so much stringer out that when he turned the boat, we turned right into the stringer and the motor prop hit it. The seventeen-inch crappie was gone, and the severed stringer was all that was left. We looked at each other and decided to go in. We only hoped the crappie had been spared so that someone else might have a chance at him.

We ate well that week: eggs and bacon with coffee in the mornings, and hamburgers, hot dogs, pasta, and fish for supper. One evening Jim cooked up a walleye that I had caught one afternoon off the point of the center reeds. We were anchored in about five feet, fishing the ridgeline we had fished the night before. The wind was not bad. It didn't take long before I hooked into a nice walleye while bobber fishing. Man, there is nothing like bobber fishing, whether it is for northerns, walleyes, crappies, or bluegills. Nothing beats it. We estimated the walleye to be around four pounds. We filleted him, wrapped him in foil, and set him on the grill. It was our version of a shore meal. The taste was excellent.

The week went fast. I envied Jim, as he had all the following week to look forward to. Friday night we settled with Daryl. We got to talk to him about the big crappie we had on the stringer. He didn't seem surprised.

Daryl knew there were big ones in the Bottle Lakes. He told us this was the place locals came for big crappie. Daryl said he hadn't gone out once that week. He thought next week looked to be better.

Saturday morning, I left early. Jim was packing his stuff to move into cabin 3. The rest of the gang would be there by noon. True to form, Wayne's group had left at midnight Friday to drive all night. Next week's weather report was favorable with good conditions. The cold front would move out, and temperatures would turn back to normal for the season.

I contacted Jim after their second week fishing. Jim told me they'd had the best fishing he could remember, with perfect weather conditions. The fishing hadn't been the best during our stay that first week, but I wouldn't have traded it for any other week I had ever spent on the Bottle Lakes. I have Jim to thank for that. I swore then and there I would try to make as many trips as I could if health and circumstance allowed. Time is too short, and friendships are too precious.

CHAPTER 23

1987: Twenty-Year Anniversary

Jim and Wayne, over the past twenty years, had somehow laid the groundwork to carve out a tradition that still stands to this day. Their resolve to head north for a wonderful week of fishing grew stronger with each passing year. In 1987, Jim decided to organize our first anniversary get-together. Rick, Jim, Michael, Wayne, and I left Prague on a Friday evening to celebrate our twentieth year. Doug would miss our trip that year. It had been a long time since I had seen Doug, and I was disappointed he could not make it. What an exciting time for us all.

I don't have a record of fishing that year, and our picture-taking was just as bad as it had been during our first years coming up to Home Bay. Imagine how stupid we were—our twenty-year anniversary, and nothing recorded. We had hardly any photos and not one journal. Except for a couple of stories to share, we treated that year just like any another year.

The most notable story from that year just happens to be one of the most memorable stories of all the years at the Bottle Lakes and one of the most memorable stories I like to tell involve crappie fishing. What is it about crappie fishing that captivates my interest? Maybe it is because crappies offer up heart-thumping action on light tackle. They are a tremendous amount of fun, and on the dinner table, they make for excellent eating.

Of all the fish I caught in the Bottle Lakes, including walleyes, northerns, bluegills, perch, and bass, crappie fishing for me was most exciting. In 1987, none of us were experts in Minnesota crappie fishing.

That year we happened to experience a crappie bite that took us until 2013 to repeat. It was a fall crappie bonanza.

During the week, we had come across a large patch of cabbage weed that existed in front of Whippoorwill Resort. Whippoorwill Resort was located next to Wambolt's, tucked into the northeastern part of Upper Bottle Lake. The resort itself was small in comparison to Wambolt's. Only a few cabins existed there, and those were small.

Daryl had told us that in the spring, boat after boat would be lined up fishing the cabbage weed beds, looking for crappies. It was a crappie spawning area. We told ourselves it might be possible that location would hold crappies in the fall. On Friday afternoon, Jim, Rick, Wayne, and I decided we were going to go fishing for crappies. Equipped with only minnows for bait, we set our sights on the cabbage weed beds in front of Whippoorwill Resort. Rick and Wayne took one boat, and Jim and I the other. Michael didn't come; he decided to visit a friend of his that lived on the Bottle Lakes.

The cabbage weed itself was a formidable foe. Getting hooked in that weed meant the immediate loss of bait and, often, the loss of one's whole rig, bobber and all. The cabbage weed does not give up its hold easily. The weed rises from the depths on sturdy canes with large, wavy leaves secured to each cane. Fishing them requires some finesse; lowering your rig in a voided area is the only way to achieve a measure of success. Even then the weed exists at various depths. One location that might be presentable could have weeds lying a few feet below the surface that cannot be seen.

After a couple of lost rigs, bobber and all, Rick and Wayne had enough of the infamous cabbage weed and decided to go fish elsewhere. Jim and I were giving it the old college try with little success. We were not to be deterred. We anchored a couple of times and drifted through a few spots, but we had no luck. A good hour must have passed since Rick and Wayne left when we decided to see if they had found anything.

We cruised up the east shoreline to where we could see Rick and Wayne anchored just off one of the reed beds. "Any luck?" we asked them as we slowly drifted by. They had these shit-eating grins on their faces, and I knew something was up. Rick reached over the side and held up a stringer of crappies. They must have had a dozen or so of the most beautiful black Minnesota crappies. "How in the hell did you find them?" I asked.

One of them shouted back, "We just kept moving to different spots. When we tried it here, we started catching them right away."

"How deep are you?" I asked. I could see they were anchored just off the reeds and fishing toward deeper water.

Rick said, "We're fishing in about ten feet, anchored in about six feet."

Jim and I decided to try to drift to a point just beyond where they were fishing and anchor. We started catching crappies right away. The action was not fast, but it was consistent. We could sit for a few minutes, and then the bobber would rise and then dive out of sight—a sure crappie hit. For me it does not get any better than sitting on top of a crappie hole when the bite is on. What a wonderful experience!

We fished in that hole until we ran out of bait. We didn't catch our limit, but we were close. Nobody, not one of us, marked the spot for future reference. In future years, we were never able to find that hole again. Year after year we fished that shoreline, hoping to come across another school of crappies, but we never could find them again. It took us until 2013 to experience another crappie bonanza, but that was in a different location.

When we got back to camp, we had the sense to take a couple of pictures of our crappies that we had spread out on the deck. (See figure 9.) Then we were off to the fish house for cleaning duty.

Our trip in 1987 went too fast. I could not believe that it was Friday and tomorrow morning we would be heading home. Back on the Musilek farm we said our farewells. None of us knew when we would be together again.

By the end of the seventies and eighties, all of us had established careers. Responsibility rests with all of us to nurture our careers, which should never be jeopardized. Those of us lucky enough to take a week off would meet at Leonard's farm on a late Friday night in September for another great fishing adventure. Those of us that could not make it were always welcomed back. Our tradition was now on solid ground.

CHAPTER 24

Leonard

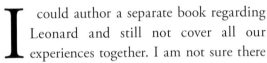

I could author a separate book regarding Leonard and still not cover all our experiences together. I am not sure there was one among us that loved to fish more than Leonard, and that included my dad. My dad loved to fish and taught me how to fish, but not out of a boat. My dad was a bank fisherman. He had no use for boats. The few times I did take him out on a boat, I always felt he was not comfortable fishing in that manner. However, give him a nice sandy beach on a sand pit lake or an accessible Platte River bank with backwater and he was in fishing heaven. Leonard loved fishing anywhere. Mostly he loved to fish out of a boat. When Leonard was with us on the Bottle Lakes, he could fish us all into the ground. After he was finished with us, he would still be out on the boat, trying to catch something.

Leonard was Jim's dad. He was also an uncle to Michael, Leo, and Rick, so he never slept! None of the Musilek clan slept, but Leonard was the worst of all. Leonard would fish all day, come in for one of Michael's great dinners, and then stay out in the middle of the night into the wee hours of the morning. Then he would come in to watch some TV before he hit the hay for a few hours' sleep. By seven the next morning, he would be one of the first to rise and wait for one of Michael's great breakfast spreads. And then he would repeat the whole thing, weather permitting. During the many years I spent fishing with Leonard, I doubt he got more than four hours' sleep in any one night.

Leonard became a regular part of our group in the late eighties, the nineties, and beyond. Our ritual was well established by then, and Leonard was now part of it. That he was a generation older than us didn't matter. He was part of our fellowship and will always be remembered as just another one of the guys that headed north year after year.

Leonard became one of my dearest fishing companions. We fished together during the day, drifting for northerns. (See figure 10.) We would fish together again at night, till the wee hours of the morning, trolling for walleyes. He loved to drift-fish as much as he loved trolling minnows at night.

There was a time when we didn't fish for walleyes by trolling at night. Daryl always trolled Rapalas at night and usually had good success. We simply resorted to the one technique that had worked for us in prior years. We would be anchored off the middle reeds or some other suitable location, fishing with bobbers for crappies or walleyes. Leonard didn't like bobber fishing. For that reason, Leonard rarely went out with us at night if our plan was to sit and fish with bobbers.

If we stayed out long enough, anchored off one of our favorite spots, sometimes we would hear Daryl come cruising by, pulling his Rapala. Daryl ran a Mercury motor that made a distinctive sound as it moved slowly through the water. It was like a *Chung! Chung! Chung! Chung!* He never tried to contact us as he passed us; he just kept going until the sound of his motor dissipated to nothing.

None of us liked pulling artificial anything except Michael. For Michael to get one of us to go out and pull an artificial lure was akin to impossible, so we anchored and fished with bobbers, all to Jim and Wayne's liking and all to Leonard's disliking. But I believe we all felt there had to be some alternate way to catch walleyes at night other than pulling artificial lures. One morning we asked Daryl how fishing was and whether he had noticed us anchored off the reeds. He said, "Yep, I seen you guys!" I distinctly remember Daryl telling us he had caught eight nice walleyes that night, all on Rapalas. He'd kept six. He said they'd been hitting well.

Well, we had a tough time telling him we caught nothing. When we voiced our having gotten skunked, Daryl gave his normal reaction to something that he thought unusual: "*The hell!*" Then, in his scratchy voice, he said, "You need to be shallower. You're fishing too deep." He told us we should "try pulling just a walleye minnow with a split shot behind the boat only a casting distance out. Five to seven feet of water is all you need at night." He said he used to do that all the time until he got sick of catching rock bass that would steal his bait. Daryl didn't like rock bass. Switching to Rapalas had solved his problem.

By the time the early nineties hit, we normally rented three boats from the resort, and now all three boats were equipped with depth finders. Wayne and I each brought up portable depth finders from home. They ran on two six-volt batteries. They lasted all week. What a difference it made to have a digital readout showing our depth. Jim also brought along his flasher, which he relied on exclusively. I don't think Jim had much use for any confounded innovative technologies already sweeping the fishing industry. As far as he was concerned, the flasher still worked just as well as anything.

Now we had the equipment to help us stay in five to seven feet of water, just as Daryl had told us to do. We decided to give Daryl's suggestion a try. We trolled the shorelines in five to seven feet of water at night and started catching walleyes using a minnow and a split shot behind the boat. What an exciting way to fish! We wondered what we might have missed in the past by not fishing in that manner.

Nobody among us was more excited about our newfound fishing technique than Leonard. Normally we didn't stay out after 10:00 p.m. We just had enough of it, and many times the bite stopped around 9:00 or 9:30 p.m. Leonard, on the other hand, never wanted to come in. But true to his character, he never, not once, complained. He would reluctantly gather his gear from the dock and make his way to the cabin for the night.

One night, that changed. I can remember coming into the large cabin where we all would normally congregate to tell our stories of the night's fishing. We would warm up with a hot cup of coffee and then attend to our fish-cleaning duties if needed. By now all of us knew how to fillet fish, and we typically would take turns in the fish cleaning house. It didn't matter how many we had to clean or who caught them; there were always volunteers to help with fish-cleaning duties.

I have always felt there is a bond between fishing and the cleaning of the fish. As with any outdoor sport, the cleaning process is an important part of the overall experience. It closes the loop between the sport and the food on the table. One way for me to help appreciate the sport of fishing was to help clean whenever I could.

As we all sat around talking that night, I looked up at Leonard enjoying his hot cup of coffee, and our eyes met. His head turned to the door with a twitch. He did that three or four times before I realized what he was asking. He wanted to go back out and troll. I thought about it and nodded. *Let's go.* I will never forget that moment. My fish-cleaning duties would have to wait until we came back in. We stayed out till well after midnight. That was the start of a long fishing tradition that Leonard and I would partake in every year—slowly trolling the shallows late at night for walleyes, weather permitting.

I learned a lot about Leonard while fishing into the wee hours of the morning. When the fishing was slow, he told me stories about WWII, during which he served in the navy. We talked about all aspects of life, from childhood memories to how we got to where we were and what the future might bring. We talked about politics, farming, growing up, families, fishing, and anything that had to do with anything. It was refreshing to get that kind of interaction from someone a generation older.

We both had to love the smell of outboard motor exhaust to have spent that much time out on the water together. At night, the air was usually calm with no breeze. Sometimes I would watch the fumes rise from the water and lift upward, radiating all through the boat. I do not believe I ever got lightheaded while running the motor. Leonard, being a farmer all his life, was used to exhaust fumes. We made for a good pair in the boat.

Leonard was fun to fish with. At night he would sit in the bow, smoking a cigarette with his line out in tow. The greatest kick I got from him was when he hooked into a fish. When he got a hit, he would feed out line, and then he would set the hook when he decided the time was right. When he felt he had a fish on, he would most loudly voice his pleasure by saying, "*I got that som-bitch!*" and the fight was on. This was my cue to stop the engine and grab the dip net.

I never knew if Leonard was going to land any fish that he hooked, simply because of his line-tying abilities. Many times I would look at his knot only to see a simple square knot, with ends dangling about. Leonard was proud to do things himself, and I respected him for that—even though I could have showed him how to tie a good fishing knot if he'd wanted. If he was like my dad, and I suspect he was, he resorted to the only knot that he knew was simple and easy to tie, even though it was subject to breaking at any time.

The other part of the equation was the line he used and how old it might have been. I never did know the condition of his line. I fell into a habit of changing out all my line before I made the trip to Minnesota, simply because one year I was snapping line with everything I set the hook into. That sealed the deal for me, and it was new line from then on.

If we landed his fish, he was the proudest man. Nothing would excite him more. After he secured his fish to the boat on the biggest stringer he could find, we would sit out there in the middle of nowhere, take a breather, and share a cup of his snapper. Snapper was Schnapps with hot chocolate. It had to be hot, hot, hot! Back at the cabin, Leonard would mix enough of his concoction to fill his thermos and take it out with us on the water. I cannot describe how fine it was.

In some years we were lucky enough to draw the week of a full moon. Leonard loved to fish at night when there was a full moon. To see the moon casting its light on the lake was both peaceful and beautiful. To our joy, sometimes the moon would rise later in the night, and we could see silhouettes of trees against the moon's lantern. Sunrises are beautiful. Moonrises can be just as gorgeous. When the full moon gained some height, the nighttime was transformed from the depth of dark blackness to a magical place where soft, gentle light surrounded all. No longer did we need flashlights to help us with proximity to the shoreline or our position on the lake. It was there all along, and all we needed was the moon to show us.

During some years, we would draw the week of a new moon, which meant pitch-black nights. Relying on a good depth finder was all important during those kinds of nights. Even though we knew every inch of shoreline, there was still a level of uneasiness regarding our position on the lake—especially after landing a fish. The boat could get turned around easily just from moving about. Righting ourselves to our direction required the use of our powerful flashlights to scan the shoreline. When we figured out where we were, off we went again, watching the depth closely.

Fishing in pitch-black darkness can be challenging, but there is no better way to see the stars. The Milky Way comes into full view without a single candle of light to obscure the experience. How lucky we were to see that heavenly layout in all its wonder while out enjoying what we loved to do. A few times, when the conditions were right, Leonard and I would shut the motor down, douse all the lights in the boat, stare up into the heavens with some of Leonard's snapper, and enjoy the stars. What a special time!

Sometimes strange things happen out on the lake in the middle of the night. One night Leonard and I were fishing late, and it was pitch black outside. I could not have seen my hand in front of me if not for the soft glow of my depth finder's backlighting function. At night, the rear running light was a nuisance, simply because if I accidently stared into it, I became temporarily blinded, so I normally turned it off but kept the front lights on. We were fishing in Upper Bottle Lake, close to the Narrows. Suddenly we heard a very loud outboard motor speed through the Narrows. We could not see it, but we heard it. It is amazing how far sound travels on a still night over water. Leonard and I heard that motor over our little motor, and then it stopped. I shut my motor off and we just drifted for a brief time. It was long enough to witness the most amazing event both Leonard and I had ever seen on that lake.

It was like a chapter out of Jules Verne's *Twenty Thousand Leagues under the Sea*. After the motor stopped, some type of watercraft illuminated itself with no fewer than ten powerful floodlights. Leonard and I stared at that thing, wondering if the world was coming to an end. We were too far away to make out what was going on. There was a lot of commotion on that craft, and then more light, coming from underneath the craft, lit up the waters to a depth unknown. That was followed by short bursts of a very loud humming noise akin to a large charge of electricity. The humming noise stopped, and then there was more commotion. Then all the lights were shut down, the motor started up, and the craft began moving to another unknown location.

It sounded as if they were getting closer to us. I hurriedly attached the rear light we had taken off. I hoped whatever it was would see us. Then it stopped again. They were somewhere on the eastern shore. The whole scenario repeated itself: the floodlights, the underwater lights, the humming discharge of electric current, and all the commotion. Suddenly whatever it was raced off to another location. The scene repeated itself a couple more times, and then the craft disappeared back through the Narrows.

We watched the whole thing from our vantage point close to the center reeds. The next morning, after talking with the guys, we arrived at the conclusion that it had to have been the DNR shocking fish for research. Later Daryl verified that is what we saw. It never dawned on us that it could have been the DNR. Nonetheless, it was very spooky since it happened in total pitch-black darkness.

Another majestic event that we witnessed on occasion was the northern lights. If it were not for fishing with Leonard late at night, I never would have seen them. I will never forget my first time seeing the event. A luminous glow that took on a greenish cast filled the northern sky. "Leonard! Look at that!" I told him. It was a ghostly sight of light shooting out into the sky and swaying left and then right, like sheets in the wind. Of all the hours we spent on the Bottle Lakes, the northern lights appeared just a few times. Even though they didn't last long, they were magical.

I consider myself a very impatient fisherman. If we were not getting hits on a regular basis, while staring into the soft light of the depth finder and listening to the tranquilizing effect of the motor, I would find myself slowly going to sleep. I can honestly say there were times I would suggest trying one more spot and then shamelessly hoping we never got a hit, just so we could go in. I knew that if Leonard or I would get a hit, we would have to be out there for at least another half hour.

When we did finally come in and we had fish to clean, I normally would go ahead and clean them even if they were all Leonard's fish. Leonard would always ask if I needed help, but I normally told him I could do it. On most years, Leonard and I would bunk in the same cabin simply because everyone knew we would come in late. Sometimes it was two in the morning before I went to bed, only to find Leonard watching some late show on his portable TV that he would always bring along. The next morning, he was up by seven, making his way to the big cabin, where Michael would serve breakfast. And so the day started early for him and ended early; only the latter was early the next morning.

That was Leonard, one of my best fishing buddies and a great friend. If Leonard could have one wish granted to him, it would be to have one more fishing experience on the Bottle Lakes, sitting in the bow of the boat with one of us running the motor, trolling a minnow for walleyes late at night under a full moon, on water as smooth as glass, his snapper by his side as he smoked a cigarette. For Leonard, it simply didn't get any better than that.

CHAPTER 25

Terry

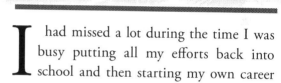

I had missed a lot during the time I was busy putting all my efforts back into school and then starting my own career in the seventies and early eighties. One person I wish I would have gotten to know earlier in those years was Terry Carlson. Terry married Leonard's only daughter, Connie, in the early seventies. He swept her off her feet, and together they moved to Pasco, Washington, where they bought a wonderful home right on the bank overlooking the Snake and Columbia Rivers. Connie and Terry still live there to this day.

Terry is a well-structured man with a full head of hair, so when the wind blows, he sometimes looks as though he stuck his finger into an outlet. He has a wonderful sense of humor and very seldom takes on a serious posture toward anyone. He is the friendliest of people, is easygoing and talkative, and loves to fish.

Terry's move to Pasco, Washington, was a dream come true for him and Connie. One of the greatest fisheries in the United States, the great Columbia River, can be viewed right out of his picture window. It stands to reason Terry took full advantage of his prize location. He bought himself a boat and learned to fish the Columbia and Snake Rivers for walleyes, smallmouths, salmon, sturgeon, and anything else that swims in that fishery. Terry often told me stories of fishing for smallmouths on the Columbia until he and his friends could not cast anymore, their arms and wrists spent in just a few hours. He told me of years when the fishing was so good in those waters that he would wear the gears down in some expensive bait casting reels, only to have to buy new ones for the next year.

In addition to the rivers, the surrounding area of Pasco is loaded with reservoirs that offer excellent largemouth bass fishing. As luck would have it, Connie loves to fish and is an avid bass angler in her own right. Terry proudly would tell me stories of how she often outfished him in bass tournaments, which they both loved to partake in. The two of them were made for each other.

Terry's love for fishing took him in many directions. He not only fished the rivers and the reservoirs in Washington State and Oregon; he would head up north into Alaska fishing on charters for king salmon. A few times, he booked trips into South America, where he fished the Amazon in search of the famous peacock bass, which is arguably, pound for pound, the hardest-fighting freshwater fish in existence. No matter where his travels took him, he was sure to experience great fishing adventures.

I first met Terry in 1989 during our trip up north. (See figure 11.) It was a long time coming, as Jim often told me about Terry and his love for fishing. I was anxious to finally get to know the man that would soon become one of my best friends. Terry could talk a person's ear off regarding fishing, and he knew what he was talking about. Some of the stories he would tell us about walleye and smallmouth fishing on the Columbia I could only dream about.

Terry is never boastful. His stories always come across in the most eloquent way, and he never brags about anything. He was successful in his career and still is one of the most down-to-earth guys I ever met. Connie is a lucky woman to have him. Some of my fondest memories on the Bottle Lakes are those of fishing with Terry. Whether fishing or just socializing, he is a fun person to have around.

CHAPTER 26

Uncle Charlie

In 1993, Terry invited his uncle Charlie to come along. We were all eager to meet his uncle Charlie and treat him to a fun time fishing in Minnesota. Terry's uncle Charlie was about thirty years senior to us. He loved to fish. He was also a man after my own heart. He loved to fish for carp, so whenever Terry and Connie would visit relatives in Nebraska, Terry would take Uncle Charlie out carp fishing.

Uncle Charlie lives in Fremont, Nebraska. Fremont had by that time grown to a sizeable community bordered on the south by the Platte River. Expansion then had to take place north and spread out east to west. Since the town lies near the Platte River, there are plenty of sand pits to choose from that host a plentiful supply of carp. Their favorite destination was the Fremont State Lakes, which are decades old, with deep, clear blue water and a great supply of carp. Terry had told me stories of his uncle Charlie catching fifteen-to-twenty-pound carp out of those pits using nothing but the fruit from a mulberry tree as bait. During a certain time of the year, normally late spring, mulberry trees are in full production. Mulberry trees are native to Nebraska, so they abound along the Platte River valley, growing wild in the sandy soil. It is quite common to see mulberry trees growing next to the water's edge near an old sand pit. Such is the case around the sand pits of the Fremont State Lakes.

That is when Uncle Charlie would take out his boat and launch it into his favorite lake. He knew where to go. He knew where to find the mulberry trees whose branches were extended out over the shore. Anchored close to the tree, he would bait a small hook with a mulberry, put on a bobber, and pitch it right under the mulberry tree. If he timed it right and the carp were feeding on the mulberry fruit floating on the water, Uncle Charlie had a good chance to hook into a massive carp. It didn't work all the time, but the results were worth the effort. Hooking into a carp in the fifteen-to-twenty-pound range is the ultimate fishing experience.

In 1993, Jim, Wayne, Larry, Leonard, Uncle Charlie, Terry, and I left Leonard's farm around midnight. Uncle Charlie experienced the long nighttime drive that Terry had described. Soon Uncle Charlie would be a direct observer to the breathtaking beauty of the Bottle Lakes. He would become an active participant in our traditional ways. In 1993, along with the rest of us, Uncle Charlie was looking forward to a fun week of fishing. (See figure 12.)

The long-range forecast for our upcoming week was not favorable. It was predicted to be colder than normal. Everyone was made aware of the forecast before we left Nebraska so that suitable cold-weather clothing was not left behind. The last time I had experienced chilly weather in Minnesota was 1984, when Jim and I stayed by ourselves.

The issue with chilly weather in the fall is that nobody was acclimated to it. Normally everyone had just experienced the sunbaked days of the summer, during which temperatures can exceed one hundred degrees with high humidity. Throw us into chilly weather without becoming acclimated, and it can feel like ten below zero. If this year was going to be a repeat of 1984, we were in for some chilly days out on the water.

During our weeklong stay in 1993, Wambolt's stove in the large cabin was working overtime. The forecast proved to be correct. The cold, chilly winds moved in from the north and stuck around for the whole week. Daryl was scrambling to start winterizing some of the cabins. The large cabin had a restroom with a shower, but the community showers were in better shape. Most of us took to the community showers to use the restroom. It turned out that year that we had one usable shower head, one sink with running water, and one stall. Everything else got shut down. Daryl was also in a noticeable hurry to get some of the unused docks out of the water. During the days, he would work on removing docks, to the exclusion of anything else.

In 1993, we were the only group in the resort. Daryl was in a bustle of activity, preparing for what promised to be a long winter. However, that didn't stop Daryl from getting out at night and pulling Rapalas for walleyes. The walleyes also felt the chilly weather coming, as the water temperatures dropped significantly. The walleyes started hitting at night, and Daryl was nailing them.

This was great music to our ears. Fishing during the day was disappointing. The northern bite, if there was one, simply shut down. Live bait has always been our traditional method to catch walleyes. The first couple of nights out, live bait was not doing the trick. Stubbornly, a few of us were ready for a change.

Leave it to Terry to organize a plan. If not for him, we would still have gone out at night and sat with live bait or pulled a small minnow behind the boat, which would have yielded us nothing. Daryl was coming in with walleyes, and Terry wanted to do the same. Daryl suggested we pull Rapalas in front of Whippoorwill Resort.

On the third night, we put Terry's plan into action. After an evening meal, Terry gathered all of us around the table and told us what we were going to do. First, everyone that was willing to pull a Rapala needed one, or at least some shallow-diving floating artificial minnow. Terry showed us all how to tie the Rapala knot—a nonslip loop knot tied directly to the lure. This allowed the lure to move freely and more naturally. I hadn't previously known the knot existed. I silently told myself, *Maybe this guy does know something about fishing.*

It was already getting dark. The forecast was not good. The lows for the night were to dip below freezing and into the twenties. That meant insulated coveralls, long underwear, a warm shirt, two pairs of socks, a good pair of shoes, hooded sweatshirts, warm gloves, and a stocking cap. The least favorable outcome from all these clothes was restricted movement in the boat.

We had rented three boats for the week, each one equipped with the usual nine-horsepower Johnson motors. Each boat had a depth finder. This year Terry had brought up Leonard's trolling motor, which he used for bass fishing in the mornings. For our little outing that night, he wanted to use the trolling motor instead of the boat motor. It was all charged up, ready to go.

Since Leonard, Jim, and Wayne would have nothing to do with running artificial lures, they agreed to go in one boat, where they could pull live bait. Logistically it is poor practice to mix up fishing techniques in the same boat. Either we would all pull artificial minnows or we would all pull live bait. Uncle Charlie and Terry manned the second boat. Larry and I would take the third. Larry was Jim's younger brother. A good fisherman in his own right, Larry volunteered to run the motor, which I agreed to without reservation.

"Out to the docks and man the boats!" was the cry. Damn, it was cold outside! The blustery air hit us as soon as we opened the cabin door. Our destination was just up the north shore in Whippoorwill Bay. We didn't have to go far.

Whippoorwill had four large pole lamps spaced along their shoreline. Over the years, we would use those lights as a guide to Wambolt's Resort. Wambolt's had lights, but nothing like Whippoorwill's. The large lights cast a soft incandescent light out over the water. We could see where we were going. Along with the depth finders, we could use Whippoorwill's docks as way points. Could it get any better than that for pulling artificial minnows? Terry was betting on a successful evening.

Whippoorwill's bay was not that large. Higher speeds than normal were needed to get the Rapalas to dive to around three feet and shake the way they were designed to do. Running boats at a slightly higher speed in a congested area would take some practice and attention from the boat drivers. Terry had more experience in that regard than the rest of us. I was glad I was not running the motor.

The bay itself was free of any drop-offs, so finding a consistent depth for a considerable distance was easy. Consistent depth is desired when pulling an artificial bait. Traversing in and out while searching for depth made it difficult to have any success using an artificial lure. In that regard, Whippoorwill Bay was as good as any place on Upper Bottle Lake.

Our walleye run started just west of Whippoorwill, which was about halfway home to Wambolt's Resort. We would head east until the bay shallows forced us to turn south for a few hundred yards. The route one way was about half a mile. Wayne's boat was running the slowest of the three, since they were pulling minnows. They decided to start on the other end of the route.

Larry and I entered the slot, with Terry behind us. Before too long, we had separated ourselves from each other to a manageable distance. Terry was running just a bit slower than we were, since he was using the trolling motor. Larry wanted to troll forward, since a little more speed was needed. This reminded me of the first night on Lower Bottle Lake in 1967, when we had five in one boat. This time we had a manageable two in the boat, and we had a depth finder. One-half mile is not far when trolling an artificial lure. Once we had finished one direction, Larry and I would pull in our lure, make a sharp turn, and then start the entire process over again going in the other direction.

The action started right away. We started catching walleyes while trolling artificial minnows. There was no single thump that I felt on the line, but there was an immediate thrashing about from the rod tip. When one of us had a fish on, the motor was shut down and we enjoyed a great fight with a beautiful walleye.

I have not forgotten how cold it was that evening on the water. It was a good thing there was no wind. Trolling at a faster pace was bad enough. There was just enough wind generated that Larry and I had our line freeze to our rod eyelets a couple of times. The other guys reported the same incident back at the cabin. The rods were covered in a thin film of frost. We kept running while the walleyes were hitting. Back and forth we went, up and down Whippoorwill's shoreline. By 10:00 p.m., we'd had enough. Three hours on that water had chilled everyone to the bone.

We all caught fish that night. Terry caught the largest walleye of the night, at over five pounds. I watched the whole thing, since Larry and I were close behind. Uncle Charlie was there with the net, and Terry was enjoying a great fight. Uncle Charlie got so cold that night that he was uncomfortable. I believe most of us were. I can honestly say it was the coldest evening of fishing I ever experienced on the Bottle Lakes. I am not sure any amount of clothing would have made us feel comfortable during that evening in 1993. Terry's plan worked, and that is what seals the memories. Yay for Terry! Yay for Uncle Charlie for putting up with us that evening!

During the rest of the week, we experienced more cold weather, but that didn't deter Jim and Larry. One evening they decided to go on a grand tour of Upper Bottle Lake at night. Their plan was to start at Wambolt's

Resort, head toward the eastern shore, and circle Upper Bottle Lake. They were not going to come in until they made the full circle, which would take a good two to three hours to complete. According to Jim's recollection of that evening, they were pulling small minnows behind the boat. Neither Jim nor Larry managed to get one single hit until they had Wambolt's Bay in sight while running down the western shore.

Suddenly Jim got a hit. He set the hook into something big. Soon Jim was engaged in a battle with a large fish. Jim, as usual, had as much line out as he could run, and it took some time to gain some advantage over the fish, whatever it was. The battle at the boat was just beginning. The fish made run after run when it saw the boat. They could see the diamond-like eyes deep in the water, reflecting off Larry's flashlight—the unmistakable signature of a walleye. They still could not make out its size. Finally, Jim began getting the upper hand, and the fish slowly came up to reveal his true magnificence. It was the biggest walleye they had ever seen. With one swoop, Larry got him in the net and over into the boat.

Back at camp, everyone else was just milling about until both Jim and Larry came in to warm up. Then they told us their story. We went out to look at that fish, and I could not believe my eyes. The walleye was a beautiful fish. Daryl had a scale in his fish house. It weighed nine and three-quarters pounds. (See figure 13.) His length was thirty and one-half inches. Jim decided he wanted to mount him. I helped him soak some towels and carefully put him in the freezer. Later, when we told Daryl about the walleye, he told us that was the biggest walleye he'd ever heard of coming out of the Bottle Lakes.

Uncle Charlie had an enjoyable time with us that year, and we had a fun time with him. I know he was glad to get home to some warmer air. Uncle Charlie never did come back with us. In his own words, "It's too cold up there!" It can be cold up north, and it was unfortunate that week—the week Uncle Charlie came—had to be the coldest week I ever experienced on the Bottle Lakes.

CHAPTER 27

1997: Thirty-Year Anniversary

1997 was the first year that the whole gang was able to get together since we started our annual fishing trip in 1967. It was our Thirty-year anniversary. During every year from 1967 to 1997, someone had been missing for one reason or another. This year all was in alignment. I cannot answer for everyone else, but for me, out of the fifty years we have been coming to the Bottle Lakes, this one was the most memorable. Michael, Rick, Terry, Leonard, Jim, Wayne, Douglas, and I left Leonard's farm at our normal Friday-night departure time, headed for an unforgettable week of eating, drinking, and fishing. (See figure 14.)

By the time we unpacked everything at the resort, the screened-in porch of the main cabin was stuffed with fishing gear and accessory items. It was hard to find a place to sit down without rearranging in some manner. A lot of the gear made it into the boats, which was developing into an issue for us. It was becoming almost impossible to move around in the boats.

We could not have asked for a better weather pattern than the one that had settled into the region for the week. The week's forecast called for clear skies and mild weather for both days and nights. I can remember that week representing some of the best visual presentation of color Mother Nature had to offer. The trees were in their prime fall color spectacle. The lake itself was mostly calm, reflecting the colors of those trees into the water, creating a scene that could not have been painted. Most of the days, we could fish in T-shirts or short-sleeved shirts. Nighttime required only a hooded sweatshirt or a light jacket. We were in the doldrums of northern Minnesota.

We had trouble with a family of otters that year. Periodically we could see the family of five swimming in line along the shorelines, with the mother and father out front and the pups behind. They were cute animals, but they were thieves. We found out the hard way that otters would ransack the bait in our trolling-style minnow buckets if we left them tied to the docks without securing the lids. Before we realized it, they would push their way through the top lid, and not a minnow could be found in the morning. That was an expensive lesson. The secret was to secure the lid so they could not push it open. This was easier said than done. Even when using wire that Daryl had on hand, the clever guys still managed to swipe some of our bait. That went on the whole week. We didn't dare tie a fish to the docks in hopes of cleaning it the next morning. The only thing left would have been the chewed-off stringer or a skeleton of the fish left behind.

Fishing was not excellent, but we still managed to catch enough for a fish fry and then some. Up to the year 1997, we had not targeted panfish as we did in the later years, so stringers of bluegills and crappies didn't make it into the boat to help fill our coolers. We did manage to catch some rock bass at night while trolling for walleyes. Rock bass are good eating fish. I rate them close to a bluegill in taste.

I can remember one exceptional fishing story that came out of that year, complements of Jim. Doug, Michael, Terry, and I decided to take an afternoon and play a friendly round of golf. On that afternoon, Jim decided to go fishing by himself. Wayne, Leonard, and Rick took another boat and went trolling for northerns. Jim's plan was to sit with his cane pole just off a point that jutted out from the eastern shore reeds.

When we returned from our golf outing that afternoon, Jim led us to the docks, where he lifted out of the water two of the most beautiful walleye I had ever seen. The colors embossed on those fish were golden brown. We took them to the fish house, where Daryl had a scale all set up. Close by was a tape measure. They were exactly six and three-quarters pounds and twenty-six and a half inches. We had dubbed them "Jim's twins" because that is exactly what those two walleyes were—twins to each other. (See figure 15.)

Jim said he motored out to his location, dropped anchor, and sat for a couple of hours catching small perch. He was using small minnows, looking for walleyes. Jim has the most patience of anyone I know when it comes to fishing. He can sit in one location for hours. I don't know how he does it. According to Jim, his bobber went down, and soon he was fighting with a large walleye. Jim described the situation as desperate, since nobody was there to help him land the walleye. However, after a lengthy battle, he managed to get a net under the beautiful fish and get him in the boat. There was still life twitching in the tail of the small walleye minnow Jim had used on the first walleye. He didn't want to waste time baiting up a fresh minnow while this beautiful walleye lay on the bottom of the boat. Without hesitation, Jim dropped the minnow back into the water in the same location before he tried to place the walleye on a stringer. Just a few minutes flew by, and down the bobber went again. Soon Jim was in another battle with another large walleye. By the time he was done, Jim had caught his twins. It was time to head back to the docks.

The significance of this story lies in the fact that we simply do not catch walleyes during the day in the fall in the Bottle Lakes. None of us, to my recollection, has ever said on any given afternoon, "I'm going walleye fishing. Want to come?" We go out for bass, panfish, or northerns, but not for walleyes. The Bottle Lakes have always been a nighttime walleye lake in the fall. Jim proved us wrong that afternoon. Catching those two walleyes during the day was about as implausible as Jim and me catching two crappies during that first trip in 1967.

It was hard to accept that the week was over. We left as usual on Saturday morning, around eight. It was very cold that morning, and the weather was about to turn nasty. A cold front had passed through the Dakotas during the night and had dumped a couple of inches of snow in the area. On our way back to Nebraska, we stopped for gas at Brookings, South Dakota, where the land was laden with snow. I remember this being the first time I traveled home on snowy roads. Nobody knew the next time we would all be together again, but I was sure that if I could make it, I would.

For the past thirty years, as far as I knew, we had all been lucky in not having any major health issues. Most of us had high blood pressure. I had a screwed-up back—something I would have to deal with the rest of my life. Nobody ever got hurt over the past thirty years we'd spent traveling I-29, which was a major miracle given our condition during those nighttime hours. We had learned a lot about fishing the Bottle Lakes. We knew every hole, every drop-off, every bar, and every weed bed in the lake. What we still didn't know was how to catch the damn crappies. We'd had no success with crappies except for 1987, when Wayne and Rick stumbled on them one afternoon. We had caught a few by accident, and Wayne and Jim would catch a few at night, but those were small numbers. We needed some way to figure this crappie thing out.

My "unsettled years" became settled in 1984, due in part to one particularly important phone call. It was my great friend Jim who made that "phone call of all phone calls." Nobody can understand how important that call was to me.

Writing about our adventures over the past thirty years brought back many memories. During this time, I had been blessed to enjoy the company of my best friends, some of which I have known since kindergarten. What started out as just an idea had blossomed into what I like to call "our yearly ritual." It was our "tradition like none other." What would the turn of the century bring to us? It was fast approaching. Michael's journals had the answers.

PART 3
MICHAEL'S JOURNALS

CHAPTER 1

The Turn of the Century

Prior to the year 2000, none of our trips were documented. If it had not been for a few pictures we had taken during the late eighties and through the nineties, most of the events during those years would have been lost to memory. What allowed me to recall the stories from some of our first trips had to do with first-time experiences. My impressions from those trips were so significant that my long-term memory could easily recall most of the events as they happened, with only small clues to help me out. A statement, a date stamp, or a photo was all I needed.

Sadly, that was not the case in the nineties. Apart from my almost total recall of my trip with Jim in 1984, the only memory stimulus I had of our trips in the nineties can be attributed to pictures. I suspect the loss of recall had to do with repetitive activities. We drove north during the night. We stayed at Wambolt's Resort. We caught lots of fish. We came home. When we repeated that every year, everything turned into one big jigsaw puzzle. Without documentation, it was impossible to order any events of significance into a proper perspective and time line.

In 1987, we had our twentieth reunion. In 1989, we had an exceptionally large group. In 1993, Uncle Charlie came with us. In 1997, we had our thirtieth reunion. Everything in between is a jumbled mess. Specific stories that could have been told were simply lost. At the turn of the century, in the year 2000, Michael started writing his journals.

Michael's journals were a form of diary and were not specific to our Minnesota fishing adventures. The diaries were a 365-day account of Michael's ventures during the year. They were not limited to just hunting and fishing but also included family gatherings.

Normally Michael would dedicate one page to one single-day activity. One-line sentences were jumbled together, rendering a small account of some highlight or specific occurrence deemed important enough to make it into the diary. Reading the journals takes some doing. Michael's cursive leaves a lot to the imagination, and sometimes finding just one word that was discernable could get me through the sentence. It was a form of hieroglyphics in which only the author could understand what was written in its entirety.

Michael documented departure times and arrival times. Michael also made sure to list those of us that went each year. He kept track of our grocery bills, what we paid for bait, what the reservations costs were, and, most significantly, how the fishing was during the week. Weather conditions were of interest, as that part of the trip was always haphazard. Some years the weather was good. Some years it was not so good. Michael also made sure to include the menu for our daily dinner meals.

Michael's journals were a priceless record of our daily activities regarding our fishing trips. Without his journals to draw on, it would be impossible to share some of our most cherished stories and memories. As I read the diaries, it took only a small entry to generate an unexpected but vivid recurrence of a given experience. Frequently I would tell myself, "Oh yeah! I remember that! I had forgotten all about it. Did it really happen that long ago?" Those experiences lost to declining memories are what I was looking for, and Michael's journals were full of them.

CHAPTER 2

Boats and More Boats

The first year we went up to the Bottle Lakes in 1967, we had one boat with one 5.5-horsepower motor for five guys. We did opt for another boat later in the week, but that one had no motor. In 1989, we rented four resort boats for ten guys.

Fishing out of resort boats year after year had led to overcrowding—not from people, but from fishing equipment. (See figure 16.) It seemed that every year, everyone had more junk to bring. Somehow all that additional equipment needed to get into the boats. Consequently, there came a time when we could not walk from one side of a seat to the other without stumbling into someone's gear. Just moving about in the boat was a chore. A typical resort boat would be loaded up with our trolling minnow buckets; our homemade rod holders; our portable depth finders; our endless supply of fishing equipment, which included tackle boxes, countless rods and reels, and dip nets; anchors; coolers packed with goodies; our transom-mounted trolling motors; fish baskets; Coleman lanterns for night fishing; and, for some of us, a portable seat that helped with tired butts. Life jackets got thrown about or became welcome seats for sore butts. Jim and Wayne even constructed a homemade rig for a lantern that somehow hung off the side of the boat while they were fishing at night. Plus our clothing got bulkier as rain gear became common attire for the boat driver. Trolling backward into wind-driven waves would soak the driver in minutes without good rain protection. Daryl had a lot of the old-fashioned metal chairs scattered about for his guests. I found out one year that this type of chair could straddle a boat seat and slide down to the floor of the boat. Now I had a comfortable boat seat with a much-needed back support. I was fishing in style for sure. Those were the good ole days—quite simple and very crowded. Of course, things had to change, and innocently enough, I was the bad boy for starting a trend—bringing my own boat!

Around 1995, I figured we needed a boat for my boys and me. Both my boys love to fish, and bank fishing was not cutting it for them. I was anxious to get a boat, so I bought the first decent one I ran across for just under a couple grand. The boat was called a Bluefin and was made by Sea Nymph. It was a sixteen-foot-long deep v aluminum design that was narrow in the beam. It had a screaming twenty-five-horsepower Johnson tiller motor on it that ran like the devil. I bought a transom mount trolling motor for it, and along with my portable Eagle depth finder, I was ready for Minnesota waters.

In 1998, Leonard decided he was going to get himself a boat. He bought himself a fourteen-foot aluminum v-haul Lund with a fifteen-horsepower Evinrude motor. It was a beautiful boat, perfect for Bottle Lakes fishing. In 1998, along with my Bluefin and Leonard's new Lund, we started pulling two boats to Minnesota for our week's stay.

There was some advantage in taking my own boat, but there were disadvantages as well. I was never comfortable getting there or coming back. I was always worried about something happening to a tire or having a bearing problem. My running lights became a nightmare every year. My lights never worked without me having to perform some sort of surgery on the entire system. I hated working on that kind of crap. I became a worrywart wondering if the engine would start or continue to perform during the week. In defense of my twenty-five-horsepower Johnson on the Bluefin, it never failed to start or run like the wind. It trolled without hiccup on low throttle, backward and forward. To this day, I consider it to be the best boat engine I ever owned.

The biggest disadvantage of having my own boat was that I always had to be the skipper. When I started pulling my boat up north, I intended for it to be used by anyone that wanted to use it, but that didn't materialize. I often told everyone to just take my boat if they wanted to go out, but nobody did. When we had only resort boats, everyone would take a boat whenever they wanted, and whomever wanted to go would go. I had hoped that bringing a boat from home would warrant the same circumstance, and then we would not have to pay for a resort boat. I was wrong. Strangely enough, if I didn't go out, my boat sat. I always had that sense of urgency to get my ass out into my boat so we could go fishing. Anyone could have taken it at any time. I would have been very cool with that arrangement. But that never happened.

When Leonard started bringing his boat, it seemed to always be in use by someone. It didn't matter the time of day or what kind of fishing was to be done; if someone wanted to go, he would go out and would take his boat. I never did understand that situation fully until I suddenly realized it had to do with family. Nearly everyone was related to Leonard, so taking his boat out was not a big deal. Mike, Terry, Jim, and Leonard all, in some manner, shared his boat. It is family ties that form the strongest bond. I was okay with that. In my case, my boat sat until I dragged my sorry, tired ass down to the boat dock, climbed in, turned over the motor, and waited for someone to come fishing.

Some of the advantages Leonard and I had in bringing our boats outweighed the disadvantages. We now had ample room to store our gear for the long trip up north. This was a huge plus for us, as we were bringing more junk every year. Most of it went into the boats. Running my own boat allowed me to control the boat in a way I felt best, depending on the type of fishing we were doing. It sounds selfish, but I never did go anywhere unless those in my boat were united in our destination and presentation. It does no good for anyone in my boat to not have some harmony of opinion. Regardless of whether I caught anything or not, the best feeling I would get was for others in my boat to have some success. That meant I was putting them on some fish. There is no greater reward for the skipper.

Another advantage was my comfort. Resort boats were not comfortable. Until I found my metal chair that I used at Wambolt's, sitting in a resort boat all day resulted in a stiff back and a sore butt. Running my own boat resulted in more room and more comfort. The resort boats didn't handle well in high waves. No longer did we have to worry about windy days on which waves could make it impossible to get onto the lake. Our more modern boats could handle the waves without issue, allowing us more time on the lake regardless of the wind.

One of the great advantages of having boats with larger motors had to do with getting somewhere quickly. There was no more putting around with nine-horsepower motors. My twenty-five-horsepower Johnson made short work of the Bottle Lakes. Except for the instability and the steep sides of the Bluefin, it was a fine boat. Even Leonard's fifteen-horsepower Evinrude was a large step up from the nine-horsepower motors of the resort boats, which meant getting to our fishing hole quicker. Another advantage was the ability to canvass more of the lake on a given day. We could skip around faster. If one hole was slow, we could get to another in fleeting time. This was important for me, as I am a very impatient fisherman.

Getting someplace on the lake fast seemed to make the lake feel smaller. On Upper Bottle, we would be at our destination in just a few minutes. In 1967, it took us up to twenty minutes just to get to the Pork Barrel. In 1967, we felt the lake to be large and intimidating. Now we could make that same trip across Lower Bottle in three to four minutes. In some respects, that shrinks the lake.

When I first bought my Bluefin, my boys and I took the boat out many times to our favorite reservoirs, only to find out the boat was not very stable in the wind. The boat, being light, long, and narrow, made for a fast skip across the lake. It was like trying to control a torpedo. Wind was a big issue for this boat. A gust of wind would tear into the bow, and if I was not paying attention, it could turn the boat a few degrees—just enough to force immediate corrections before the wind could flip me. I have no problem going fast, but not in an unstable boat. I always watched out for the wind direction when I was heading across the lake. I quickly learned to throttle down if heading into the wind or, most importantly, dealing with a brisk broadside wind, which was most dangerous.

The coup de grace for that boat happened in the year 2000 in Minnesota. Not only was the boat hard to handle in the wind, but it was a major chore just to get in and out of the damn thing. (See figure 17.) One slip could send someone falling backward or, worse yet, forward into the water. It happened to Doug that year. One of my best friends lost his footing and fell between the boat and the dock, right into the water. Doug was lucky to escape getting badly hurt. A bang on the head or a gash would have sent him to the hospital. It was after that very episode that I vowed at once to sell that dangerous boat and get myself a safer one.

After Doug's incident at the dock, I decided to start looking for another boat. After a little research and talking to a few people, I knew I wanted a late 1980s or early 1990s Lund, preferably a tiller style, no less than a sixteen-footer with a wide beam and a Johnson motor on it. I do not know why I wanted a Johnson except that my limited experience with motors had been with Johnson motors. I had a price in mind, but the other requirements were more important to me. In 2001, after the year's fishing was over, I was able to sell my Bluefin. Then I set out in search of my newest used boat.

Week after week, I searched the ads in the papers. I looked at many boats over the course of many months, but nothing suited my fancy until one Sunday afternoon in the spring of 2002, when I saw a listing for a boat located in Omaha, Nebraska. I drove over that very day. I knew right away it was the boat I was after and paid the guy his asking price. The boat was a beautiful 1989 Lund Predator 1650 with blue trim that had a Johnson forty-horsepower tiller motor sitting on it. I still fish out of that boat to this day. (See figure 18.)

By the time 2008 rolled around, Michael bought himself a boat—a red Lund fourteen-footer on the same line as Leonard's, except Michael had a twenty-five-horsepower Johnson on it just like the one I'd had on my Bluefin. Now we had three boats that we pulled up every year. The vehicles and boats were packed with gear. It was more gear than we needed, but we felt we still required it. Did we need a dozen tackle boxes, five to six rods and reels apiece, enough clothing to last a whole winter, food that would feed an army, and enough coolers to pack out an elk? Probably not! In addition, we had five-gallon buckets to deal with, a dozen or so trolling-style minnow buckets, battery chargers, backup batteries, and more. By the time 2008 came around, just bringing up unnecessary equipment was not enough. We required more. Could it get any better?

In 2011, Wayne decided he'd had enough and bought himself a brand-new beautiful black seventeen-foot Lund Rebel that had an eighty-four-inch beam and a new four-stroke sixty-horsepower Mercury tiller motor on it. The boat was decked out with two depth-finders that Wayne, to this day, still does not know how to operate, and an ultramodern front-mounted

Minn-Kota trolling motor that does everything except catch the fish. (See figure 19.) In our later years, we would pull up north my Lund Predator, Wayne's Lund Rebel, and Michael's Lund. In 2012, Michael lost his boat to an accident and purchased a 1989 Lund along the same lines as my boat. He still fishes out of that boat to this day.

CHAPTER 3

Getting There

etting to Park Rapids year after year was an adventure itself. We could have made it easier on all of us if we had not been in such a damn hurry to get there. But as it was, tradition, more than anything else, played a great part in our departure plans year after year. Aside from our first three or four trips back in the late sixties and then, most recently, the last few years, our plans never changed. We left at the same time from the same location and drove the same roads.

In the seventies and eighties, Jim's tradition was to leave on a Friday evening close to midnight. Jim's only requirement for those planning on coming would be to gather in Prague, Nebraska, at the bar where plans were made spontaneously as to available transportation, which was always an issue. Most of the other important considerations would be improvised over the course of the trip. The caravan would normally depart just after midnight.

Eventually our departure materialized into something grander than just leaving from the Prague bar. By the early nineties, we had grown into a tight-knit group. Jim, Mike, Wayne, Leonard, and I became regulars. Doug, Terry, and Rick came when they could. Sometimes Jim's brother Larry would come along. One year, Terry's uncle joined us. There were others: Chris, who was Leo's brother, would come occasionally. Jim's business partner, Kevin, would sometimes make the trip with us. Consequently, instead of meeting at the bar, our place of gathering needed to be a little more refined. That place became Leonard's farm, which was just a mile outside of Prague.

Year after year, those that decided to come would gather at the farmstead around ten thirty or eleven on Friday night. Everyone was excited to meet. For some of us, this was the only time of the year we got together. Plus we were all very anxious to get going.

During the late eighties and early nineties, before we started pulling boats, gear space was limited. We had to make do with the space Wayne had in his pickup and what space Michael had after seating four normally large men in his Blazer. The nice part of using those two vehicles was that we had no worries about anything getting wet. Wayne had a full shell on his pickup, and Michael's Blazer was waterproof already. Our constant reminder to us regarding anything about our trip has always been that if we did it in 1967, we could do it now.

Since I missed most of those years, I am not able to write about the unavoidable events that had to have happened to those caravans. When I talk to Jim, Wayne, and others who went during those years, nobody can remember anything. I do not blame them, but I know there had to be some situations they got themselves into simply because fate, destiny, or bad luck made it inevitable, regardless of how careful they were. Getting to Park Rapids then became one of our most revered conversation starters. The drive up north was so profoundly honored by us that we would ask ourselves every year, "I wonder what will happen to us this year?"

For Instance, in 1992, I didn't come, for reasons I cannot remember. That year Wayne had an unfortunate incident. He lost the front left wheel assembly on his pickup—not just the tire; the whole damn wheel flew off. Nobody got hurt, thank God. They were all lucky! When something like that happens, the whole caravan stops until everyone can move on once again. Luckily they were able to find a garage in a nearby town with a mechanic willing to mend the situation. However, the garage didn't open until early Saturday morning. The worst part of the ordeal was that it happened while they were still in Nebraska. In Wayne's situation, it took the whole Saturday to get things fixed. That meant another four hundred or so miles to go once they were up and running. That year they didn't arrive in Park Rapids until early Sunday morning, at which time everyone was spent. That little incident tapped into precious fishing time.

There simply was no easy route to get to Park Rapids. Our route was set from year to year in the eighties and nineties. We would head out from Leonard's farm to Fremont, Nebraska, where we would pick up Highway 77 and take it all the way to Sioux City, Iowa. It was the same exact route we took during our first year back in 1967. Then we would take I-29 and head straight north until we got to Fargo, North Dakota. At Fargo, we would pick up Highway 10 east through Detroit Lakes, Minnesota, and then to Park Rapids. That route never changed for years.

One year Wayne decided there had to be an alternate route off I-29 instead of going all the way to Fargo. Of course, tradition dictated everything we did during those years, and our paradigm was hard to change. But anything that would take miles off our travel was well worth pursuing. Prior to Wayne's stirring of the pot, our paradigms were so imbedded that we simply did not look at a map to find alternate routes. But leave it to Wayne to change all that. And he found one that worked well; our alternate route cut about forty miles off from the route through Fargo.

Our new exit was Wahpeton, North Dakota. Somehow from there we had to get to Detroit Lakes and then to Park Rapids. Detroit Lakes then became our waypoint, but getting there took some doing. Out of Wahpeton, the route became twisted. When traveling through Minnesota, there is not a straight three-mile section of road anywhere. This was also true with Wayne's new route. Twisting and turning was the norm. Where is the next turnoff? What highway are we on? Do we turn left or right? Now which way? These are all questions we asked ourselves during the first few years traveling our new route until we became comfortable with it.

I-29 was not a favorable highway for gas in the middle of the night. Whoever drove had to make sure to fill up in Fremont before we set out. Normally our next stop out of Fremont would be Brookings, South Dakota, about 213 miles out. One year I was driving my small Ford Ranger pickup that had an 18-gallon gas tank. I pumped in 17.7 gallons of gas in Brookings that night. It was the closest any of us ever got to running out of gas.

From Brookings, gas was not much of a problem, but fatigue was! Going down I-29 in the middle of the night is something you must experience to believe. There are miles and miles of nothing but straight road void of any significant traffic. To make matters worse, sections of the interstate were always getting resurfaced or completely torn out to make ready for resurfacing. We never could get from Sioux City to Wahpeton without running into construction. Construction took place both in South Dakota and North Dakota. Barriers that usually diverted the traffic to single lanes ran for miles.

I developed a great admiration for those truckers that ran at night, but they were not running on empty regarding sleep—at least I hope they weren't. As for us, we normally had just spent the day working. The evening was set aside for final packing and then a late-night drive to meet at Leonard's farm at a time we all should be going to bed. But our adrenaline was flowing, and the excitement of once again venturing north gave us our second wind until we hit the wall around three in the morning.

From 3:00 a.m. to around 5:00 a.m. was the most dangerous time. If I were driving, the interstate would turn me into a zombie. Normally the radio would be on softly. My companion in the cab was worthless, because he was fast asleep. I found myself staring out into the night, watching the white lines whiz by. I didn't know it, but that action was slowly hypnotizing me. The monotony of I-29 made all the miles look alike. At three in the morning, even approaching headlights were few and far between. My eyes would start to burn, so I would have to blink often. I started having difficulty focusing. I changed positions in my seat constantly, trying to get comfortable. Opening the window helped, but then the heavy eyelids would hit again. I wanted to yawn all the time. I wanted to rub my burning eyes all the time. Nothing helped. I was fighting a losing battle. I started daydreaming and having wandering, disconnected thoughts. Suddenly the hypnotic state would hit—the condition I was trying to avoid. I was under a spell and felt drugged. I know there were times when I dozed off while I was just staring straight ahead without blinking. Then, suddenly, I would come out of it. I knew something had happened.

One of the best ways to help us with monotony during those wee hours was to call for a piss stop. We would find an off ramp along the way, get out, and take a piss. We could walk around and take in the clean, fresh air, which usually had a chill in it. If the night was clear, we could look at the stars that filled the sky. Sometimes I would find myself just staring out for a brief time into the endless blackness of the night. A short piss call can go a long way in reviving the body in the middle of the night.

It was important for us to all stay together like a moving caravan. Our band was tightly knit, so if something happened to one of the vehicles, the others could help. We prided ourselves in staying together. In the nineties, nobody had a cell phone. Nobody had CB radios. Visual sight was our only means of keeping up with each other. Staying together was so important to us that Michael bought a pair of two-way analog radios one year—one for the lead truck and one for the rear truck. Those radios helped us keep open communication within the caravan. The range was no more than two or three miles, but they did the job. Later in our years, cell phones and then smartphones allowed easy communication between all of us. We lost some nostalgia when we started using smartphones. The trip was not as exciting, because it was not that important to stay together anymore. We could be twenty miles apart and could still stay in contact with everyone if something happened.

Sometimes, in the middle of the night, even the best-thought-out plans didn't work regardless of whether we had radios or not. One year Leonard and I were in his pickup, pulling up the rear. Michael and Wayne were in front, blazing the way to Brookings, South Dakota, which was our normal stop for gas. That year Leonard decided he wanted to drive from Fremont to Brookings, and then I would take over from there. Since north of Brookings was the "hit the wall" time, Leonard wanted nothing to do with that next stretch of road. After we passed Sioux Falls, South Dakota, we had another ninety miles to Brookings. I decided to take a nap. I told Leonard, "Those taillights up ahead are our guys. Do not let them out of your sight."

He told me, "Okay! Yeah, I see them."

I've always had a tough time sleeping in a car or truck, but for some reason that night I fell into a deep sleep. When I awoke, I didn't realize how much time had passed. I can remember waking up and seeing Leonard staring straight ahead. The truck was still purring down the road. I pulled out my thermos of coffee and poured myself a cup. After gathering myself, I asked Leonard, "How much farther to Brookings?"

He said, "We should be there anytime."

I checked the time, and things were not adding up. Normally we would pull into Brookings around two thirty or three at the latest. It was well past three thirty. I could see a few taillights in the distance. I asked Leonard, "Are those our guys up ahead?"

He said, with bloodshot eyes, "Yep! That's them up ahead."

I asked, "Are you sure?"

He responded, "Well, I think so."

I asked Leonard another question: "Did we pass Brookings?"

He was not sure. The taillights up ahead disappeared. That was when I knew the lights Leonard was following were not our guys. Then I realized what had happened. Leonard had somehow just kept right on going and never stopped in Brookings.

Now our guys were behind us and were wondering what had happened to us. We were now a good half hour to forty-five minutes ahead of them, and they had no way of knowing it. I broke the news to Leonard, who took it all in stride, and I never made a big deal out of it. It could have happened to any of us on that crazy road at three in the morning. I told Leonard to pull over the next chance he got, and we would change drivers. *He has to be dead tired*, I thought to myself, but true to Leonard's character, he never complained. After changing drivers, we decided to just keep going until we came into Detroit Lakes, where we normally stopped for breakfast. We would wait for the others at our usual greasy spoon in downtown Detroit Lakes.

Around 7:00 a.m., Leonard and I walked into the restaurant looking like a couple of zombies with bloodshot eyes. Around seven forty-five, sure enough, our gang came walking into the restaurant looking just as bad, all of them with bloodshot eyes. We were all looking forward to one of the best breakfasts this side of Michael's. We were tired and really needed something in our stomachs after surviving the long haul from Leonard's farm. The guys wanted to know what had happened to us. When we told them, we all had a good laugh over coffee or milk, bacon and sausage, eggs with hash browns, and Wayne's biscuits with gravy, all with warm, buttery toast. Year after year, that breakfast was a "pump me up" for sure and was one of our most prized traditions.

Apart from getting lost a couple of times by taking wrong roads, if we survived the night, the morning hours normally took care of themselves. If we made it to Detroit Lakes and filled up our empty stomachs, there was nothing else in the way to test our resolve to get to Park Rapids. It was just a straight shot east of about forty miles.

When we took the Wahpeton exit from I-29 to head into Minnesota, some transformation took place that reenergized all of us. Those guys that were sleeping woke up. We all wanted to talk again. Our breakfast only made it better. We watched the sunrise and experienced the world around us waking up. We were anxious again.

Heading north in the middle of the night was okay when we were young. As we grew older, the drive north became harder on us. It wore on our patience, and we started getting that look in our eyes that brandished mood swings. But nobody ever complained or let loose with some senseless outburst bound to be regretted. We were all tired, and being of great friendship, we would never let an uncharacterized statement or action threaten that bond. We continued our traditional nighttime adventure until 2011, when we decided to head north on Saturday morning. It was one of the best decisions we could have made.

In the year 2013 Michael, Terry, Jim, and I decided to stay for two weeks instead of our traditional one-week stay. We found out that a two-week stay was the perfect fishing vacation. We never felt obligated to put in as much time on the water as possible, which was the case during a one-week stay. I cannot describe how fine it felt come Friday night to know I had another week of fishing ahead of me instead of packing up for our trip home. For some of us, a two-week stay became another tradition.

CHAPTER 4

Eating Like Kings

Dining was important for us during our weeklong stay in Minnesota—so much so that missing a meal was considered very impolite. Unless someone had a particularly good reason, missing dinner was not cool. More than anything else, our quality of sociability was based upon camaraderie and good fellowship. One way to reflect those values was to sit down to the dinner table and enjoy a delicious meal. It was our time to get together with everyone on the trip, to talk about the day, and to poke fun at anybody about anything. We would laugh, drink what we wanted, discuss topics of consideration, and reminisce about past trips. It was so important that even if the northerns were hitting, we would still come in to eat at the proper time. If we were sitting on a school of crappies and the time for dinner approached, we went in without hesitation.

Going out to a bar or to a restaurant for dinner was not our way. Dining, for us, was a gathering of all in the main cabin around a large dinner table. To accomplish that, we needed a good cook. We were lucky in that regard, as Michael is one of the best culinary artists I know of. He could have easily started his own restaurant. Michael taught himself everything he knows about cooking simply by just getting in there and doing it. Over the years, Michael has made some of the most memorable meals for all of us to enjoy. It didn't matter what food we would bring from home; Michael always found a way to transform those ingredients into something fine.

Before we checked in to the resort, we would stop to buy our groceries for the week. During our extravaganzas in the grocery store, all of us would normally follow Michael around, because Michael had the all-important list of items we would need for the week. The list was all-important but not inclusive. If anyone wanted anything, we just pulled it from the shelf and put it into the cart. The whole mess, sometimes two and three carts packed full of food, would go through the checkout, and we would divide the total among everyone regardless of how much or how little we would each eat during the week. It was our way of managing those kinds of issues. According to Michael's Journal in 2000, we paid $285 for groceries. In 2006 we paid $382. There were years when we spent less and years when we spent more. I cannot remember a year when I did not pay more than $50 for the week concerning groceries.

The equality of division among us didn't hold true for our spirits. We felt as though our liquor had personal connotations and we should all oversee our own purchases. Most often, however, those of us that enjoyed good wine would buy a few bottles to be shared with anyone.

The cuisine that Michael liked to prepare most favored wild game plates. Michael loves sports of all kinds, indoor and outdoor; however, I suspect hunting must sit at the top of the list for him. Michael has hunted all his life, and in Nebraska there is good hunting; white-tailed deer, mule deer, wild turkey, duck and goose, pheasant, quail, grouse, and a good supply of rabbits can all be taken in Nebraska if you know where to go and are lucky enough to get permission.

Michael hunts them all, and he knows how to cook them all. Every year Michael would kill a wild turkey and bring it up for one of our meals. I would swear we were having Thanksgiving early. In a way, we were celebrating a Thanksgiving among ourselves. The turkey was as juicy and tender as any domestic bird I have ever had. He would prepare all the fixings: cranberries, mashed potatoes and gravy, dressing, sauerkraut, corn, bread, and fine wine. It was tough to go out fishing at night after one of those meals. One could not get a better meal in a restaurant.

Deer loins were another favorite meal for all of us. If prepared properly, and Michael always did it properly, one cannot tell a filet mignon from a deer loin. Juicy and full of flavor, complemented with a fine wine, deer loin was one of my favorite meals.

Some of the best meals I can remember came from Terry. For many years, Terry would bring over fresh salmon he would catch out of the Columbia River. Terry had a way with salmon. Sometimes he brought the best smoked salmon I ever had. Or he would make a smoked salmon dip that could not be bought in the finest stores. Some years he would grill salmon with a sauce glaze for a meal nobody could buy at the finest restaurants. Sometimes we would have pasta with a smoked salmon alfredo sauce that was to die for. How lucky we were to experience the taste of fresh salmon cooked to perfection in various dish arrangements.

One night would be chili night. Michael normally would bring his favorite pots and pans to cook in. Chili went into a large camp pot, which was an old large pressure cooker without the lid. All the hamburger or meat that went into that chili was processed deer meat. One could not tell it from beef hamburger. Michael's chili is as good as it gets.

Every good cook needs a good assistant, and that job went to Doug. Douglas was a wonderful cook in his own right, often bringing his own dishes of quail and sometimes pheasant. Michael and Doug together would transform those dishes into meals to which no price could be attached. Most years Doug would make the most wonderful, biggest plate of nachos I have ever seen. Doug grew his own peppers, which he put into those nachos. Everyone dived into them, and they were devoured in no time. The plate was a full meal in its own regard.

Doug helped Michael with the preparation and serving of most meals. In the first years we came up to the Bottle Lakes, Mom used to tell me I had lost ten pounds simply because of our eating habits. Well, Michael and Doug turned that around, to the joy of us all. I swear I would thereafter gain ten pounds over the course of the week.

Another traditional dinner we normally had one night was a fish fry. (See figure 20.) Oh my God! Talk about the best eating fish there is, fresh from the cold, clear depths of the Bottle Lakes. Traditionally, Tuesday night was designated as fish fry night. Our number-one priority regarding fishing would be to catch enough fish for that special night. Everyone contributed their catch for our fish fry. If one person had caught all the fish by Tuesday afternoon, too bad; they would all get eaten by everyone else. That was just the way we handled it. All types of fish would get fried up: northern pike, walleyes, crappies, bluegills, rock bass, and sometimes bullheads. There was not one of us that didn't like to eat fish. Everyone ate until he was full, and we had some powerful eaters.

Jim was the gatekeeper for our fish. His job was to monitor our catch and make sure we were never over the limit on any species. Jim also handled the packaging of our fillets. He was so diligent in his methods that if someone else froze a package not to his liking, that person had Jim to answer to. I was often on the receiving end, as my packaging skills were very lame.

Jim took his job seriously in that regard, but never with demeaning behavior. We needed someone like Jim; otherwise, we would just have had a jumbled-up mess of frozen packages of fish that would have been impossible to pack into our coolers with any orderliness.

Jim also monitored our fillets so that we had enough fish to eat for our fish fry. He had a good understanding of how much fish he should set aside, all based upon the number of guys we had that year. Some years we would end up frying everything we had accumulated up to Tuesday afternoon. If Jim decided we had too much for the meal itself, the rest would get frozen for distribution when the time came. One year we experienced such bad fishing that we didn't have a fish fry until Thursday. It took us that long to catch enough fish.

Along with getting our fillets ready for the fish fry, it was also Jim's responsibility to score the northern fillets. Scoring northern fillets is a technique we learned from the preparation of carp in Nebraska. Carp is an excellent fish to eat if prepared correctly. In Nebraska, fish fries of predominately carp have been taking place in small bars across the whole state for decades. The secret to preparing a good piece of carp is to get rid of the Y-bones that sit above the rib section of the carp. By making diagonal cuts spaced close together where the Y-bones are located, the knife cuts through the Y-bones. This technique is called scoring. When the scored rib sections are deep-fried in hot oil, the bones still found in the cut sections are turned to chips. Then the whole strip, bone and all, is eaten.

Northern pike also have Y-bones located along the backbone, just above the rib cage. Those Y-bones are dangerous to anyone that does not know they exist. They are very slim and very sharp. Worst of all, they are pliable. They can be bent, flexed, or twisted without breaking. It is almost impossible to chew one up. Sometimes they are not even noticed in the mouth until swallowed, and then the nightmare begins. And to make matters worse, they just happen to be imbedded in the best part of the fillet. So eliminating their existence is priority number one for any person serving up a delicious fillet of northern pike.

One way to get rid of the Y-bones is to cut them out during the fillet process. That type of preparation does eliminate them totally. However, that process is also a total waste of meat. We decided to take the technique used for carp preparation in Nebraska and apply it to our northern fillets. The results were positive. Scoring the fillets with about quarter-inch spacing is all that is needed. Not only did we now get good, crisp strips of northern meat, but the Y-bones were also cooked right out of existence. To take this one step further, if we kept the belly meat in place during the fillet process and carefully cut out the ribs, we could score only through the backbone meat that included the Y-bones and keep the whole fillet intact, held together by the belly and rib meat. Then we could section the fillet into two-to-three-inch-wide strips. The whole strip would go into the fryer, resulting in a delicious mouthwatering fillet of northern pike, free of Y-bones.

Jim held the added responsibility of scoring our northern fillets, and there was nobody better than Jim in handling a knife. Give him a razor-sharp Rapala fillet knife, and he could shave off the top layer of dead skin from your hand without you ever knowing about it. He was that good. Aside from the northern pike, Jim also sectioned out two-to-three-inch widths of walleye fillets. Sometimes we had crappies and bluegills to fry up. Michael sat by along with the rest of us until Jim gave him the prepared platter of raw fish. There was a pecking order to our fish fries. Michael fried them up, but only after Jim prepared them.

Michael used a deep kettle fryer filled with oil that sat on top of a propane burner. We never battered our fish. We only used a special flour coating. The coating made the fillets golden brown, which complemented the fresh taste of the fish. The spices in the flour were almost nonexistent. Unlike some of the shore mixes, this coating was smooth and never objectionable to the palate.

Michael cooked and cooked until all the fish Jim had prepared went through the fryer. The completed fillets were put into a large pan and set in a warm oven until we could all sit down together and have one of the most delicious meals anyone could muster up. On a personal note, I'd like to state that northern pike is the best eating fish there is.

While Michael was frying, other activities were taking place. Those guys who were not part of the cooking crew set the table and made sure all the amenities were taken care of, which included everyone having a place to sit. Our fish fries also included fried cubed potatoes mixed with cubed onions. Jim and Doug did most of that preparation. Along with potatoes, we normally had pickles of diverse types, rye bread with caraway seed, Michael's homemade tartar sauce, and a bottle of beer. I was not a beer drinker, but on our fish fry night, no respectable person of Bohemian ancestry would turn down a cold bottle of beer. It simply went with fish.

Everyone took turns doing dishes. It was our policy that the cooks never did dishes. We tried to uphold the principle that because they made the food for us, we should clean up for them. In my own regard, I always tried to thank the cooks. They cooked for us, so I felt I should thank them for it.

CHAPTER 5

Breakfast

Evening meals were not the only time hungry men needed food. Someone said, "Breakfast is the most important meal of the day." I believe most of the guys in our bunch tend to believe that, and I think that was especially the case when we were in Minnesota fishing. And I am here to say there is nothing like one of Michael's breakfasts. Now, I must admit, breakfast was a meal that we had to work up to. Nobody had any breakfast until Michael came in from his routine morning bass fishing outing with Terry. Sunrise in the fall took place around 7:00 a.m. Michael and Terry would be out bass fishing at 7:00 a.m. If the weather was good and the wind was barely kicking in, then breakfast had to wait. Priorities took precedence over hunger. Most of us knew how to cook breakfast. After all, it was just eggs, bacon, hash browns, coffee, and toast. However, Michael just had a way with it.

Another reason we waited, and the real reason to be patient in the mornings, was our policy to all eat together. It was important to us for dinner, and it was just as important to us for breakfast. It was sacrilege to not have Michael cook breakfast for us, so we sat around drinking plenty of freshly brewed coffee, impatiently waiting for our cook, who was out on the lake bass fishing.

Brewing our coffee was a process we took very seriously. Each cabin had a Mr. Coffee brewer for the guests to use. I would not give a rat's ass for one of those. The best coffee we could ever muster up was brewed using an old-fashioned stovetop percolator. An electric percolator was just as effective, but traditional as we were, the stovetop percolator made for a strong, full-of-flavor cup of coffee.

When Leonard and I used to stay up till all hours of the early morning, getting up to go bass fishing was next to impossible for me. I would not have gotten any sleep. I thought that since we had to wait for Michael and Terry, I could finally get some time to sleep in. Silly me! The whole Musilek clan was up stirring about. Plus Michael's entrance and exit from the cabin just to get going at 7:00 a.m. was like a bull in a China cabinet. No one could sleep through that commotion. So I just managed to drag my ass out of bed and join those sitting around starving and drinking coffee.

Of course, we were not without our sense of humor. Not everything was taken seriously all the time. We took our fishing seriously, but we had fun doing it. Dinnertime was always respectful, cordial, and fun, with plenty of pomp and circumstance. Breakfast, on the other hand, was the time to whip out everyone's sense of humor. It was important for all of us to have a sense of humor. No one survived our band without it. Anyone that acted like a big baby, felt he was above occasional ridicule, or could not handle having a sarcastic remark thrown his way didn't belong with us. We all knew how to take a good ribbing, and we all knew how to dish it out. Those that did not never came back.

Sarcasm was our main tool, and there was no one better at it than Terry! He is the funniest of guys. If we got him going, he could make us laugh until our sides hurt. Since Michael was our chief cook and was also our camp boss, the target of our witty language most of the time was none other than Michael. It made for some very funny moments.

One such example involved eggs. This priceless episode still gets me to laugh every time I see a fried egg in front of me. One morning the kitchen was filled with excitement. Michael and Terry had finally had their fill of bass fishing. It was breakfast time. The bacon was prepared and set on the table, all wrapped neatly in a paper towel to keep warm. The toast was made and buttered to perfection. Our hash browns were golden brown and ready to eat. Everyone was scurrying about, pouring a good cup of hot coffee or a glass of orange juice, anticipating our great meal. All we needed now were the eggs—the final piece of our scrumptious breakfast.

Most of us liked eggs cooked over easy. This is a challenging task for anyone to carry out when there are five or six guys sitting around the table waiting for eggs, and we all wanted to eat together. Consequently, it was Michael's way to make our eggs in one big cast-iron skillet. That way they would be done all at one time. That means up to twelve or more eggs were cooking at once. It was impossible to turn all twelve eggs at the same time, so Michael would put a lid on the skillet, allowing some of the steam to cook the tops of the eggs without having to turn them. This is a form of steam basting. It is also hard to control the outcome. It was hit or miss for over easy eggs.

Michael's way to serve eggs was to have each one of us bring his plate to the stove to receive his portion. Normally everyone got two eggs. In single file, we made our way to the stove and stuck out our plates. It was a form of food line. Michael would cut out two eggs with his spatula and place them neatly on one of our plates. Then we would go off to the table to find our seat and get the rest of the food on our plate.

Once everyone was seated, we dived in. The first thing out of Terry's mouth was, "What the hell; these things are like hockey pucks!" Terry looked at me and asked, "What's your eggs like?"

I said, "They're pretty hard," knowing all along where this was going. Nobody else commented.

Michael is a gentle giant. He has not a mean bone in his massive body, and his sense of humor is just as big. Michael heard all this commotion about his eggs and promptly stood up, grabbed Terry's plate, marched down to the garbage bag, and scraped the eggs in. He then brought the plate back to him without saying one word. He sat down, and we continued to eat our breakfast. Everyone had a great laugh, including Terry. Michael let the scenario play out for a brief time, knowing he had gotten the upper hand. After a few minutes, halfway through our meal, Michael, with his kind heart, went back to the stove and made Terry two of the most perfect over easy eggs he could ever hope for. What a special moment! Terry's sarcastic comment was truly one of the great ones of all time, and this is one of the funniest moments I can recall during any breakfast meal we ever had.

Everyone drank coffee in the mornings except for Michael. He simply did not like coffee. I am not sure he knows how a percolator works. I, for one, never could understand it. Everyone that Michael grew up with enjoys good, full-bodied coffee. Michael's drink of choice in the morning is milk—God-awful milk! In fact, if he is not drinking beer or having a fine glass of wine for his evening meal, he will pour himself a glass of God-awful milk! I personally cannot stand milk. It smells awful, and the taste lingers far too long. The aftertaste sours my breath. To make matters worse, it upsets my stomach and gives me the runs. Why would anyone want that?

Michael's love of milk and my intense dislike for the drink made for some fun ribbing between us during mealtime. All in playful harassment, I would provoke Michael with persistent annoyance on the subject. But alas, the dreadful drink always occupied precious space in the refrigerator, and Michael made sure he had plenty of it.

One year, those of us that drink coffee took for granted that good ground coffee would somehow magically get to the cabins. Unless one of us brought coffee from home, we made sure to get our coffee in Park Rapids during our grocery run. Next to bacon, it was the most important grocery item, except for milk. Michael always made out a list of items he needed for the week's meals. Over the years, I never knew Michael not to have a list; and I would bet one hundred dollars that over the years, coffee was never on that list. I would also bet, double or nothing, that milk made the list.

On Sunday morning, the first thing we all wanted was a good cup of coffee, but there was none to be had. Coffee hadn't made it into the grocery cart. Five guys sat looking at each other, blaming one another. We had taken our coffee for granted. One of us should have put coffee into that cart, but it hadn't happened. However, in our refrigerator sat two one-gallon milk cartons taking up precious space. I suspect that if we had looked at the dates on those cartons, we would have found them to be the freshest of the lot. I cannot help believing that when Michael found out about our little ordeal, he had a little grin tucked away somewhere we didn't notice.

Another item that I can say with assurance never made it onto Michael's list is candy. Anyone that knows Jim, Terry, or me realizes that we love candy. It really does not matter what kind of candy; we love it all. Michael, on the other hand, is not a candy lover. We had to make sure multiple bags of candy made it into the grocery cart, because candy was not on the list.

There is nothing like having some candy in the pocket to nibble on when out on the lake.

One of the more desired pieces of candy that we all like is licorice. I simply adore licorice. Twizzlers, Crows, and Good & Plenty all make my list. Most of the time, if I am out on the water, I will have some combination of those candies in my pocket. Terry also loves licorice, which, innocently enough, led to one of the great moments we all laugh about when we talk about candy—especially licorice.

Terry, Douglas, and I one afternoon were drifting for northerns in Lower Bottle Lake. It was a beautiful afternoon full of sunshine with just enough breeze to allow for drifting. I had brought along a bag of Twizzlers that we were sharing by passing the bag back and forth between us. Terry unexpectedly told us about some licorice he had brought along with him. Into his coat pocket went his hand, and out of his coat pocket came out a large bag of licorice. Terry told us, "You need to try a piece of this licorice I picked up in Washington. It is the best I ever had."

Oh boy, I thought to myself, *I cannot wait to try that licorice.* He presented the bag to both me and Doug. We reached into the bag and grabbed a piece. Each was about half an inch in diameter and about one inch long—a swirled piece of solid black licorice. The taste was incredible—beyond delicious. Terry was right; it was the best piece of licorice I ever had, and it was the only best piece of licorice I ever had. Into the pocket went the bag, never to be seen again. Because we are exceptionally good friends, I cannot let Terry live that one down. I needle him every chance I get about the one and only greatest piece of licorice I ever had. Doug just laughs at the whole thing when we bring that story up. The sad part of it is that I never did find out who made the licorice.

At the end of the week, most of the food was gone. When Saturday morning's departure came, what was left was put into remaining coolers and distributed back home. Nothing was thrown away. For our trip home, Michael would put together a special treat for all of us. Each vehicle got a lunch box filled with sandwiches, chips, and maybe an apple. How could it get any better!

CHAPTER 6

The End of Wambolt's

Sometime during the week of our stay in 2002, Daryl and Rosemary approached us with sad news. They had put the resort up for sale. That year, 2002, was the last year he was going to keep it open. In fact, we were Daryl and Rosemary's last guests. (See figure 21.) They both were over seventy by then, and they had decided it was time for them to retire. We didn't know any details about the future owners. Daryl was not optimistic that the resort would still be run as a fishing resort. Anyone buying Wambolt's would have to sink a lot of money into it if they wanted to keep running it as a fishing resort. Among all of us, we were betting the place would be sold and sectioned off into lots.

The news left us with heavy hearts. Jim had been coming to this resort for twenty-five years. Most of us had been coming here since the end of the eighties. I think we all looked at each other with doubt in our eyes as to the continuation of future trips to the Bottle Lakes. Our yearly ritual was in jeopardy. Daryl could see the trouble in our eyes. That was when he told us about Whippoorwill Resort, which was just east of Wambolt's. He suggested we talk to the owners before we leave for the week. He had been suggesting Whippoorwill to his guests throughout the summer, and Whippoorwill was glad to accommodate them.

We all knew about Whippoorwill Resort. Some of the best fishing in the Bottle Lakes exists in front of the resort. Just ten years ago, Whippoorwill Resort had a few small cabins painted light blue. They looked to be in bad shape and in need of an upgrade. The owners of the resort lived in a larger cabin that was also painted a light blue. That was all that stood on the resort—a few cabins and a small house. Al and Marty bought the resort and immediately started updating.

Prior to 2002, if we found ourselves fishing in front of Whippoorwill Resort, it was easy to see that the new owners were making improvements. We noticed that the small cabins had been upgraded to be larger and more attractive. A deck was built on each cabin facing the lake. Some of the cabins were upgraded to three-bedroom units. Those that had only one bedroom were upgraded to two-bedroom cabins. All the cabins were resided and painted a more interesting reddish brown instead of the pale blue. New roofs replaced the old ones. The new owners had built themselves a beautiful two-story house on the eastern end of the resort. They also put up a large pole shed next to the house. They upgraded another offset building behind the cabins into a recreation center. They were turning this place not into a fishing resort but a family resort. Little did we know that the transformation we were seeing would be part of our not-so-distant future.

We wasted no time, and one evening before supper we drove down to Whippoorwill, which was only a mile or so down the road. We had some hope! When we turned into the resort, there was not much going on. We thought they had closed for the year. The first thing I noticed was a nice launch site for the boats. Things were looking up. The front door to the house was open, so we just walked in. Inside was a neat little office. It was nothing big but was nicely set up. Soon the owners of Whippoorwill Resort, Al and Marty, came through an entrance from their private quarters and greeted us.

We introduced ourselves and told them about our situation at Wambolt's and asked whether they could help us out. I held my breath until they answered. When I heard their answer, I was suddenly flooded with relief. They told us that they were sorry about Wambolt's decision to close, but they said it was a windfall for them. In past years, they had struggled to fill the resort. Now it appeared to them the resort would be full in the coming season. They would be happy to accommodate us.

We spent a considerable amount of time talking about our tradition and what it meant to us. They seemed to be impressed by our ritual and told us that many of the guests coming from Wambolt's had similar stories. However, they thought our story was the most impressive, given the number of years involved. We started discussing dates, cabin prices, and how they ran the resort. Marty had a large chart pinned to the wall. On it was the upcoming season's layout: weeks by column and cabins by rows. From where I stood, the damn thing looked plum full. When we left that evening, our names were on that chart. We had booked two cabins for the last week in September 2003—cabin 1 and cabin 3. Marty wanted a contact address. I gave her mine. She told me brochures were being reprinted for the coming season and the price of the cabins would be on them, that they would be sent out when she received them. Once I received the brochures, she wanted a fifty-dollar deposit sent in for each cabin, which I told the guys I could handle.

I cannot speak for the rest of the gang, but when I left Whippoorwill that evening, I felt we were all in for a slight change. It was a kind of reality check. As far as we were concerned, Wambolt's was the ultimate fishing resort. We'd had it so nice for so many years. Now it appeared we had secured another place to keep our ritual alive. That was all important to us. However, we knew right away Whippoorwill would not be the same as Wambolt's. Al and Marty would not be the same as Daryl and Rosemary. We would have some adjusting to do. We all owe Whippoorwill Resort some gratitude for allowing us to continue our traditional fishing trip on the Bottle Lakes. It was, after all, the last resort on the lakes.

CHAPTER 7

Whippoorwill Resort

No more could we just call up Wambolt's and book cabins a couple of weeks before our trip. Jim used to do that with Daryl and Rosemary. Daryl didn't care, and for Jim it was tradition. That all changed at Whippoorwill Resort. Around April of 2003, I received the brochures that Al and Marty had told us about. They had booked us for two cabins during the last week in September. For six guys renting two cabins, our price would be $187 per person. That price was in line with what Daryl used to charge us at Wambolt's. However, there was one significant difference: most of the time, Daryl had boats, motors, and the gas we used mixed into the bill. He also had all the bait that we used factored into the bill. If we took those items out, Wambolt's was a cheaper stay. However, who could challenge a $187-a-week bill for what we got out of the week? Not one of us could stay a weekend in Chicago for that price.

On Friday, September 26, 2003, Rick, Leonard, Wayne, Jim, Michael, and I left Leonard's farm around 11:30 p.m. Leonard pulled my boat with his pickup, and Michael, in his Blazer, pulled Leonard's boat. It was grand to see Rick once again. It had been a few years. I was hoping to see Terry and Doug once again, but they could not make the trip. Maybe the following year we would all be able to get together once again. This year, however, we were off to a new adventure staying at Whippoorwill. I think we were all wondering what was in store for us.

The nighttime drives were getting harder and harder for all of us. I started wondering to myself when we were going to end this madness of driving at night. After our Detroit Lakes breakfast, we headed out to Park Rapids. Our first stop was the grocery store, where our food bill for the week was $177. Once we got our licenses and our alcohol, we headed out to the resort. When we arrived around eleven thirty Saturday morning, Al and Marty were all ready to check us in. Our cabins were ready.

During our check-in, Al and Marty told us some incredibly sad news. Daryl had passed away just six months after he closed Wambolt's Resort. He had succumbed to throat cancer. Rosemary had passed away shortly afterward. The news of their passing took away some of our enthusiasm. They didn't know whether Daryl had the condition prior to his retirement. Daryl and Rosemary had sold the property the previous fall for an undisclosed amount. They didn't live long enough to enjoy the money.

As I had feared, Whippoorwill Resort took some getting used to. We had to make some adjustments, and for some of us, traditional ways were in jeopardy. First, the check-in at Whippoorwill was more formal. We also had to make sure we checked in our vehicles with license plate numbers. They didn't permit smoking in the cabins—something Leonard was going to have to deal with. The cabins didn't have screened-in porches, but only decks with rails. That might seem insignificant; however, with no screened porch, we were now forced to carry our fishing equipment in and out of the cabin every night. The fish cleaning area was small and amounted to a small room in which three people could not fit. Plus, by some reason, it sat just off from the owner's home. The beach was manicured almost daily by Al—a far cry different from Wambolt's, where reeds and natural aquatic vegetation lined the beach and grew in abundance. The docks were all metal, and of most importance to us, they didn't sell bait.

The resort didn't have a fisherman's appeal to it. Wambolt's had truly been a fisherman's resort. Whippoorwill looked to be more pleasing and more agreeable to family-oriented clientele. The interiors of the cabins had a nice layout with pleasant décor, and the furnishings were more modern than anything Wambolt's had. It felt as if we had taken a step up in class, which is something we all needed to get used to. None of us needed a class adjustment to have an enjoyable time. That was evident just by our staying at Wambolt's. We only needed someplace to sleep, a decent kitchen, a place to eat, a place to clean up, and the desire to be left alone.

The question of bait came up right away. While we discussed the bait issue, it became clear that neither Al nor Marty had any interest in fishing. I could only assume both had had to make some personal attitude adjustments due to the influx of fishermen from Wambolt's that had taken over their resort. Al told us of a wholesale bait company just east of Emmaville where most of the fishermen went to get bait. Al told us to just turn into the drive by the red mailbox. We knew exactly where it was. However, none of us could recall a sign that would indicate to us that one of the biggest wholesale bait distributors in central Minnesota existed in the area. We simply could not believe we had driven past that place all these years without realizing its existence.

Now we knew why it had taken Daryl so little time to get the bait we always asked for. Daryl would scream off in his beat up old white Ram and in twenty minutes be back with our bait. I swear that at times I wondered where he went that could offer him so much bait in so little time. Well, it was just a couple of miles up the highway. Since Daryl sold bait at Wambolt's, the prices he charged were retail oriented. Daryl was also being charged retail from the wholesale distributor, but with one major change: Daryl was receiving three to four times the quantity he requested from the wholesaler. When we purchased one dozen chubs from Daryl, he had three more dozen sitting in his holding tank. It was all a numbers game.

When we got settled into the cabins and launched our boats, off we went to check out the bait store. We drove up the highway, and sure enough, up on the hill stood the red mailbox. We pulled into the drive and entered a scene that Stephen King could have used in one of his books. There were john-style flat-bottom river boats everywhere, bait traps stacked everywhere, cars and pickup trucks everywhere, and larger trucks used to transport bait to retail locations in and around Minnesota lined up three to four deep. A large two-story private residence sat back in the trees a good distance from the main yard. The house was old and in dire need of paint.

Three dogs came barking from out of nowhere to greet us. Domesticated ducks and a few geese roamed freely among the piles of bait traps scattered about the property. Chickens roamed freely throughout the property. To the right side of the yard, another single-story building stood in rough shape. A door led us to the inside, where about two dozen concrete holding tanks were lined up. The floor was wet with water runoff from countless aerators running in the tanks. The unmistakable stench of dead fish filled the interior.

There was no activity, so we assumed nobody was around. Just then a short, round lady came in and asked if she could help us. We told her we were looking for bait. "Well we have plenty of that," she told us. "What would you like?" she asked. We gave her our list. She grabbed a couple of five-gallon buckets, made her way to the holding tanks, and started pulling out minnows. After she was done, what we got was close to four times what we had asked for. She never counted anything. The total bill was thirty-five dollars. We had enough bait to last us the week.

Back at camp, we struggled to figure out how we were going to keep all this bait alive. We had six trolling-style minnow buckets available. They would have to do.

The forecast for the week included some periods of moisture along with unseasonably cold temperatures. Frost warnings were issued for our area for the middle of the week. Forecasted temperatures for the week suggested forties and fifties with the lows hovering in the lower thirties. The last time we'd experienced a cold stay like that was 1993, when Terry's uncle Charlie was with us. Since that year, we had been lucky on weather. We felt this year might be different.

Al was scrambling to get the cabins that were not rented winterized. We were the only guests they had for the week, so we had the resort to ourselves. "Ourselves" is a relative term. Since cabin 1 was just a walk, skip, and a jump from the owner's home, we never felt as if we were alone. Al was constantly walking about, both in front of and in back of our cabin. In some respects, I wished we had cabin 7, which existed clear at the other end of the resort, where being left alone would be guaranteed simply because of its location.

Regardless of the cold temperatures, fishing turned out to be particularly good. The northerns were hungry and of decent size. The ones we kept were between twenty-four and twenty-eight inches, which made perfect fillets. Everyone contributed to our northern catch. We cleaned twenty-five northerns that week. We took home our limit of eighteen, and the rest we cooked up for our fish fry. The walleyes were not great in numbers but were decent in size. The longest was twenty-four inches. Every one of them was caught during the night. We cleaned twenty-six walleyes that week and packaged eighteen for our trip home. The rest were mixed in with the northerns during our fish fry. Jim and Wayne picked up three crappies while fishing at night and about one dozen bullheads. According to Michael's journal we caught ten bass on the week, all of them released. That number seems low simply because it was so cold in the mornings that Michael normally was the only one that went out.

The weather forecast turned out to be true. The resort experienced two hard freezes during the week, getting down to around twenty-five degrees. During the day, we normally had sunny skies. Temperatures in the forties can feel much colder out on the water. It was important to dress well. It was especially important at night, when the cold evening air could chill us through to the bones.

Our first stay at Whippoorwill was okay. The cabins were roomy and had good facilities. The decor was nice—too nice for a bunch of fishermen. We made sure we cleaned everything up before we left early Saturday morning. Before we left, Marty asked about next year. She said she could reserve the same cabins if we wanted. We told her yes. She told me to expect a brochure once again around April. At that time, I could send in the deposit, assuring us a place to stay the following September.

It appeared that we had secured another resort on the Bottle Lakes to continue our tradition. What the future years would bring was anyone's guess, but for now, we were content. This was the third resort for us on the same lake. We were hoping Whippoorwill would be available to us for many years to come. Al and Marty were responsible for making Whippoorwill Resort into a very respectable place. It didn't have Wambolt's old artistic charm, but apart from a few run-ins regarding some rules, we all enjoyed staying at Whippoorwill Resort.

CHAPTER 8

Bass Fishing

The Bottle Lakes had become a great largemouth bass fishery. During our early years, to our disappointment, the Pork Barrel was closed to fishing in the spring. It was a bass spawning area. Those years gave rise to the great largemouth fishery it is today. I would bet there could be a bass in that lake weighing close to eight pounds fifteen ounces. That weight just happens to be the state record for largemouth bass. We just have not run across him.

Largemouth bass in Minnesota do not get as heavy as those caught in the south. The season is short, the waters are cold, and the competition for food is great. What they do not have in weight they make up for in strength. They will simply pull your boat around.

It took me many years to accept the idea that getting up early in the morning to go bass fishing was worth it. It was impossible for me during the years when Leonard and I would fish into the early-morning hours. During those years, at sunrise, Terry and Michael would go bass fishing. If Terry was not there, Michael would go himself. Consequently, if Michael was not around, sometimes Terry would go himself. (See figure 22.) Whatever the case, they always seemed to come back with wonderful stories concerning the bass they had caught and released.

The inevitable time did come when Leonard's senior years started to slow him down. Staying out till the early morning hours gave way to short episodes at night during which one or two hours of nighttime walleye fishing was all Leonard wanted to do. It was not Leonard's fault; his age was impeding his ability to enjoy what he loved so dearly. It was a sad time for me. Even though the change was gradual, we could see it coming.

Over the course of those few years when Leonard no longer wanted to stay out late, Michael and Terry somehow got me to go bass fishing. All it took was one morning of persuasion. Michael pounded on my bedroom door. "Get up! Let's go! Terry's already at the boat!" I somehow dragged my butt out of bed at a time when I was sleeping the hardest. *Can this be worth it*, I asked myself? I did remember the largemouth bass Jim and I had caught back in 1984. Had I forgotten what it felt like to tangle with Minnesota's largemouths? Eventually I would find out. That morning, however, the only thing I found out was what it is like to be a third party in the back of the boat while fishing with Michael and Terry.

When I finally got myself ready, the three of us got into Leonard's boat, and off we went. When we reached our destination, I found myself in the back of the boat. I knew immediately it was not going to be easy. Michael was up front running the trolling motor, and Terry was in the middle. Terry was no slouch when it came to bass fishing. He could hold his own being second in the boat. He knew more about bass fishing than Michael and me combined. Having three in the boat, all fishing for bass, can be a little challenging.

As the morning sun slowly rose in the east, watching those guys catch one bass after the other got a little sickening. I had to listen to their constant gibberish. Terry was yelling out, "Michael, hit that point." Then Michael would yell out, "Terry, try that small opening; I missed it." Wham! Terry had one on. My job was to get the net and try to land the poor bastard. Then, of course, they were all over themselves after I netted it. "Wow look at the shoulders on that one! What's the length?" Terry asked.

Michael pulled out his board. It measured nineteen and a half inches. One of them suggested, "Let's take a picture." Out came the cameras. I had to take the pictures! After they were done with their ceremony, the bass got released. It was that way the whole morning. I believe that between them, they caught well over twenty bass. I caught nothing. I suddenly found myself wanting breakfast. When 10:00 a.m. came around, in we went for a little R & R. I was sure they needed it.

Terry told me I was using the wrong plastic. I had on a purple spotted creature. It worked great in Nebraska, but in Minnesota it was worthless. Neither Michael nor Terry was using any kind of weight, and I wondered how the hell they got such good casting distance. I was using the same reel Terry had, but he could outcast me by several yards. I needed to put a weight on my creature just to get it out into the reeds where it belonged. The issue with that, according to Terry, was that the bait was sinking too fast.

Both Michael and Terry were using Senkos made by Gary Yamamoto. Terry had introduced them to Michael years ago. Green-pumpkin and watermelon-black flake were their colors of choice. The Senko is designed to flutter down backward when it hits the water. Because we were fishing shallow in the reeds, we didn't need a weight. The Senko product itself is heavy, which allows greater casting distances. The first chance I got, I made sure to buy a package of each color. I could not believe the difference that bait made in casting distance. I could spot cast that bait just as well as they could. I started catching my share of bass, even though I was in the rear of the boat most of the time.

Just because I started catching my share of bass in the rear of the boat didn't mean I could be not be outfished just like before. One morning during our first week in 2013, I decided to go bass fishing with Terry and Michael. We would be fishing out of Michael's boat. Since I had started using my own boat for bass fishing, it was a rare opportunity for me to fish with those two guys in the same boat. The morning was foggy with no wind—perfect conditions for bass fishing. Michael would run the trolling motor, and I volunteered to run the outboard, which put me in the back of the boat. I knew the situation I would be facing with Terry and Michael. I had experienced the inevitable outcome before. It would be a tough go for me just to get a hit. They are two of the best bass fishermen I know. We were all going to throw Senkos.

Sure enough, according to Michael's journal, the bass quit hitting around nine thirty. Michael logged, "Don never got a hit!" I remember it well. Repeatedly, I noticed a promising spot coming into my casting range. Before I knew it, *Plop! Plop!* Michael or Terry had it covered. All I heard all morning was "Fish on." Just like before, I had to take the pictures, I had to net their fish, and then I had to listen to all their gibberish while they were beating their chests. Then, the phrase I hated the most came flying out of one of their mouths: "Your turn, Don!" Between Michael and Terry that morning, they boated and released fifteen bass. The biggest was twenty inches, caught by Terry. I never had a hit. The last time this had happened to me, Terry told me what I was doing wrong. Either I was using the wrong bait or I was presenting what I had in the wrong manner. This time, however, I knew my trade. I knew how to catch bass. I simply was up against the best. I kid about the whole experience, but I would not trade any morning of fishing with Michael and Terry in the same boat. It is simply so much fun. They taught me so much about bass fishing.

In 2002 Michael landed one of the biggest bass we ever caught out of the Bottle Lakes, and he got him on a spinner bait. Michael and Larry, Jim's younger brother, decided to fish the east shoreline. About fifteen feet from the boat, he hooked into a monster largemouth. According to his journal, "It immediately went right under the boat." I can only guess that bass must have pulled the boat around just a bit. Larry did his job on the net, and into the boat came the largemouth. Michael wrote in his diary, "I had to sit down after that one." They came back to camp to show everyone the beautiful largemouth and to take pictures. (See figure 23.)

Michael decided he wanted to get this big boy mounted. We had been coming to this lake for years, so he felt a trophy mount should be in order. We took the bass into Emmaville for an official weigh-in. His weight was six pounds nine ounces. It was 22.5 inches long with a 16-inch girth. Michael won $250 that year in the resort fishing contest with his bass.

I told Michael about a taxidermist in Lincoln that was as good as anyone. Getting this bass to Lincoln safely, without damage, required a little doing on our part. First we needed a donation of a large towel. As it turned out, we needed two towels. After saturating the towels with water, we placed the large bass flat on its side, being careful not to damage the tail or any fins. We carefully wrapped the bass in the soaked towels and transferred him to the freezer. It was important for the bass to remain flat until frozen solid. The water-soaked towels kept the bass from dehydrating. When we left on Saturday, the bass barely fit into the longest cooler we had, but it worked. Three months later, Michael had his beautiful largemouth hanging on his wall.

Fishing for bass in the mornings is a most rewarding experience. Normally the weather was good with no wind. If the weather was bad, we simply didn't go. Around 6:45 a.m., I found myself along with Terry and Michael, staring out the cabin window at the lake, trying to decide whether we should go. When conditions were right, off we would go to dress up for a morning filled with bass-fishing adventure.

Venturing out before sunup can be the most beautiful part of the day. It sounds strange for me to say that, because all my life I just hated to get up early. Bass fishing in Minnesota changed my attitude. Now I look forward to it. No more did Michael have to pound on my door. I was hooked.

Sometimes the mornings were foggy. For me those mornings were the best time to be out on the lake bass fishing. We knew the lake and we knew where to go and how to get there. Once we were close to a favorite spot, the boat motor was shut down, and in went the trolling motor. Creeping up to the reeds on a foggy morning is like being in a void in which nothing exists. We knew the reeds were out there, but where? Then suddenly, barely visible through the misty fog, we would see small slivers of reeds just ahead. The trolling motor slowed to a crawl, pulling us along in two to three feet of water. We tried to make little noise as Michael maneuvered us into casting distance. By then a good many reeds were visible, beckoning us to test our casting ability. The bass were in there, feeding in the reeds and taking advantage of the low light conditions. Everyone was ready for the first cast. Proper etiquette in the boat suggested Michael cast first, then Terry, and then me.

Michael's reel zinged out. *Plop!* Then Terry let it fly. *Plop!* His worm would land right next to a taller reed. It was then my turn. I would let my green pumpkin Senko test my reel. I would watch the Senko fly through the air with ease and land right in the middle of a small void between two patches of reeds. It could not have been in the water for two seconds before I felt the gentle thud on my finger. I would set the hook, and the whole area would boil into a big frenzy. "Got him!" I yelled. There would be no need for the net; he was one I could handle myself—a sixteen-inch Minnesota largemouth bass.

Over the years, that scenario repeated itself countless times. There were mornings when the bass were hitting so fast that one of us would run out of Senkos, but that didn't matter. We were not above sharing. We could not waste a morning if the conditions appeared inviting and the bass were hitting. It was too much fun.

All of us caught our share of largemouth bass over the years. If I were to guess, I'd say we boated and released hundreds of bass. The Bottle Lakes are a great fishery for largemouth bass. But smallmouth bass also exist in the lake. We typically do not target smallmouth bass but occasionally will pick up one while fishing for largemouths or walleyes. Sometimes a smallmouth will hit one of the large chubs we use for northerns. This happened to Wayne one sunny afternoon while fishing for northerns with his cane pole. He thought he had hooked into a monster northern pike. The great fish had his pole bent over double and led him around the boat several times before we were able to land it. To our surprise, it was an exceptionally large smallmouth bass. I was in the boat that afternoon along with Jim. The bass measured over twenty inches and weighed close to six pounds. Michael and Terry also caught many smallmouths over the years.

An interesting story came forth one morning during the second week in 2013. Terry and Michael went out bass fishing on a beautiful morning. They decided to head down into Lower Bottle Lake to hit some of the vast reed lines associated with that part of the lake. There was a small bay in the southeast part of the lake. At the entrance to the bay, a small point existed that held good reeds. Terry and Michael tried it.

Michael sometimes likes to flip a brush hog. He had one tied on that morning. The point was a perfect spot to flip, since it was very deep with a steep incline just off the weed beds. Michael hooked into a bass. He yelled to Terry, "Fish on!"

Just then, Terry yelled, "Fish on!" They had a rare double—two fish on at the same time. When Michael netted the bass, they found out they had no double but had hooked the same bass. That bass had taken Michael's brush hog and then gone after Terry's Senko. Terry's Senko ended up hooked in the side of the fish's lip. Michael's brush hog was hooked in its lower lip. That bass was hungry.

In 2014, Terry and I decided to try a different lake for bass. We selected Potato Lake, which was a large body of water, long and narrow, close to the Bottle Lakes. Unlike the Bottle Lakes, which resemble more of a bowl shape, Potato Lake has two long fingers that lead into the main body of the lake. Potato Lake's real estate was some of the most sought after in the Park

Rapids area. Real estate on that lake was almost untouchable. Although Potato Lake was a good walleye fishery, some investigation revealed it had good numbers of bass.

The weather showed favorable mornings in the middle part of the week. Wednesday morning, we pulled my boat. Terry and I headed out to Potato Lake. We used the public boat launch located at the far end of the north arm, away from the main body. Out on the lake, we realized its size. The small finger we were going to fish seemed to go forever. Wild rice and tall reeds lined the shoreline as far as we could see. It was impossible to select a starting location, so instead of cruising endlessly, we decided to jump right in and start casting.

It didn't take long before Terry caught a nice sixteen-inch bass. I followed with a couple of smaller bass. We were protected down the north shore from what little wind there was. Onward we went, picking up a bass here and there, but nothing in the eighteen-to-nineteen-inch range. But man did they fight! The bass looked like footballs, with very wide shoulders and deep bellies. It was becoming clear to us that it would take us all morning to canvass all the shoreline, so we started skipping less favorable spots for areas that we considered more favorable. Finally, we could see the end of the arm that gave way to the main body of water.

One small section of that distance, not one hundred yards long, rewarded us with some of the best bass fishing I had yet to experience. When we approached the area, it appeared to be nothing different from what we had been fishing. This area, however, had various-sized boulders scattered about the bottom that we could see just below the surface. They were deep enough not to have to worry about the boat or trolling motor, but they were visible in the clear waters. If we accurately cast up to the reeds and then let our Senkos drop down among the boulders, before we knew it, *Wham!* Bass on!

We started picking up bass every other cast. The action was so fast Terry started to giggle. We must have caught a dozen bass in that area and missed countless strikes. It was good that we had plenty of Senkos on hand. One issue with a Senko is its lack of tear resistance. Normally the whole thing was ripped to shreds after one or, at best, three hits, requiring a fresh one to take its place. Given a bass bite like the one we were experiencing, it didn't take long for us to go through a whole lot of Senkos. By the time we were done, we had caught and released over twenty bass, all of them healthy, fat, and full of fight.

Our time to get off the lake had arrived. It would be scandalous to miss Michael's breakfast, and we were getting hungry. We headed for the dock and were back in camp just in time for bacon, eggs, hash browns, toast, and coffee. We made it back to Potato Lake the next morning, where Rick joined Terry and me for a wonderful time catching bass. We caught and released another seventeen nice bass.

Those of us that like to fish for bass look forward to this wonderful experience every morning. If the weather is favorable, those that venture out have a good chance of hooking into a fabulous Minnesota largemouth bass.

CHAPTER 9

Northern Pike

Ever since we first tangled with a great northern pike in 1967, my admiration for this great fish has grown. I love to fish for crappies, bass, bluegills, and walleyes, but I must put the northern pike on a higher pedestal. They own the lake and are at the top of the food chain. They are ferocious fighters and when hooked will provide the angler with an unforgettable battle. Northern pike can generate great bursts of speed and power in an instant and will twist and shake all the way to the boat in their resolve to free themselves. They attack with fierce intensity and will knock the rod out of one's hands if it is not well attended. The great northern pike is a fierce competitor and, if prepared properly, one of the tastiest fish on the dish.

My ability to catch northern pike had improved year after year only after I started using ⅜-ounce jigs whose hooks were constructed of a heavy-gauge wire. A decent-sized northern will make mincemeat of any artificial bait if it is not constructed well. Normally I would tip the jig with a large four-to-five-inch chub, hook it through the lips, and fish it just above the weeds in ten to fifteen feet of water. If the winds were favorable, I would drift fish, regulating my depth with the trolling motor. If the conditions were calm, I would use my transom trolling motor and back-troll. Speed and depth were at my discretion. It took some practice to keep the jig out of the weeds, but once I had the technique down, the northerns were jumping into the boat. An entry in Michael's 2000 journal states, "Don came in with thirteen northerns. The largest was thirty-two inches." This happened once again in 2014; three of us in my boat alone brought in thirteen northerns. I caught eleven of them.

Prior to using jigs, we would pull lindy rigs tipped with a large minnow or chub. Sometimes we would pull Little Joe spinners tipped with a large minnow. The results didn't come as fast. There were days when I found myself trolling backward for hours without a hit.

Jim and Wayne, on the other hand, would normally find a large weed bed and anchor in about ten to fifteen feet of water and still-fish for northerns using a bobber and a large chub on a bare hook. Over the years Jim and Wayne grew to love fishing for northerns using sixteen-foot cane poles. They were made of fiberglass and had a few eyelets running down the pole. Normally a pole of this length would require some sort of reel placed at the base. Both Jim and Wayne used old baitcasting reels to handle the line. Watching them tackle a broad-shouldered northern was a real treat for all of us. The entire process went something like this: Once they were anchored, the collapsible cane pole was extended out some sixteen feet, which required some maneuverability within the boat. After the bobber was set to the desired depth, they would attach the bait and stand up in the boat. Then they would pull out enough line to make a reasonable fly-rod-technique cast and, they hoped, get the whole damn works out into the water. The final arduous task was to sit and wait.

Some measure of patience is required to sit in the boat and wait while holding on to a sixteen-foot cane pole. Patience of that kind I do not have. However, those two guys could sit in a boat for hours and never experience a bite. When they did get a hit and that bobber disappeared into the depths of Bottle Lake, it was time to look out for some fun. (See figure 24.) Many times, anglers in other boats would stop and watch either Jim or Wayne battle a northern. They could see the cane pole doubled over in a perfect bow, wondering what in the hell was going on. An angler could land any kind of fish equipped with such an instrument. If the line didn't break or the pole itself didn't snap, in the end, the fish had no chance. Jim and Wayne were masters at it.

Michael loved to pull either a spinner or lures for northerns. Since everyone else would rather fish with live bait, Michael had a tough time finding anyone that was willing to go out with him and troll for northerns in that manner. Consequently, Michael would have to succumb to the status quo or simply go out himself.

There is no doubt that the Bottle Lakes host a good northern pike population. We also knew that the Bottle Lakes host northerns that can reach incredible sizes. We proved that to ourselves back in 1970, when both Jim and I latched onto something so large we could not imagine it. We never saw either one of those fish, but I am not sure we wanted to. Ever since our 1970 confrontation, over the years we would occasionally hook into something excessively big, but we never got a chance to see the fish. It took us until a sunny Wednesday afternoon in 2001 to finally come face-to-face with the largest fish any of us had ever seen. The recipient of this encounter was none other than Wayne, who was fishing out of my boat for bluegill.

CHAPTER 10

A Lunker Story

I n 2001, five of us were able to make the trip. Jim, Michael, Leonard, Wayne, and me. We struggled all week to catch anything. Even the northerns were not hitting, which normally was not the case. The northern fishing was so bad we didn't limit out by week's end.

Wednesday afternoon was calm and clear. We were tired of putting in hour after hour on the lake, trying to catch northern pike that were hard to come by, so we decided to go bluegill fishing. We ended up in one of our favorite spots on the eastern shoreline. It was a small bay where the depth was no more than twelve feet and the water was full of weeds. It was also full of bluegill. We started catching bluegills one after the other. We were selective in what we kept. The action was fast and exciting.

If there is one fish that goes through a frenzied fight when hooked, it is a bluegill. It turns, runs, twists, and shakes. Then, near the end of its ordeal, it will swim in a circular pattern until taken aboard. No self-respecting king-of-the-lake northern of gigantic proportions could ignore the commotion set forth by this kind of frantic fight for freedom. So, out of the depths from somewhere near, one such northern cruised into the bay that afternoon to find out what was going on.

We were fishing for about one hour when suddenly I saw a flash just near my bobber. I thought nothing of it. Wayne was fishing out of the rear of the boat. I was watching him bring in a bluegill. As Wayne was struggling to get this one over the side of the boat, up came the biggest

246

damn fish I ever saw in my life, and he made a lunge at that bluegill just as it broke water. With his mouth wide open and teeth exposed, he missed. Thank God he missed. It would have taken Wayne right into the lake with the bluegill.

It was *Jaws* in 2001—a northern at the top of the food chain. Wayne turned back at me, as white as a sheet, with his mouth stuck open. I swear he could not talk. That whole encounter had occurred right in front of him. The fish had almost hit the motor; he was that close to the boat. It took us a while to gather ourselves, and then we went back to catching bluegill. I must say I was just a bit nervous knowing the owner of that bay was out hunting. It could not have been five minutes later when it happened to Wayne again—the same thing. This time the bluegill was just under the water, and the massive northern made a lunge and missed once again.

Wayne yelled, "Christ Almighty! Did you see that? He tried for it again."

I told Wayne, "Yep! I saw it!" The length on that fish looked to be as wide as my boat.

Well, Wayne had had enough. In the well-spoken words of Wayne's perfect prose, he made it clear to me: "I'm going to get that fucker!" Wayne put his bluegill rig down and picked up his northern rig. He had an open-faced reel attached to a stout rod. He dug around his tackle box until he found a large red-and-white Daredevil spoon. He attached a steel leader, secured his spoon, and let it fly out into the bay.

I was closely watching Wayne make his first cast when suddenly he hooked onto something. A northern smacked his spoon and started peeling line off his reel. After a couple of runs and some turns, the large northern made its way back to the boat. Wayne told me to get ready; he was coming up. Get ready for what? If this was the same northern, my not-so-big dip net was no match for that fish. I was preparing myself for an encounter we could not win. Slowly Wayne was gaining, and suddenly, just like a submarine rising from the depths, up came this massive northern. I told Wayne, "There is no way we are landing this fish." He had to be fifty inches long. It could have been a muskie. I could not tell the difference looking down into the water. When this fish saw the boat, he spit out the spoon and slowly descended out of sight as if nothing had happened. Wayne lifted his rig out of the water with a dejected look, and that was that. I told Wayne,

"It's a good thing he let go. I didn't want to deal with that fish." It was absolutely the biggest fish we ever saw.

Besides Wayne's tangle with the unimaginable, we had other encounters with massive northerns. We never saw any of them. Normally those encounters would happen while fishing for panfish with ultralight gear. It happened to me three or four times. But ultralight gear was no match for these rulers of the lake. All I got back was a mangled panfish and a feeling of amazement in trying to realize how large a fish could have done the damage.

Over the years, the largest northern any of us ever landed was thirty-nine inches long. In fact, every northern we ever landed over thirty-five inches was caught in the same year. That year was 2008.

CHAPTER 11

2008: Big Northerns

Our trip in 2008 was destined to be an exciting time. Finally, we had hit a year when the old gang would be together. When the time for departure arrived late Friday night, Michael, Jim, Wayne, Leonard, Terry, Rick, Doug, and I left Leonard's farm around 11:30 p.m.

Our ability to deal with the nighttime drive up I-29 was deteriorating. Even our Detroit Lakes breakfast was not enough to revitalize our bodies, which were growing old. I could tell it on everyone's face. Exhaustion and the lack of sleep continued to take a toll on our functionality. Mistakes and sometimes forgetfulness could be the outcome. If tradition would not get in the way, we could leave Saturday morning and say screw the nighttime drive. We could enjoy a nice drive north during the day and get a good night's sleep; then we would be in much better shape come Sunday.

Driving at night was a great adventure in our earlier years, but it had grown to become a burdensome obstinacy. A good example of my growing concern is taken from Michael's journal that year involving Doug. This incident stemmed from lack of sleep and our bodies' inability to function without it. Doug tripped on the dock while trying to shut off Jim's and Wayne's lights, which had been left on in the resort boat after we all came in from fishing Saturday night. Firstly, the lights should not have been left on, and secondly, it is easy to trip off those docks when tired, especially at night. Into the lake he went, headfirst, tackle box in hand. Doug didn't get hurt, and we did manage to retrieve the tackle box, which was full of water. I blame the nighttime drive for the incident. How many more clues did we need?

We had so much fun that year laughing and joking around. The week had turned memorable, with excellent food and good company. Michael had prepared meals mostly of wild game. Terry made one of his famous salmon meals to die for. Douglas brought with him pheasant and quail breasts that he cooked up in mushroom gravy. I had not had a pheasant-and-quail meal since my high school days. Put a nice bottle of wine to that meal and *wow!*

The forecasted weather for the week called for moderate temperatures in the fifties and sixties. Wind was going to be a factor for us all week. Sunny skies were predicted, with no rain in the forecast. As nice as the weather was, we were experiencing a disappointing fish bite that year. The walleyes were not hitting, and the northerns were stubborn. Those that we did catch were big.

For some reason, the big northerns were in a feeding cycle. Wayne was fishing by himself one afternoon with his cane pole when he caught two northerns. One was thirty-nine inches in length, and the other thirty-seven. Landing fish like that is tough with two people in the boat. Wayne landed both by himself. Wayne said each northern pulled the boat around. Doug brought in a thirty-nine-inch northern that same afternoon while fishing in an entirely different location. (See figure 25.) Late that week, Doug caught and released another northern of thirty-seven inches on a Lindy trolling rig. For our fish fry and for our fish we took home, the northerns were fat and healthy. Every northern we cleaned had a decent-sized perch sitting in its stomach—a good sign that the Bottle Lakes were healthy.

After that year, we started to realize that northerns of that size should be released back into the lake. They are too big to eat, plus they help to control the balance of the lake. They give anglers a memorable fishing experience. Why deny that to someone else! Why take them out? In subsequent years, we never kept a northern over thirty inches. Our group slot limit became twenty-two inches to thirty inches. We agreed to release everything else.

Right or wrong, that was our decision. Little did we know that the Bottle Lakes were undergoing a transformation of much importance. The significance of this transformation directly affected the quality of the northern pike population. The lake was filling up with small northerns. Over the years after 2008, it became increasingly difficult to catch quality northerns over twenty-two inches. Northerns between twenty-six and thirty inches were hard to come by. That trend continued; there were afternoons when Terry and I would go out drifting jigs for northerns and go through three dozen chubs. They were all lost to small northerns. Sometimes those afternoons would produce very few decent-quality northerns, and we would have to settle for twenty-two-to-twenty-four-inch fish if we were going to have a fish fry. This was the case not only in my boat; Wayne and Michael struggled to catch decent-sized northerns as well.

Not only were the northerns getting smaller, but we had also noticed a puzzling lack of small perch under the docks swimming in and out of the protection of the weed beds. Perch would sometimes be a bothersome presence when we were targeting crappies or bluegills. Gradually we had noticed that the annoying perch were not annoying us anymore.

Shortly after 2008, we started to see a lack of perch in the stomachs of the northerns and walleyes we were cleaning. It was an alarming sign that something was happening to the perch population in the lake. In later years we noticed that the stomachs were usually empty. Were the small northerns decimating the perch population in the lake and, of more serious consequence, the food chain itself? If that was the case, the Bottle Lakes were going through an ecosystem change right under our noses.

The trend in small northern populations taking over the Bottle Lakes was happening across central Minnesota. The trend caught the attention of the DNR, and the DNR finally decided to change the regulations regarding northern pike possession limits in central Minnesota. This is a move I applauded with enthusiasm, as nothing more important needed to be done by the DNR other than finding ways to remove the population of small northern pike taking over the lakes. A possession limit of three was raised to ten. Slot limits were introduced. I believe these measures to be important in getting the lakes back to producing quality northerns and, of significant importance, to help bring back the perch population.

CHAPTER 12

Fun with Walleyes

N one of us were particularly good walleye fishermen. We knew of only three ways to catch walleyes: still-fishing with minnows at night, pulling minnows at night while trolling in shallow water, or pulling an imitation minnow, such as a Rapala, in shallow water at night. The latter was Michael's preferred way of fishing for walleyes, but none of us except Michael were fond of pulling artificial lures. Consequently, that method of fishing was normally associated with a last-gasp effort when the other two methods were not working. The only year we really had good luck with artificial minnows occurred in 1993, when Uncle Charlie came. In later years, Michael and I would sometimes pull Rapalas at night with minimal success. If the walleyes were not hitting at night, we were out of luck, as we were not experienced enough and had never been shown methods of catching walleyes during the day. Plus none of us had the desire to experiment during the day, simply because the week went so fast. We devoted our daylight fishing to panfish and to northern pike.

Walleye fishing in the Bottle Lakes sometimes can be a tough proposition. The lake itself is not favorable as a walleye fishery. The vegetation itself is abundant to depths of twenty or more feet. There are few rocky ledges in the lake, and the floor of the lake is vacant of boulders of any significance. The only feature the Bottle Lakes has that would be favorable for walleyes is the depth. The Bottle Lakes are deep, with one hole in Lower Bottle Lake of 110 feet.

The Bottle Lakes are not only deep but are some of the clearest lakes in the Mantrap chain. It is for that reason that the lack of light at night will bring the walleyes into shallow water to feed. During the day, they just sit on the floor of the lake or hide in the deep weeds that surround the lake.

If the walleye bite was on and the locals got word, boat after boat would venture onto the Bottle Lakes to take advantage of those rare times. The locals knew that the Bottle Lakes lacked walleyes in quantity but made up for that in quality. The Bottle Lakes produce decent-quality walleyes. Jim managed to catch one of the largest walleyes ever caught out of the Bottle Lakes. It measured thirty-one inches long and weighed close to ten pounds. When Daryl, the owner of Wambolt's Resort, heard about that walleye, he could not believe the size and thought it to be the largest he had ever heard of coming out of the Bottle Lakes. Daryl was an avid walleye fisherman. He told us how to catch walleyes at night by pulling a small minnow in shallow water. That was exactly how Jim caught his walleye. Daryl also told us about pulling artificial minnows at night. But beyond those two methods and still-fishing at night on the drop-offs, we had no clue.

Our lack of knowledge regarding walleye fishing during the day didn't prevent us from catching plenty of walleyes at night utilizing the three methods we knew. We were good at it, and hooking into decent-quality walleyes at night is as good as it gets when it comes to heart-pounding action. In past years, Leonard and I would stay out for hours at night, back-trolling for walleyes. We would bring in a few nice-quality walleyes if the weather permitted. Jim and Wayne had success still-fishing for walleyes.

Michael and I one evening had one of the best times fishing together that I can remember. According to Michael's 2001 journal, we had an excellent walleye bite that year. One evening in 2001, after a wonderful fish fry, Michael and I decided to head down into Lower Bottle for some walleye fishing. We wanted to pull small minnows in shallow water. Leonard wanted to go himself that evening in his own boat. Since there was no wind and the night was clear, we felt confident Leonard would be okay. He vowed to stay just in the confines of Wambolt's Bay. Off we went, not knowing that we were about to experience one of the best walleye bites we had on record. It was pitch black outside. Since we were into a new moon cycle, the stars were out early, proud to show us a beautiful display of the heavens.

The action started at once. Back and forth we trolled the south shore reed line in Lower Bottle Lake. On every pass, we would pick up a walleye or at least have a hit. We were catching fish of various sizes, but we kept only those between sixteen and twenty inches. Everything else was released. Fishing for walleyes in shallow water is exciting. The hit is strong; the fight is intense. Each time we caught a keeper, we would stop and have a toast to ourselves. Michael would pull the thermos out, and we would share some of his snapper. Man was that good! It was one of my most memorable nights fishing with Michael.

When we came in, Leonard was already in the fish-cleaning house. In some respects, he outfished us, at least in size. He had boated a nice three-and-a-half-pound walleye, along with a rare nighttime northern of four pounds. Soon Jim and Wayne brought in their catch. In total, we cleaned seventeen walleyes that night, every one of them a sixteen-to-twenty-inch beauty.

One walleye story that seems to generate a lot of dinner table laughter happened in 2008. The walleyes were not hitting that year. We cleaned very few walleyes that year. This story took place on Friday just before we were going to pull in the boats for the week. Leonard and Terry were fishing together that afternoon out of Leonard's boat. It is a well-known fact that Terry and Leonard, when paired together in the same boat, make up one of the most competitive duos on the planet. They each want to outfish the other, all in father-in-law and son-in-law tradition. Normally Terry would get the upper hand on Leonard, and that didn't change that afternoon. Terry was one person that was hard to beat when it came to fishing.

When Leonard had his gear all in and they were about to head back to camp to pull the boat, Terry decided to make one more cast. They were drifting chubs for northerns that afternoon. That one last cast amounted to a big heave of his chub and a slow retrieve back to the boat. Well, as luck would have it, Terry got a hit. After a long fight, Leonard had to be the one to net one of the largest walleyes we had seen come out of the Bottle Lakes in years—a 7.5-pound twenty-seven-inch walleye. They took some pictures, released the fish, and came back into camp to tell the story. All Leonard could say was, "What a lucky SOB!" The significance of that story lies in the fact that this fish was caught in full daylight. Very seldom were walleyes caught during the day in the fall. The last time this had happened, Jim pulled in his twins. This time it was Terry's turn, and poor Leonard had to witness it.

2008 was a pivotal year regarding the quality and quantity of fish we were cleaning. In future years, not only were the northerns getting smaller, but the walleyes were getting frustratingly harder to catch as well. Those walleyes that we did clean were void of anything in their stomachs, just like the northerns. There were times when we would go out at night and not get one single hit. Even Wayne and Jim were finding it difficult to catch walleyes at night while still-fishing in their favorite spots. Michael would find himself pulling artificial minnows around without a single hit.

By the time 2015 came around, we were all getting pissed off at the walleyes. I found myself not even interested in venturing out at night. For the first few nights in 2015, we would go out and pull the same minnow around for an hour and never get a hit. That got old fast, especially for an impatient fisherman like me. Something had changed regarding the walleyes, but none of us could figure it out. Even Terry was stumped. What could be more enticing to a hungry walleye than a fat, juicy minnow swimming around in the shallow water? Terry and I decided to try another area—someplace we had never fished before. We had been hitting the same old spots year after year, with the results in decline. But there were very few spots on the Bottle Lakes that we had not fished. However, I told Terry there was one spot that I knew about on the eastern side of Lower Bottle Lake's south shoreline that we should try. One night Terry and I headed to Lower Bottle to tangle with some walleyes.

It was a spot we had never considered in the past, but now we wondered why. It was perfect for walleyes—a rock-covered bar with a steep descent into very deep water. Next to the shore, the depth was a dangerous one foot of water filled with rock debris of assorted sizes. The bar was void of all vegetation, and our trolling slot zone was very narrow. I wanted to target three-to-five-foot gradients, but it was hard to maintain any consistency. If I drifted out of the zone, we found ourselves in deep water. If I accidentally got into two feet of water, I knew one-foot-deep water was close by. There were no reeds to guide me, so close attention to the shoreline and the depth finder was mandatory. The length of our troll one way didn't exceed 150 yards. The end of our troll in one direction was dictated by a line of reeds that started at the south shore reed line. The end of our troll in the other direction was dictated by a point that led to deep water. It was this deep point, filled with vegetation, where we first started catching fish back in 1967 in the only manner we knew how at that time, right under the boat. Little did we know that one of the best walleye spots in the lake was just around the bend. It took us forty-eight years to try it.

By the time Terry and I were ready for our first troll, it was past 7:30 p.m. Into the slot we went, back-trolling live walleye minnows just behind the boat. I got a hit almost immediately but missed him. Before long Terry was yelling "Fish on!" What sweet music that is! In the net and into the boat came a nice eighteen-inch walleye. We trolled that area back and forth for the longest time. On every pass, we either got a hit and missed it, caught a walleye and released it, or put one in the live well. By 9:00 p.m., the action had stopped. We decided to make a pass down the south shore reed line, heading west.

Terry tied into a nice fish—one worthy of dealing with his drag. A lengthy fight was taking place. I had the flashlight cast into the water and my dip net in hand. There he was. I could see his diamond-like eyes reflecting the light. He was a decent-sized walleye. Well, long story short, we lost him at the boat. I failed to get him into the net at the right time, and with one swish of his powerful tail, he was gone. Terry didn't say much, but we both knew I had lost that fish for him. That is my greatest fear when I am responsible with the net—losing someone else's fish.

Onward we went down the reed line with not another hit. We made a long turn and made our way back up. Soon we were trolling in the zone down the rock-covered bar, but the bite was off. Our window of opportunity hadn't been long. When we were in it, it was exciting. We brought home six beautiful walleyes that night, threw back three more, lost a couple, and missed a lot of hits. It was a walleye bite at its finest. When we returned to the docks that night, the other boats had caught nothing. We returned to that same spot a couple more nights during the week but didn't experience the same fast and furious bite. Our fiftieth year would be 2017, and it was fast approaching. The year 2015 was the last time we experienced a good walleye bite anywhere on the Bottle Lakes.

In 2016, eleven of us caught a grand total of two walleyes. Furthermore, we stayed two weeks. Two walleyes in two weeks! An interesting story emerged in 2016 regarding our disappointing walleye fishing. One day during our first week's stay, we saw a mouse running about in the kitchen during breakfast. The owners gave us two mousetraps. In ten days, we had caught a grand total of four mice. By the second week's end, we had caught more mice than walleyes. Our mouse count was four. Our walleye count was two. It was not that we just gave up on the walleyes; I pulled the same minnow one night for two hours and never got a hit. It was the same scenario for all of us.

Regardless of what the walleye fishing was like in 2016, we felt that 2001 was one of the best walleye bites we could all remember. But little did we know what the future would hold for us. The year was 2007, and those of us on that trip would be rewarded with one of the best years we ever had walleye fishing or, for that matter, fishing in general. We experienced not only walleye quality but also walleye quantity. According to Michael's journal, not only did we have an exceptional walleye bite in 2007, but it was our best fishing year ever. Ironically enough, it was also our fortieth anniversary of heading north.

CHAPTER 13

2007: Our Best Fishing Year

F inally fall was upon us once again. The blazing heat of summer had finally given way to some more tolerable temperatures in September. Football season was in full swing, young kids were back in school, and for those of us who could make it, another fishing trip up north was just around the corner. On Friday, September 21, 2007, at approximately 11:00 p.m., Jim, Wayne, Michael, Leonard, and I left Leonard's farm once again for our long drive up north. This year represented our fortieth year heading north to the Bottle Lakes. How lucky we all were to experience such a tradition!

We had no problems getting to Park Rapids that year except for the normal lack of sleep. According to Michael's journal, our only concern was the twelve miles per gallon his Blazer was making while pulling my heavy boat. Breakfast at Detroit Lakes hit the spot once again. I hope that little restaurant never closes. It restores our fuel that lights our fire. Next stop, Park Rapids and the grocery store. With only five guys that year, our grocery bill for the week was $208. Michael's guess was closest at $195, but there was no reward for that. What a shame! After we bought our licenses and liquor for the week, it was off to see our beloved Bottle Lakes.

Our routine was getting to be *quite* the routine. I suspect that if someone wanted to, they could set their clocks to our movements. We leave Prague between eleven and noon every year. We drive to Brookings for gas. Around 7:30 a.m., we pull into Detroit Lakes for breakfast. Then, about 10:00 a.m., we arrive in Park Rapids at the grocery store. Next we get our licenses, and we then stop for liquor. We fill up the trucks and boats with gas. Then we head to the resort around 11:30 a.m. We check in with Al and Marty. We unload the groceries, make the boats ready to launch, launch the boats, secure the boats to the docks, get bait from the wholesaler, put the bait in the water and balance out the minnow buckets, unpack the groceries, arrange the bedrooms, and put out our toiletries. By two thirty Saturday afternoon, we were done with moving in. In previous years, we would waste no time to head out fishing.

A couple of issues over the past years had started to weigh heavily on a few of us: fatigue and tiredness. I could have gone to bed for the duration of the day and then the whole night. Not wanting to be a wussy, I normally would whip up some stored adrenaline that would allow me to get out and do some fishing in the afternoon. This year, however, the evening was out of the question. That was also true for Jim and Wayne, but for some of us, this whole business of weariness simply did not apply: Leonard and Michael! I wish I knew their secret.

The weather forecast for the week was favorable but unseasonably warmer than what we had seen in recent years. Normally the lows at night would dip into the forties. That week the predicted nighttime lows were in the fifties. Daytime highs were to be in the sixties and seventies, with lots of sunshine and breeze.

The weather pattern had put a hold on the trees showing off their fall colors. Whatever triggers that event simply hadn't happened yet. When it does, the colors in the maples and birch trees are breathtaking. Reds, oranges, crimson, yellows, and bronze colors take over the landscape. Add to that the dark green foliage of the pines, and we are blessed to see some of the most beautiful scenery God has to offer.

Saturday afternoon, after all our camp chores were done, we all headed out to fish for a couple of hours. Michael set out to Blue Lake for a visit with his friend Paul and his wife Paula. (See figure 26.) Whatever fear I had from 2006, and in some respects the previous years, that fishing might be getting slow in the Bottle Lakes was unfounded in 2007. It started right off with Jim and Wayne bringing in three northerns all over thirty inches in length. They had also released two others that were larger. Leonard and

I also brought in a couple of northerns over twenty-five inches in length. We could have had a fish fry that evening.

I was shot. Wayne and Jim were shot. After our evening meal of ham and bean soup, we hit the hay. When Michael got back from his visit, he took Leonard out walleye fishing. Remember: Leonard had already spent a couple of hours on the lake with me. His endurance never ceased to amaze me. They really tied into the walleyes that night. Michael himself caught six and kept five of the most beautiful walleyes. Leonard caught two. Together they cleaned seven walleyes. Michael wrote in his diary, "The evening was one of the best walleye bites I ever witnessed." Plus it was Michael's first time he had caught his limit of walleyes in one evening—and the rest of us were in bed!

Our fishing luck continued, and one night we went out after walleyes with all three boats. I volunteered to go out myself to maximize our efforts. Jim and Wayne took the resort boat, and Michael and Leonard took the other boat. I caught three beautiful walleyes. Michael and Leonard caught eight. Jim and Wayne caught six and released three more. It is fun to go out when we can be selective about the size because the bite is on. Wayne really hit the jackpot that night, catching three that were over twenty-six inches.

The year before, in 2006, there were ten of us that made the trip. The five of us caught more fish in 2007 then the ten of us caught the year before. It was not even close. Even after our fish fry, we were taking home a full limit of walleyes and northerns. The northerns were nothing to sneeze at. They averaged between twenty-six and thirty-three inches. Other sizes were released. One night Michael, Jim, and I went after bullheads. We caught fifteen. One afternoon Michael and I went bluegill fishing. We caught twenty-five nice bluegills. The only species that we didn't have any success with was crappies. We could not get a crappie to hit. We didn't do much bass fishing in the mornings because of windy conditions, but I suspect that if we had worked at it, the bass would have been hitting as well. In 2006, so many of us caught so few. In 2007, so few of us caught so many. That year, 2007, was our best year fishing the Bottle Lakes. It was hard to explain among us why the fishing in 2007 was so exceptional, especially since the years after 2008 were so poor.

CHAPTER 14

Crappie

I n 1967, Jim and I ventured out to find some crappies. On accident, we managed to catch two of the largest crappies either of us had ever seen. Since that time, Jim and Wayne had managed to catch a few crappies at night while still-fishing for walleyes. It was not until 1987, on our twentieth anniversary, that Wayne and Rick managed to find a school of crappies stacked up in the weed beds on Upper Bottle's east shoreline. Jim and I joined them, and we were all catching crappies until we ran out of bait. The ironic part of this story was that it happened on Friday afternoon. We were not able to go back out and see if we could find them once again, because we were leaving the next morning. We cleaned close to thirty crappies that afternoon. In future years, we could not find a single crappie on that shoreline. And if there is one elusive fish in the fall, it is the crappie. It was not until 2006 that we finally found some crappies. Leave it to Jim to find them.

In 2006, our trip to Park Rapids was a wet one. It rained all the way up to the lakes and continued to rain all day Saturday and into the night. Sometime in the early Sunday morning hours, the rain quit. The first boat out held Kevin and Jim. Kevin was Jim's business partner, and he sometimes joined us for a week of fishing. Their plan was to cruise down to the east shoreline and still-fish for northerns. For them to get to that location, Kevin needed to cross the sunken island in the middle of the lake.

The sunken island was just that—an area the size of a few football fields long and only one hundred yards or so wide. Its shallowest depth was about nine feet. In fact, there were about three humps on the island, each around nine feet deep. From nine feet, a gradual deeper gradient surrounded the island until a max depth of around thirty to thirty-five feet could be found. The island was full of weed beds. The weed beds were packed so tightly that many times I lost nice northerns there simply because they would bury themselves down into the weeds before I could react fast enough. There was no way to get them out.

Once they started over the island, Jim suddenly hollered at Kevin to stop. Something had caught Jim's eye. Thousands of minnows or baitfish were breaking the surface on the northern side of the island. Jim wanted to stop, anchor, and drop a minnow in the water. While he was doing that, Jim noticed the telltale sign of crappies feeding on the surface. Crappies are the most exciting fish. Since their eyes are pointed upward, they attack from the bottom up, like some monster charging out of the depths. When they hit a minnow that is just under the water, their tail breaks the surface, causing a small splash. Unlike a northern pike or largemouth bass, which can cause an explosive attack on the surface, a crappie splash is very subtle.

Sure enough, the crappies were there. Kevin marked the spot, and by the time they were ready to come in, they had boated nine of the most beautiful crappies we had seen in years, all over fourteen inches in length. The next morning, Michael and Kevin went out to the same spot and caught five more in a couple of hours. Later in the week, Doug and I took my boat and went back to the island. We scanned the bottom structure until we found a large bed of vegetation in thirteen feet of water, with the tops at nine feet. We dropped the anchors and fished that area for about three hours in the afternoon. The weather was cold and raw, with a slight breeze coming into us from the north. We ended up boating six beautiful crappies. I decided right then I was going to mount three of them. When we got back to the dock, I saved three of the biggest ones: a fourteen-incher, fourteen-and-a-half-incher, and one incredibly beautiful fifteen-inch crappie. I individually wrapped them in a soaked towel and put them in cabin 2's freezer. On Friday, Michael and I went hunting for a nice birch tree spread I could use for a mount. Back in Lincoln, I commissioned the same taxidermist that had mounted Michael's beautiful largemouth. The result was marvelous. I could not have asked for a better display.

In 1987, on a clear Friday afternoon, we found a crappie bonanza. Since that time, we had caught a few crappies at night, and then in 2006 we had found crappie on the sunken island. The crappies were of excellent quality but not quantity. It took us until 2013 to finally find another crappie bonanza.

On Monday in 2013, the weather report called for beautiful skies and hardly any wind. Terry and I decided to take advantage of the smooth conditions and head to Upper Bottle's south shore for an afternoon of bluegill fishing. Tucked into a small bay that gave way to a shallow bar, we could normally find nine-to-ten-inch bluegills in eight to ten feet of water, hiding in the abundant weed beds that existed all up and down the bar.

My way of finding bluegills required some backbreaking work, primarily from the guy in the front of the boat. Anyone who came bluegill fishing with me knew what was in store for him. My front anchor was twenty-eight pounds. My rear anchor was twenty pounds. Lifting that front anchor was hard. Many times, the anchor had to be pulled out of the weeds and then lifted with twice the weight of weeds on the other end. It was not an easy task. Lately it had been requiring two guys to pull that anchor in—a sign of old men doing something they should not be doing.

I had often said that I was an impatient fisherman. Just because we found a nice little hole with weeds all around in eight feet of water, that didn't mean that was the spot. If we had no action in ten to fifteen minutes, up came the anchors, and we would look for another spot. By day's end, sometimes my fishing partner in the front of the boat was sick of putting the anchor in and taking it out a dozen times.

During one of my constant moves looking for bluebill, Terry and I accidentally ended up on the shallow bar that existed off the south shoreline. My depth finder showed no more than four feet, but to my surprise we came across a large patch of cabbage weed dancing just below the waterline. Cabbage weed! I could not believe it. I had not seen cabbage weed since 1993, when Uncle Charlie was with us. In those years, Whippoorwill Bay was full of the stuff. However, that weed gradually disappeared to total nonexistence in the early 2000s. I told Terry, "Look at that cabbage weed!"

Terry and I decided to find water about ten feet deep next to the patch of cabbage weed. We dropped anchor and sat there fishing for bluegills until Michael and Jim showed up. "What's happening?" they asked.

We yelled back, "Nothing!" We told them about the cabbage weed close by in four feet and pointed out the direction from our boat. That was music to Jim's ears. They decided to cruise up on the bar and find the patch. When they did, Michael headed north into deeper water until they hit about six feet and dropped anchor. Jim was in the bow of the boat—a perfect spot for him to launch his cane pole into deeper water. They had anchored within casting distance of our location.

It didn't take long until Jim's bobber disappeared. Up came a beautiful Minnesota black crappie. I was not sure who was more excited, Jim or the rest of us. Cabbage weed equals crappies! Crappies equal cabbage weed! A few minutes went by, and Jim landed another, and then another. Soon Michael got the hint and started casting a slip bobber close to where Jim was fishing. In came another crappie. They had found them—the elusive fall crappies.

Terry and I could not take it any longer. Off came the piece of night crawler, and on went a small crappie minnow. I have no use for a slip bobber. I would rather use a stick bobber set high up the line with a small split shot and small hook. Besides, my Johnson Century reel can outcast any open-face reel made on the market. I had no problem launching my bobber and minnow close to Michael's boat. Terry, a fan of slip bobbers, followed suit. Before long, all four of us were catching crappies.

We sat there for close to two hours catching crappies until Terry realized we needed a fish count. The limit was ten crappies per license. My livewell was full, so we decided to count them out. Jim and Michael did the same. When both boats had twenty, we stopped fishing and headed back to the resort. We had some cleaning to do. This marked the first time for all of us that we were able to catch our limit of crappies. We still have not repeated the feat. (See figure 27.)

The next year, in 2014, we managed to find another spot that yielded us another crappie bonanza. On Thursday afternoon of that year, we all decided to make a day of it fishing for panfish. My boat partner for the day was Charlie Brown.

Our first thought was to head up to the southern shore and fish for bluegills or crappies. It was the same location where, just a year prior, Terry, Michael, Jim, and I had limited out on crappies in one afternoon. Michael and Doug had taken up berth on one location on the south shore, while those in Wayne's boat found another spot. They were primarily looking for crappies. Finding a bed of panfish is often a hit-and-miss prospect. Charlie and I moved often, but we could not find a good spot. We decided to move and try fishing the sunken island. We told the other guys where we were going. Their biggest mistake that day was that they didn't follow us.

Once we found the island, I was looking for nine to ten feet of water. When the depth finder lit up, we dropped our anchor. I started right off with a bobber and night crawler, just to test out the bluegill situation. Charlie decided to put on a small crappie minnow. Charlie likes to get his bait out a considerable distance from the boat. He let it fly as far as he could, to a point where it was almost impossible to see his bobber.

I was fishing about as deep as I could while still managing a decent cast. If I stood up in the boat and raised my rod tip to the point where the bait was dangling above the water, I would let my trusty Johnson Century do the rest. I figure my bobber was keeping the bait about seven to eight feet down. The bluegills started hitting right away, but they were small.

Suddenly, Charlie's bobber disappeared. It was so hard to see his bobber that I had to second-guess myself. Charlie saw it disappear also, and he set the hook. In came a beautiful Minnesota black crappie. Charlie was so excited, and so was I. I had not expected a crappie. Sometimes the larger bluegills will also hit a small minnow.

Into the livewell the crappie went. Soon Charlie was fighting another, and then another. It was time to get my night crawler off and put on a minnow. Charlie was fishing much shallower than I was. I decided to decrease my depth by a foot or so. Out flew my bobber, a few yards from the boat. I checked my depth finder, which still showed nine feet of water. Suddenly my bobber lifted and then fell sideways. A second later, it slowly started going down. That was the distinctive crappie hit. Up came another crappie.

We had no way to tell the other guys what was happening. Nobody had a cell phone on him. It was not our practice to take phones out on the water. The only way to let the others know the crappies were hitting would have been to lift anchor and get them. I was not going to do that. It had been my experience that if we found them, we should not leave them. Jim knew I didn't sit in one location long if nothing was happening. They should have gotten the hint simply because we hadn't moved for a couple of hours.

We sat out there until we ran out of bait. With our minnows gone and suppertime approaching, we had a lot of fish cleaning to do. Up came the anchors, and we headed back to camp. The other two boats came in shortly after. We cleaned eighteen crappies that evening before supper, all of them twelve to thirteen inches long. It was one of the best crappie afternoons I ever experienced. When the other guys came in, I am not sure what they were thinking. I know Jim wanted to kick himself for not suggesting they come check us out. The next day, Doug, Jim, and I went back out on the island. I had set a buoy marker on the spot where Charlie and I were the day before. We ended up cleaning another twenty-one crappies.

For me, a good crappie bite is better than anything. The action is fast and heart-pounding. There is nothing like seeing a bobber lift, then lie down on the water, and then disappear. It is the distinctive crappie hit. The next year, in 2015, the crappies were back on the sunken island. It is not easy finding crappies in the fall. We now had a few spots that we could check out. If the weather was decent and there was a small chop on the water, we might tie into another school of crappies. I hope that is the case, since fishing for northerns and walleyes had been becoming a burden, and I would just as soon sit out on the island and watch my bobber disappear into the clear blue water of the Bottle Lakes and hopefully pull in a crappie slab.

CHAPTER 15

New Owners for Whippoorwill Resort

A couple of months after our stay in 2009, I received notice from Marty and Al that they had sold the resort to a couple out of Colorado: Connie and Mike. When I read their notice about the resort being sold, I must admit I had a bit of a chill run through me. I didn't know what that meant for the future of our traditional fishing trips. This could all end very soon. A month or so after receiving their notice, I received a brochure from Connie and Mike introducing themselves as the new owners of Whippoorwill; they included some reassuring words that they fully intend to continue running the property as a resort. There would be some scheduling changes, but nothing that would indicate a major change to the business plan Marty and Al followed. They would still offer off-season rates, which was welcome news to us. Some resorts simply close after Labor Day and do not take advantage of the great month of September, which a lot of fishermen look forward to. Connie and Mike planned to keep the resort open through September, but with one guideline not to be negotiated on: the resort would close October 1. Nobody was to stay after that date. For us, if October 1 fell during the week, we would have to back up our weeklong stay to the previous week if we wanted to keep our Saturday-to-Saturday tradition alive.

That whole October 1 drop-dead date didn't sit well with some of us. Jim especially loved to fish into the first week of October simply because he felt the fishing was better. That was not going to happen with Connie and

Mike. I understood their position, simply because Connie and Mike were not going to stay at the resort over the winter. They already had a winter home in Colorado. They wanted to get everything winterized during the first week of October and then get the hell out of Dodge before the first snowfall or hard freeze set in.

Another change to Marty and Al's business plan was their requirement of a hefty deposit for each cabin. Marty and Al needed $50. Connie and Mike needed $150 per cabin. Worse yet, the deposit had to be in hand before December 1 of the current year to reserve the next year's cabins. That required many of us to think ahead about next year's trip sooner than what we were used to. There are few people that can plan one year ahead of time. Most of us cannot plan one month ahead. These were all small, trivial changes if it meant Connie and Mike would keep the resort open. I was determined to honor whatever changes they made, just to keep our tradition alive.

Connie liked to take pictures. There is not a more picturesque place in Minnesota for subject material like the Bottle Lakes in the fall. The colors are beyond description. Connie was an instant hit with our bunch of raggedy guys. One of the first encounters the guys had with Connie was regarding a picture-taking session. She wanted everyone to gather on the resort's pontoon boat so she could take a picture of our group for their website. That picture still exists on Whippoorwill's web page.

Next year was 2010. We would get to meet the new owners of Whippoorwill. We would catch one of the biggest fish we ever saw. And a few of us narrowly escaped a brush with tragedy when tradition came face-to-face with the angel of mercy.

CHAPTER 16

2010: A Shocking Story

D id we ever expect to continue what we had been doing for the past forty-three years and get away with it? We had seen all the signs. We had seen all the warnings in advance. We had talked among ourselves about imminent danger. We could see it in our bloodshot eyes. We could tell it in our demeanor. We could feel it in our fatigue, but we were not listening to the messages our bodies were sending out, informing us of potential peril just around the bend. Was our tradition so solidly imbedded into our souls that all the cautionary warning signs in the world could not stop us? We had built up such a strong resistance to change that simple, sensible alternatives could not break our paradigm. It would take something much more than talk to change our way. It would take a face-to-face encounter with the angel of mercy, and we would have to hope she showed pity on us. Such an encounter took place in the early morning hours of September 25, 2010.

We had been traveling at night, leaving Leonard's farm on Friday night for years. Nothing changed in that regard for 2010. We were all excited to get back to the beautiful Bottle Lakes once again. Plus, we would get to meet the new owners of Whippoorwill Resort, Connie and Mike.

Our old gang was back that year: Terry, Rick, Jim, Wayne, Michael, Doug, Leonard, and me—the best group of guys in all the world. Wayne pulled Leonard's boat with only Jim to keep him company. Michael drove his Blazer with Doug and Leonard to keep him company. Terry and

Rick decided to drive from Washington and meet everyone at the resort Saturday morning. The small caravan started out around 11:30 p.m. in a pouring rain.

That year my boat was all tucked away at Whippoorwill for the summer. When my boys and I were there in the spring, I was allowed to store my boat at the resort until the coming fall. I had a prior commitment that year that prevented me from traveling with the guys. I was staying in Waseca, Minnesota, and would meet the gang at Whippoorwill Saturday afternoon. I can remember having a tough time sleeping that night. By the time I did fall asleep, it was past midnight. I slept in late that morning and didn't get a good start out of Waseca until well past 10:30 a.m. I had a four-hour drive ahead of me that would put me into the resort around 3:00 p.m. What a beautiful drive it was to Park Rapids! Then it was on to Whippoorwill, where I could not wait to meet the old gang once again.

Something was amiss when I got into camp. This situation, whatever it could be, appeared to be serious. All the signs of fear and shock were written on everyone's face. They were all sitting around on the main cabin's deck, staring out into space. Nobody said a word. *Not much of a reception*, I thought to myself. They all looked as if they had seen a ghost. I glanced over to the docks and noticed that only Leonard's boat was moored. I made a quick peek to see if my boat was where I had left it in the spring. It was still there. "Where's your boat, Michael?" I asked.

After a long pause, Michael said, "We wrecked it." That was the only response I got. I glanced at Terry. He was shaking his head in disbelief about something I have yet to understand. Finally, some conversation started up about an accident. I could tell it was hard for them to talk about it. Doug finally broke the ice and volunteered to tell their story, which left me in shock. He told a story of near disaster that had occurred on I-29 north of Sioux Falls, in the middle of a downpour, at two thirty in the morning.

Interstate 29 from Sioux City, Iowa, to Fargo, North Dakota, was always in some degree of repair. I cannot remember a time when it was not. It was one of our jokes we would make among ourselves just before we would leave for our trip: "I wonder what section they are repairing this year?" In 2010, the sections being repaired were between Sioux Falls, South Dakota, and Brookings, South Dakota. We had traveled down this road enough to know that if a section was slated for repair, the first targeted segments of the road were always the bridges and small viaducts. There were a lot of viaducts down I-29 that were no more than small overpasses crossing a valley or creek bed.

The method the crews would use to direct traffic across these overpasses was to set concrete dividers down the center, forcing single-lane traffic to one side or the other, depending on which side they were working on. The concrete dividers were extremely dangerous if they were set too close to the center line. This was especially true at night. Add to that a downpour of rain, the pulling of a boat, and the onset of fatigue at 2:30 a.m. A recipe for disaster could not have been drafted any better.

Doug was driving in relief of Michael. Michael's Blazer was leading the caravan down I-29, with Wayne's Tundra running behind them. Wayne was a driver that didn't like to tailgate cars in front of him, so he kept a good distance apart from Michael's Blazer, respecting the weather they were driving in. Wayne told me, "The conditions were horrible! It was raining so hard I could barely see." Apparently the repairs being made to the viaduct were on the inside lane, forcing all traffic to cross the viaduct to the outside lane. It is hard enough to get through a single lane like that during the day. At night it is a dangerous situation.

Wayne said to me that he suddenly saw headlights right in front of him, and then they disappeared. In perfect Wayne prose, he shouted out to Jim, "Holy shit, did you see that? What the hell happened?" Wayne went on to say, "I immediately hit the brakes." The next thing he remembered seeing was Michael's Blazer stopped perpendicular on the right side of the road. Michael's trailer was still attached to the hitch with the boat still intact but flipped over sideways, having ended up backward in the ditch.

Doug continued the story. I sympathized with him. I am sure he was struggling to postulate a sequence of events over and over in his conscience regarding what had transpired and how he had managed to save everyone's life that morning. He was going through that whole scenario one more time for me. Doug remembered going over the viaduct in a pouring rain. Not only can the rain hamper visibility, it can cause some hydroplaning of the tires against the road. Doug had thought he was getting too close to the concrete dividers, so he compensated to the right with the Blazer. However, Michael's lighter boat didn't follow. Instead the boat wheels continued their outward movement, and the small amount of whiplash from Doug's move to the right sent the left wheel of the trailer up against the concrete divider. Suddenly a dangerous situation developed.

The design of those dividers worked against Doug. The dividers had a very wide base and then curved upward to a rounded point much narrower than the base. Because of that design, the side of the divider was curved. Once the tire contacted the divider, it simply followed the contour upward to a point where the boat flipped onto its side. Doug felt the impact and hit the brakes. Hitting the brakes caused the boat to go faster than the Blazer. It must have been like the fishtailing of a motorcycle's rear tire. Anyone that has ever ridden a motorcycle can relate to a fishtailing story. Suddenly the boat was screeching down the road parallel to the truck, only backward. Leonard told me that he was sleeping in the backseat when the accident happened. When he opened his eyes, he could see the boat out his window; it was sliding backward down the road, parallel with the truck. Somehow Doug maintained enough control of the Blazer during a 270-degree spin down the road that he didn't flip the vehicle. It was during that spin that Wayne saw the headlights shine in his direction and then disappear. After I heard all this, I had to sit down in welcome disbelief that nobody had gotten hurt—not one scratch. I am no doctor, but I could still sense some shock and fear among all those that were involved. Luck was with them that night. The angel of mercy took pity.

If Michael had been pulling a heavier boat, an accident like that would have flipped the truck, and then, I believe, something far worse would have happened. But Michael's boat was light. It stayed on the boat hitch during the whole mishap. The boat itself flipped, but it didn't have enough torque to flip the truck. A heavier boat would have. The lighter boat contributed to the accident, but it also spared a worse outcome.

Once all those involved gathered themselves, they crawled out of the vehicle only to see just how fortunate they were. The boat was still attached to the trailer, flipped onto its side. Somehow it had stayed hitched to the truck. The trailer hitch itself was bent, but it hadn't disengaged from the ball. The boat trailer's tires were still inflated and functional. Everything that had been in the boat was scattered all over the ditch and the highway. The motor's lower unit had sustained a lot of damage and been rendered useless. The side walls of the boat were bent inward. The first thing the guys did was flip the trailer, with the boat still attached, back onto the tires. That took some horsepower. There is something about Michael's strength that is scary. If he is called upon to conduct some feat of strength, he transforms himself into a small bull. Michael and the rest of the gang flipped the boat like an over easy egg. Then they moved the truck and the boat off the highway and tried to find as much gear as they could from the nearby ditch. The truck sustained minor damage to the rear fender and bumper.

Desolation on I-29 at 2:30 a.m. is common. Only one car came across the accident. It was a couple of guys going nowhere, and they stopped to offer their assistance. Michael had decided right away he didn't want to report anything to the police. During this time, poor Leonard was trying to salvage his tackle box, which had been thrown open in the ditch. His tackle box was a prize possession for him that included everything old: old lures, old hooks, and old line. If it was in Leonard's box, it was old. But that didn't stop him from cherishing all those possessions accumulated over the years that only a tackle box contains. I still have the same jig Lou sold me in 1967 for walleye fishing located in my tackle box somewhere. After a quick search of the ditch, Michael wanted to get out of Dodge. They threw what they could back into the boat, and off they went very slowly down I-29 until they found the first exit. The time was close to 4:00 a.m., and it was still raining.

Douglas saved their lives that morning. Somehow he managed to keep control of the truck; that could not have been an easy task. I believe a combination of circumstances prevented a worse outcome: (1) Douglas maintaining some measure of control, (2) Michael's boat being light enough that it didn't flip the truck, and (3) the rain making the road slippery enough that the truck simply slid down the pavement instead of rolling over. The rain might have been the reason for the accident, but the wet conditions just might have saved their lives.

From what I could gather from those involved, the story above is close to the actual events. When Michael took the first exit off I-29, they noticed a large parking lot nearby that was owned by a trucking company. They unhitched the boat and left it parked on their lot. Nobody was around, and everything was closed for the night. Michael left them a note to call the resort the following afternoon. When they were finished telling their story to me, Michael still had not heard from the trucking company. Later that afternoon, Michael did get a call, and he explained to them what had happened and that he was making plans for someone to get the boat and trailer.

What a colossal lesson for us. There was nothing stopping us from simply leaving on Saturday morning after everyone got some sleep, except our unwillingness to see what was before us. It took a brush with disaster to open our eyes. That was the last time any of us traveled down I-29 at night again.

In 2011, we decided to take I-29 out of the equation. Our new route took us east of Sioux City on Route 75 and then Route 60 into Windom, Minnesota, where we picked up Route 71, which took us all the way into Park Rapids. The trip was shorter in distance but took about the same amount of time. Plus, it was safer. We finally got to travel during the day, free of exhaustion. Our demeanor had undergone a drastic and far-reaching change regarding our ways of thinking and behaving. We could enjoy heading north once again instead of facing the dreaded nighttime trip that was nothing more than a bad hallucinatory experience.

CHAPTER 17

Waldo 2010

The year 2010 was a pivotal year for us. We would meet the new owners of the resort. The guys that were driving up at night escaped a brush with disaster. Then, on Sunday evening during our stay in 2010, one of our grandest fishing adventures was about to take place. Michael's journal for 2010 mentions it only in passing simply because Michael was in a different boat at the time. It was too bad all of us could not have witnessed the unimaginable. Three of us did: Terry, Doug, and me. Few of us in our bunch can generate more excitement when it comes to fishing than Jim and Terry. When it comes to fishing, those two are the absolute best. I had Terry in my boat that Sunday evening.

This amazing story had its beginning in 2005. One evening in 2005, Michael and I took my boat and went out walleye fishing at night. Our plan was to pull minnows in the shallows while fishing the west side of Upper Bottle Lake. This location was full of underwater vegetation. The evening was just beautiful. There was no wind to speak of, and the temperature was pleasant. We were in a new moon phase, so it was pitch black outside. We trolled back and forth without having one hit. Around 10:30 p.m., we decided to troll back to the docks by way of Wambolt's Bay. I had on my rear white boat light that stood high on a five-foot pole. The white light cast a glow across the water for a considerable distance simply because it was pitch black outside. Within Wambolt's Bay lies a large bar, which we were slowly approaching. If those not familiar with the area enter it unexpectedly, they could find themselves in dangerous one-foot water a good distance from the shore. I was trying to stay in about three to four feet.

Anybody that runs a boat while trolling at night realizes that scanning ahead and sideways is a mandatory duty. Lack of concentration for just a second or two can turn into trouble quickly. Since I was trolling backward, my area of concentration was behind me and to the sides. I cannot describe how spooky the area suddenly had become. It seemed as if we had entered a forbidden domain where nothing existed. There was no doubt we were on the bar. Our depth was only three feet, and the color of the water had changed to a lighter brownish cast due to lack of vegetation on the bar. Suddenly I noticed a large, dark shadow approaching out of the darkness toward the rear of the boat. *Damn, a log*, I thought to myself. However, we had never seen a log in this area before. When I realized what it was, I hollered out, "Michael, look at that!" It was the biggest fish I had ever seen—much bigger and much wider than the one Wayne had hooked into a couple of years before. This thing must have been fifteen inches wide and several feet long. The giant shadow passed on the right side of the boat and then disappeared. Michael and I looked at each other but didn't say much. We knew it was a fish, but what type of fish? I cannot understand how an angler could land something like that. I cannot fathom seeing something like that out of the water. This fish ruled Wambolt's Bay and was out hunting when our paths just happened to cross. We wondered if he might have been a bit curious about our lights. We continued our troll back to the docks.

That Sunday in 2010, the wind was blowing out of the southeast all afternoon right into Wambolt's Bay. Fishing was not great all day. In fact, nobody had caught anything except for a couple of small northerns. We were hoping for better luck that evening. After a great dinner of Michael's excellent chili, we left the docks around 7:30 p.m. The sun had set long ago, and with overhead cloud cover, the Bottle Lakes turned dark and dreary—perfect conditions for the beasts of the lake to be out hunting.

Terry suggested we troll walleye minnows into Wambolt's Bay along the shallow bar since the waves were being pushed in that direction all day long. We started a slow back-troll out in front of Whippoorwill's docks on our way west into the gloomy dark waters of Wambolt's Bay. Doug and I were using normal monofilament line with a small split shot and a walleye hook. Terry was using one of his casting reels equipped with twenty-pound fluorocarbon line to which he attached about eight feet of six-pound monofilament leader line. He was using a small number six wide-bodied walleye hook pulling a two-inch-long shiner minnow. He had set a small split shot about two feet up from the hook to help keep the minnow below the surface of the water.

When we approached Wambolt's from the east, the resort was pitch black. There was not one light visible across the whole property. The wind blowing through the whispering pines seemed to warn us not to invade the privacy of the bay. From the water, we could barely make out the worn and weathered cabins sitting up on the beach, tucked back among the trees. The rest of the buildings that were set deeper into the property remained invisible. It was an indefinable sight for us, as years before we had walked those very acres, enjoying wonderful times. From the confines of our boat, I could see the reflection of my rear white boat light bouncing off one of the windowpanes of the first cabin we passed. It was an eerie sight that made my imagination wander—a faint false image of some apparition. I wondered how many ghosts lived in those cabins. I would dare anyone to pick out one cabin and stay the night there alone, with no light source, and not get the shit scared out of him.

The docks Daryl used had been removed long ago. No longer could I rely on them for guidance. This was especially true of the last dock to the northwest. I often would use that dock to remind me to turn south before I ran into shallow water. Now I had to rely on my depth finder. I was running in three to five feet when I heard the two-foot warning from my depth finder. We were approaching shallow water. I quickly turned south until three feet appeared once again. When I completed the swing to the south, the ends of our fishing line were now making their swing behind the boat. It was during that swing that Terry yelled, "Fish on!"

No two words can generate more excitement in a boat than "fish on." Doug and I quickly brought our lines in, and I made a quick reference of our location on the bar. The waves were coming broadside to us, but we were far enough away from the shoreline that landing a small walleye would not be a problem. I put the throttle in neutral and got the flashlight out. Douglas manned the net and was ready when Terry was.

Terry made some comment like "This one feels pretty good!" I had the flashlight shining in the water, trying to find Terry's line angle. The fish was close to the boat, but we could not see any glaring diamond-like eyes that would indicate a walleye. Terry was gaining line steadily, and then he said, "Okay, get ready." Doug made ready the net. Terry's rod was in a good bend. We could tell this fish might be bigger than normal. I continued to scan the water surface for any sign of a fish. Nothing! I was watching Terry's line angle, which now went straight down. Then everything changed. No longer was Terry's rod tip above water. He had to put most of the rod down into the water just to keep his rod from breaking. Terry yelled, "Christ, this thing is under the boat!" Then he said, "He's not stopping. I cannot turn him." That fish decided to just keep going right under the boat and out toward the open water behind us. By now Terry's reel was all the way down to the water surface, his rod bent in a large bow under the boat.

Terry's drag was working steadily. He was constantly fidgeting with it to allow the fish to take what line he wanted. I watched Terry's reel strip out line smoothly at a constant rate—nothing fast, nothing slow. Wherever this fish was headed, he was not in a hurry. I was starting to worry about our drift. I made another glance to the shoreline. We were still okay. Suddenly Terry yelled, "I'm starting to gain some line back. I think he turned." Sure as hell, Terry was picking up line back onto the reel. Doug was ready with the net. It appeared the fish would surface on Doug's side. Doug suddenly put the net down and cried out his paraphrase of one of the greatest cinema lines of all time: "You're going to need a bigger boat!" I had the flashlight shining in the water. What appeared just below the waterline on the starboard side of the boat startled us all. None of us were prepared for it, but there it was—the biggest northern or muskie any of us had ever seen in our lives. We didn't know for sure which species it was; we knew only that it was too big for us to handle.

When he saw the bright light from the flashlight, that fish made an abrupt turn right back under the boat and again started heading out to open water behind us, this time with more authority. Terry had to get his rod tip down quickly to prevent a busted rod. The reel was stripping out line much faster than on the first run. Terry looked at me and asked, "What do you want to do?"

I thought to myself, *We have no chance to land him.* "Can you turn him?" I asked. That was somewhat of a stupid question given the size of this thing.

Terry said, "There's no way!"

My head was spinning as I tried to decide our next play. We had two choices that would be dictated by the fish: turn the boat and follow him, or, if Terry could turn him, make one try with my dilapidated net to boat this guy. There was no way I was going to put my hand in that water and try to gill this fish. He would have taken me right out of the boat.

Terry was holding his own. Terry's reel was peeling out line against the drag. Just when I was going to take the throttle out of neutral and turn the boat, Waldo turned and decided to come back toward the boat once again. Terry yelled at me, "I think he's coming back to the boat!" I could not believe it. Terry was getting line back onto the reel.

Doug and I traded the net for the flashlight. I told Terry, "If we get a chance, we will have one crack at this." The time was near. Terry was yelling at me to get ready. I told Terry, "Do not worry about the fish or the net; just concentrate on your rod. I'll handle the fish." I don't know why I said that; it just seemed to be the right thing to say at the time. There was no way I was going to handle that fish. My net was just a normal twenty-two-inch aluminum net that can be purchased at any sporting goods store. Fish like this have nets like mine for breakfast. I figured we had no chance in hell.

Suddenly he came into view. My heart was racing. Terry yelled out, "Holy shit, look at the size of that thing!" That was an understatement! Douglas was trying to keep the water illuminated so we could see what was going on. Terry somehow guided him toward my end of the boat headfirst. It was a brilliant maneuver; that meant I could try to get his head into the net first. I dared not put my net into the water slowly, as that would have spooked the massive fish. When he was within reach, I decided to quickly get the net deep and at the same time charge the net into his head all in one full sweep and, with any luck, lift him into the boat. To my surprise, he somehow got tangled in the net and was not able to escape. I started to lift him over the side. As I was lifting the net, the aluminum handle gave way against the weight and bent the net back toward the water. We were about to lose him. I quickly grabbed the other side of the net, and with one heave I lifted him over the side and onto the boat floor, with half of the fish still tangled in the net.

Lying on the floor of my boat was the biggest muskie any of us ever saw. That fish was so pissed off. I doubt he knew what happened until he was in the boat. In a violent fury, he started thrashing about. I didn't want him to get hurt, so I threw myself down over him until he calmed down. That is when fish die; they hurt themselves thrashing in the boat, and I did not want that to happen to this fish.

During the ordeal, Terry's line broke. He managed to save his rod, which was a small miracle in itself. *Now what?* We all sat there staring at the crowned king of the Bottle Lakes. He had to be the king. I could not conceive of a larger fish swimming those waters. I asked Terry, "Do you want to mount him?"

Terry said, "No!"

Neither did Doug. I wanted nothing to do with him. In my mind, a fish like this needs to be released back into his kingdom.

We all decided to let him go. Terry, however, was adamant he wanted a couple of pictures. Our problem was that nobody had a camera. *Unbelievable! No camera.* My head started spinning again. *How are we going to get back to camp and take some pictures before he dies on us?* I would not be able to forgive myself if that were to happen. Our decision needed to be made fast. I knew from reading about large fish like this that they cannot survive out of water long. My livewell was not large enough to host him. However, the water was cold, and he hadn't put up a battle at the boat, which had saved some of his strength. So I cranked up the motor and made a full-speed dash back to camp. By now the large fish had calmed down. He was still moving his gills, which was a good sign. He was bleeding out of one side of his gill plate, which was a bad sign. When we docked, I took the flashlight and inspected his gill. There was Terry's small hook, stuck onto one of the gills. We had no choice but to leave it alone. Nature would take its course regarding that hook. I am sure this fella had dealt with bigger hooks during his lifetime than that little walleye hook.

Terry raced down the dock to get his camera. When he came back to the boat, Terry wanted a picture with the fish held up. The problem was that Terry had shoulder trouble and was not going to hold this fish, so I volunteered. I carefully placed my left hand just inside his gill plate and cradled his tail with the other hand. (See figure 28.) I didn't want to lose my hold and risk him getting hurt. I knew that if I dropped him, he would die for sure. Terry took the picture. We decided to try to get him to the grass on the shore under the large floodlight. Since I had the fish secure in my arms, I decided to make a dash for the beach while cradling him in my arms. If that fish wanted to, he could have had his breakfast right then with one bite out of my armpit.

My head was racing again. I knew Waldo had been out of the water for over fifteen minutes. We had to get these pictures taken quickly or risk losing the fish. I found myself constantly checking his gills for expansion. He was still gasping, which was a good sign. Terry took three pictures very quickly. I wished we had more time. It would have been nice to set up a decent pose to show just how massive this critter was. We improvised in one of the pictures, with Terry placing his hand next to Waldo for scale. (See figure 29.) Time was running out on the life of this great fish.

We had another dilemma before we released him. We needed to get some measurements. Implausible though it sounds, nobody had a tape in his tackle box. I had a tape on the interior port side of the boat, but there was no way I was going to risk carrying that fish back to the boat and trying to get him and me into the boat without hurting ourselves just for a measurement. Something else had to work. Good fortune came our way once again when Doug found a long, straight two-by-two lying next to the cabin. We put the stick up alongside the fish that was now looking very still on the grass and made a mark at the tip of his tail. We could measure that later. I grabbed hold of Waldo in my arms once again and made a dash to the dock, where I could get him into some deeper water. There we would try to resuscitate him and, I hoped, save his life.

Another dilemma arose. How were we going to hold this fish up and try to push water through his gills without him slipping out of our grasp? Waldo was just too big for me to handle with just my hands. I could barely get both hands around his tail. I knew that if he slipped out of our grasp, he would sink to the bottom and die. We would not have a way to retrieve him from under the dock. My head was spinning again. *A stringer. We need a stringer.* I told Doug to get into the boat and get a stringer that I knew was in the side compartment. When Doug returned, I drove the needle of the stringer through the bottom lip of the fish and told Terry to grab both ends and lift his head if he started to sink. I laid myself down on the dock and, with both hands around his tail, started to sway his tail section back and forth, at the same time pushing him and pulling him through the water to get some water flowing through the gills. With Terry on the stringer and me on the tail end, we were able to keep the great fish upright, which was most important. At first there was no response. Minutes flew by, and still there was no response. I feared we were too late. Then I felt a sudden surge from his tail. It felt like a muscle twitch. He started to move his tail by himself. There was hope. The surges became stronger and stronger. I could see his mouth expanding and contracting just below the waterline, sending lifesaving water through his gills. Soon his whole body was in a surge. He started tugging at the stringer that Terry was using to hold his head up. This fish was done with that stringer. I knew I would not be able to hold on to him if he had a sudden urge to just get on with it. He would slip from my hands, and then the only thing holding him would have been the stringer. I am not sure Terry could have kept a decent hold on that stringer if this massive fish decided he'd had enough of us. We needed to get that stringer out of his lip. I asked Doug to get my knife from my tackle box and sever the line. With the knife in hand, Doug cut the stringer and pulled out the strand from his lip. It worked, and none too soon. The fish was getting frisky and ready to go. I let his tail free of my hands, and that was the last we saw of him. My God! The three of us will never forget it.

The waves were crashing into Whippoorwill's shoreline. We waited a good fifteen minutes and then combed the beach, looking for any sign of Waldo. If he perished, he would wash up on shore. To our relief, we found no sign of Waldo. I hoped the king had returned to his lake unharmed, only needing a toothpick to get that irritating hook out of his gill.

We were done fishing that night. There was still time to venture out, but nobody wanted to go. We retreated to the deck of cabin 3, where we sat with a beer in disbelief over what had just happened. But it had happened! Somehow, Terry had managed to hook into a fifty-one-inch muskie. That is the length we measured from the stick. I had often stared at the tape on the side of my boat, which stretched to fifty-six inches. I could never conceive of a fish long enough to call for such a tape to even exist, but now I know.

We sat on the deck, reliving the whole experience, trying to understand how this fish had managed to get caught. Most muskie fishermen use lures ten inches long their whole lifetimes and never catch a muskie like this one. Terry did it with a number six wide-bodied hook on a walleye minnow. Most fishermen use thirty-to-fifty-pound-test line just to get one of these massive bodies close to the boat. Terry did it with twenty-pound line and eight feet of six-pound leader line. Most fishermen try for muskies during the day. Terry caught this one at night. Most muskie fishermen are sitting in boats over deep water. Terry managed to hook this one in three feet of water. Most muskie fishermen use seven-foot heavy-duty rods. Terry managed to catch this one with a six-foot medium-strength rod.

That evening, Leonard, Rick, and Mike went to Lower Bottle to fish the flat bar on the east shoreline for walleyes. Wayne and Jim decided to go sit for bullheads. When they returned, we told them the story of all stories. I know they wished we could have kept Waldo on a stringer for them to see that great fish, but I had decided not to. I didn't want to risk that great muskie hurting himself while tied up at the dock. Plus, I didn't know if we had a stringer strong enough to even consider such a plan. So we let him go.

Rick brought his laptop that year, onto which Terry loaded the four pictures from his camera. At least the guys had them to look at and decide for themselves the size of what we'd had to deal with. The fish itself was not handsome. It was a fearsome-looking fish. His teeth had to be a half inch long and could tear a walleye in half with one bite or inhale a twelve-inch walleye for supper in one gulp. The only beauty he possessed was in his massive appearance. Everything else I would categorize as ugly. He was an ugly fish. There were no markings of any kind on him, just a basic brown color from head to tail. We did some research on what we might have caught. It was a muskie, but what kind of muskie? The best we could determine was that he could have been a clear muskie. Clear muskies are that—clear with very few markings. They are especially void of any markings in the late fall. Also, there was a great chance he was a she, and the fish was approximately seventeen years old. At fifty-one inches, that fish was all we could handle. An estimation of weight, just using length, was around forty pounds.

Michael and I believe that we met Waldo on the same bar in front of Wambolt's in 2005 while trolling for walleyes in shallow water. My rear running light cast a faint illumination around the boat—just enough to notice a large shadow just under the water going in the opposite direction. It might not have been the same fish, but I believe it was.

When we got back home after our trip that year, I decided to send an article about our story to about four different fishing magazines. Not one magazine found it worth their time to consider publishing such a story. I believe the editors could not find themselves to believe it. This one, however, was true, right down to the last swish of Waldo's tail as he left the dock.

CHAPTER 18

Leonard's Last Trip

The year 2011 was bittersweet. It would be Leonard's last trip with us. Leonard's age simply caught up with him. Leonard was suffering from dizzy spells that had started earlier in the year and were becoming more frequent as the year went on. He didn't want to be a bother to us. Leonard made the best of it in 2011. We did manage to get him out fishing occasionally, which I am sure he appreciated, but I could tell it was not the same for him. He found it difficult getting on and off the dock because of his dizziness. Most of his evenings were spent inside reading or having a nightcap with someone. He enjoyed spending the time with all of us, just visiting and looking forward to Michael's breakfasts and dinners. Leonard always discussed with me how we should all appreciate what Michael does for us when it comes to eating. As for me, I try to always thank Michael for our meal when we are finished. All of us appreciate what he does for us.

In 2011, after the previous year's nearly fatal accident, we decided to not go knocking on the devil's door again but leave earlier, on Saturday morning. For forty-three years, those that made the drive during the night somehow survived without a major incident. In choosing to leave early Saturday morning, I would like to think we had gotten wiser in our older age. I am not sure I would have opted to drive during the night if the consensus was to do so. I simply would have gone myself the next morning. Everyone agreed that an early Saturday morning start was in our best interest.

CHAPTER 19

Curtis and Charlie

Wayne called me one afternoon in the spring of 2011 wondering about room for Curtis on our trip in the coming fall. Curtis worked with Wayne at Burlington Northern Railroad in Lincoln, Nebraska. I guess the two of them had started talking fishing, and that had gotten Curtis interested. Wayne mentioned Minnesota, and that was all it took for Curtis to ask if he could join us in the coming fall. It was unlike us to refuse anyone that wanted to go if they accepted our rules: never, ever complain, and accept our policy of splitting everything right down the middle. The deal was set; Curtis joined us that fall.

Curtis didn't know any of us except for Wayne and Charlie. Little did he know he was being thrown into a mix of guys that were seasoned veterans when it came to fishing. By now there was not one hole, not one weed bed, not one snag, and not one square foot of water we didn't know regarding Bottle Lakes. Plus, every one of us had been fishing since we were kids. Curtis, on the other hand, knew nothing about fishing. However, nobody was more determined to learn. Curtis hadn't had the opportunity to grow up with friends that liked to fish or to be taught at an early age how to fish. I doubt Curtis had ever been fishing before. There are a couple of defining characteristics I should mention about Curtis: he never got pissed, he never got disgusted, and he never gave up. At least that was what I saw from his behavior that week at Whippoorwill.

Curtis was a large man both in stature and size. Consequently, he had a bottomless pit when it came to eating meals. We came to find out Curtis was the most powerful eater we had ever seen. There were no more problems with leftovers when Curtis was around, and that made Michael happy. Keeping Michael happy was all-important to us. Michael, in his old age, was getting grumpy when it came to leftovers. Curtis solved all that. By the end of the week our motto was, "Leave it for Curtis; he'll eat it." And he did!

Whatever skill Curtis had regarding eating, he left it at the table when it came to fishing. Curtis knew nothing about fishing. Before he came to Minnesota with us, he went to Cabela's and bought out the store. He had three full large boat tackle boxes full of crap. Every design of lure, jig, hook, and weight Cabela's had to offer lined his tackle boxes. Curtis could have started his own tackle shop if he'd wanted to. He'd bought three rods and reels, all of them useless. The reels had line counters on them. The rods were built for tuna. I wish I would have known he was going to do that; I would have gone with him and told him what to buy. Nonetheless, he was stuck with what he bought and had to make do with it.

Curtis started out fishing with Wayne and Jim. I do believe they tried to show Curtis a little bit about fishing. But Wayne and Jim like to use their cane poles when still-fishing, which is something they do most of the time during the daytime hours. Curtis didn't have a cane pole, so he was forced to deal with his ocean rods and reels. Also, Jim and Wayne have more patience then a cat staring into a mouse hole. I doubted Curtis had that kind of patience and felt that what he needed more than anything was some fast action. A couple of days had passed, and every time I trolled past Wayne's boat, there was Curtis, sitting in the same pathetic position, trying to catch a tuna using a bobber the size of a softball. The week went on in that manner until Terry and I got to discussing Curtis one afternoon while trolling for northerns. We decided Curtis needed a change and a little more help. I thought Curtis should come fish in my boat for an afternoon and we could go drifting for northerns. Terry agreed. On Wednesday afternoon, Curtis, Charlie, and I went fishing.

I stuck Curtis in the middle, between Charlie and me. Our destination was the eastern shoreline, where we could make a long drift and Curtis could get used to handling a jig and a minnow. We told Curtis to get rid of the tuna rod and reel, and we equipped him with an easier-to-use medium rod with an older baitcasting reel.

The wind was perfect. A nice, cool, gentle breeze from the south was strong enough to push us along. I always used a transom-mounted trolling motor to control my depth when I was drifting. My speed was dictated by the wind. Curtis wanted to know everything I was doing regarding the trolling motor and my depth control. I told him just to concentrate on his rod and reel and his line angle. Those were top priorities. I wanted him to catch a fish.

Trial and error are sometimes the best teacher. The more chances Curtis had to land a fish, the better he would become. We had so much fun that afternoon. The northerns were in a biting frenzy. When we exhausted our minnow supply, we had boated thirteen northerns. To Curtis's delight, my livewell was full of beautiful northern pike. We had plenty of licenses to go around, so I was not worried about the possession limit. That afternoon was one of the best northern bites I could ever remember. Curtis had missed a lot of hits, but he was experiencing what it was like to get hits. I could tell Curtis was loving it. I tried to appease some of his frustration over the past days by telling him our story from 1967. It was not until Thursday afternoon of that week, in that year, that we caught our first northern. We had nobody to show us how.

Charlie Brown was our second newcomer that decided to come with us that year. Jim had known Charlie ever since high school. I got to know Charlie through Jim. We became instant friends. Charlie waited until he retired to make his first trip with us. He loved to fish, but over the years his job and family life came first.

Charlie is one of those amazing men who have that uncanny ability to know how things work. He knows a lot of stuff about a lot of stuff. If I were broken down on a highway, I would want Charlie to be with me. A good example of Charlie's ability to diagnose a problem occurred in 2015 when Doug, Charlie, and I decided to head into Lower Bottle Lake for some walleye fishing at night.

CHAPTER 20

How Stupid Can I Be?

In 2015 I had purchased a brand-new forty-horsepower Evinrude to replace my forty-horsepower Johnson. The Johnson's lower unit was leaking oil, and I didn't want to mess with it, so I went ahead and bought the Evinrude. As with most things that are new and modern, some level of understanding from the owner was required. This engine has a key start instead of the old push button that was used on the Johnson. The issue with the key is the alternate shutoff located on the throttle handle. If the operator uses the alternate shutoff, the key is easily forgotten and stays in the on position. The manual says to turn the key to the off position when not in use, since the key engages a lot of electrical crap in the engine itself and the battery will run down in fleeting time. So far, I have obeyed that rule.

Another rule not to be dismissed is the checking of the oil reservoir. The Evinrude was designed to have the oil reservoir as an integral part of the motor located inside the cowling, as opposed to an external reservoir. Somehow the gas-to-oil ratio is measured as it is injected into the cylinders. If I remove the cowling, the reservoir is in an accessible location and the oil level is easily visible. Since the engine was new to me, I didn't know how often I would have to check the reservoir. During the first week, I ran the motor without ever checking the oil level. Everything was running fine. Consequently, I didn't feel a need to check the oil for our second week's stay. That ignorance was a serious mistake.

One evening Charlie, Doug, and I decided to go troll the area Terry and I had fished the week before in Lower Bottle Lake. The evening was beautiful. It was not too cool, and the wind was minimal. The motor ran fine that evening, but the fish were not hitting, so we decided to head back to Upper Bottle Lake. After a few more passes, I wanted to try another spot. I used the key to start the motor, and it kicked right off. The issue was getting the motor to run at higher RPMs. I had no issue getting the motor into gear, but I had no power when I opened the throttle. It just stayed in idle mode, and no matter what I did, I could not get any more speed out of that engine. *Now what?* I thought to myself. *This is a brand-new engine and should not be doing that.* Charlie thought I was missing some detail, but he could not understand what. We finally put the engine in forward gear and decided to limp back to the docks in idle mode.

I was a nervous wreck. I was considering the worst scenario. I believe myself to have always been a pessimist in character, and I could not understand an optimist's point of view. I had always thought about the worst so that when the worst did happen it was not such a blow. I could then say, "See, I told you that would happen!" instead of "Damn, I cannot believe that happened!"

If we continued to have some power, I was not going to call anyone to come tow us in. At the docks, when everything was secure, Charlie and I made our way back to the cabin. Charlie wanted to know if I had a manual for the engine. I did, and it was in the boat—a fine place for it to be for sure, since I never gave a thought to looking at the manual while out on the lake. But little good that would have done me, since I hate manuals and engines of any kind. I would not have known what to look for anyway. Charlie was adamant about seeing that manual, so out to the boat I went, and I retrieved the manual for Charlie to read.

There we sat in the cabin, Charlie sitting in his easy chair under light, reading the manual from cover to cover. It had to be one hundred pages long. Curtis was already in bed. I was getting ready for a shower and then it would be off to bed with me, since I was useless at that moment, thinking about my motor. Then Charlie asked me a question: "Belik, when was the last time you checked your oil reservoir?"

"Not since I bought the engine back in August."

"I think you're out of oil."

My heart skipped a beat. I knew from experience that if Charlie was on to something, I could bet he was on the right track. Charlie is one of those guys that just knows stuff. He went on to read me the lines out of the manual about the internal oil reservoir. Charlie had diagnosed the problem. After more in-depth study on the manual, we came across a failsafe condition that the motor will put itself into if the oil reservoir is brought down to a dangerous level. A sensor goes off that will prevent the motor from running any higher RPM than idle speed. There is just enough oil left in the reservoir to get you back to dock, but only at idle speed; otherwise the engine freezes. And that is exactly what had happened to us. "Tomorrow we will pull the cowling and check the reservoir," Charlie told me. Charlie was betting it was close to bone dry.

The next morning, after a very restless night, Charlie and I made our way to the boat and pulled the cowling. There was the oil reservoir, with not a drop of oil in it. The only oil left was in the supply line, and that could not have been much. I was incredibly lucky. If not for Charlie, I could easily have ruined that engine. Our next move was to head into Park Rapids and buy some expensive Evinrude oil. When we got back, I filled up the reservoir, and the motor fired right up. I took it for a spin, and it was running at full throttle right away. Thank you, Charlie! What a lesson I learned that day!

CHAPTER 21

Towing Duty

The year 2004 was the first time I had to offer up my Lund Predator to towing duty. Up until this year, we never had to get a boat towed off the water because of engine trouble or some other issue. The inevitable had to happen at some time, and one evening two lost souls became stranded out on the water at night with no way to get back to camp.

One evening, Jim and Kevin decided to pair up in a resort boat and troll for walleyes. Wayne decided not to go out that night and went to bed early. He was in dire need of some sleep, instigated by a terrible hangover he was fighting because of his having gotten completely shitfaced the evening before. I do not think Wayne felt good the whole next day. None of us drank to excess often; however, sometimes we would reserve one night out of the week to just sit around a nice campfire and let it all hang out. We never got rowdy or loud, but we could become merry and have an enjoyable time laughing and listening to stories old and new.

Leonard and I paired up to troll for walleyes. Michael decided to visit Paul and Paula. They were alumni friends of his that lived in the area on another lake. With Wayne sleeping, the cabins were quiet. Leonard and I stayed out on the lake until well past 11:00 p.m. When we came in, we decided to wait on cleaning duty until Jim and Kevin came in. From our deck, we could see a light blinking on and off out in the distance for the longest time. We thought nothing of it, assuming only that it must have been Jim and Kevin trolling along the center reeds. When Michael got back to camp around eleven thirty, he asked about Jim and Kevin. We told him they were still out, as we could see their lights in the distance. Michael thought that to be suspicious and wondered if they had tried to contact us using the two-way radios Michael had brought. Jim and Kevin had taken one, but we were not receiving anything from them. That is when Michael found out that Wayne had shut down the radio in the cabin just before he hit the hay. When Michael tried to reach them, sure enough, we found out about the rest of the story. They had run out of gas, and since they were not getting any answer back on the radio, they had tried sending an SOS signal with their flashlights, which was what Leonard and I had been seeing all along; we hadn't put two and two together. We got into my boat, and off we went to the rescue. Of course we took all sorts of shit from them, especially about the radio being off. However, they should have known better about the gas and kept an eye on the gas consumption. That was the first of many tow duties I had to perform in the coming years.

Around August of 2013, Curtis gave me a call and told me he had bought himself a boat. He wanted to pull it up that year. I had not seen the boat, but Curtis assured me it would work well. Sure enough, when the group for the second week of 2013 drove up from Nebraska, Curtis was pulling his boat.

It was a decent-looking boat that had a twenty-five-horsepower Johnson on it. Sunday morning, he was anxious to get it into the water and fire it up. Unfortunately, when he finally got it started, it was firing only on one cylinder. It was a twenty-five-horsepower motor running like a five-horsepower motor. It is very frustrating to haul a boat all the way to Park Rapids, put it into the water, and then find out the damn thing will not run. That was Curtis's situation on Sunday morning. Curtis decided to run the motor on one cylinder.

Curtis was a conscientious guy that didn't want to cause any trouble for anyone. When we decided to all head out that Sunday afternoon, he decided to head out by himself. Curtis had a plan to get to the southern shore, where he could drift the eastern shoreline with a favorable wind and not have to use the motor that often. Terry and I went straight to the center island, looking for crappies. Wayne, Jim, and Charlie decided to still-fish with bobbers in Wambolt's Bay. Michael and Doug decided to drift for northerns. Curtis was off to the south shoreline.

Two hours into the afternoon, just by chance, I happened to glance across the water to see if I could find Curtis. Terry and I could barely make out a small boat that appeared to have the oars out. Sometimes my eyes can play tricks on me. The southern shoreline was a good distance away, but the more I stared at the small craft, the more I realized it was Curtis with oars out, trying to make his way back to camp.

I told Terry, "Christ almighty, Curtis has his oars out! We need to pick up anchor and go help him!" When we approached, the cowling on the motor was off and he was dead in the water. We tied on, and I pulled him back to camp. Well, that was the end of his motor. We helped him pull the boat and take off the motor. Curtis decided to rent a motor from Mike and Connie for the rest of the week.

My next encounter with lost souls happened in 2015, when Michael needed a tow.

CHAPTER 22

A Lesson Learned the Hard Way

In 2015, Michael engraved into the annals of our fishing trips a fascinating story. One of my greatest fears has always been running a boat at full throttle on the open water at night. Unless I am sure about what lies between me and my destination, an open-water ride at night is chilling. Furthermore, even if I am sure what lies ahead, there is something scary about the feeling of movement and not seeing where I am going. The Bottle Lakes can instill that type of insecurity in me regardless of how many times I have crossed its waters at night.

There are certain areas on the Bottle Lakes that require precaution. The Narrows, for example, is a no-wake zone. Another area is the shallow bar in Lower Bottle that guards Home Bay Resort. Anyone that does not know that bar exists runs the risk of driving a boat right up onto it and suffering extensive damage, if not worse. The most notable precautionary location on Upper Bottle is the center reeds. It is a bar that extends out to form a point and cuts Upper Bottle in half. The bar is loaded with reeds and is one of our prime spots for bass fishing in the mornings.

All of us that run boats at night realize we must pick up Whippoorwill's floodlights, which will help guide us home regardless of our location on Upper Bottle Lake. They are noticeable from the Narrows. The precaution lies with the center reeds. Anyone who comes through the Narrows and makes a direct bearing for the lights will run into the reeds. Consequently, it's mandatory that the boat driver bear right a considerable distance and then head for the lights to be assured of clearing the reeds.

One evening Terry, Jim, and I were shot and really had no interest in venturing out to fish for walleyes. We were in those later years when the walleye fishing was miserable. Michael, however, wanted to go pull artificial lures. Michael was a diehard fisherman when he wanted to be. Since none of us had any interest in fishing that evening, Michael went himself. I was never keen on anyone going out by himself at night. Michael assured us there would be no problem. Michael, like Jim, was not afraid of anything. At approximately 7:30 p.m., Michael cranked up his boat, and away he went to troll the totem pole in Lower Bottle.

The totem pole was a location on the southeastern shoreline of Lower Bottle Lake. Some of the very first homes built on the Bottle Lakes exist on that shoreline. A crafty homeowner decided to carve out a totem pole out of one of his tree trunks. The pole stood a good fifteen feet high and could be seen a considerable distance away. The totem pole was there in 1967, and Lou had told us it was one of the oldest points of interest on Lower Bottle Lake.

The southeastern shoreline was very shallow where most of the private boat docks stretched out a good distance from the shore just to reach three feet of water. There exists a shallow bar all along the southeastern shoreline. The bar maintained a consistent three to five feet of water depth for hundreds of yards before dropping off into very deep water. It was one of the best places on the Bottle Lakes to run artificial lures, since the depth was so consistent.

Michael's boat was powered by a fifty-horsepower Johnson. The boat screamed down the water and disappeared into the darkness in a matter of seconds. The rest of us went back into the cabin and played a couple of games of pitch. Nine thirty sneaked up on us quickly, and I decided to take a shower and make ready for bed. While I was taking my shower, Connie and Mike got a call from one of the lakeshore residents saying that one of their guests was in trouble in the center reeds. He needed help. The only guests they had at the resort were us. It had to be Michael. Right in the middle of my shower, Connie and Mike started pounding on the cabin door. Terry let them in and told him Michael had gotten himself into a situation in the middle reeds. Terry quickly got me out of the shower, and in a matter of minutes I was ready to go rescue Michael.

Connie and Mike told us Michael was okay but needed help getting his boat out of the center reeds. I thought, *The center reeds! What the hell was he doing in the center reeds?* We also came to find out that one of the residents in Lower Bottle Lake had heard the commotion and called the police. It is amazing how far sound travels over open water on a calm night. Connie and Mike, upon receiving a call from the police, told them the situation was under control and that everything was okay. We were all relieved Michael was not hurt, but he needed help to get his boat out.

Jim and I headed off into the pitch-black darkness toward the center reeds of Upper Bottle Lake. Terry and I both had cell phones, so he stayed back at the cabin just in case there were new developments he needed to pass on about this amazing story.

Michael had the whole neighborhood on alert, the police on alert, and Whippoorwill notified, with me and Jim coming to the rescue. When we pulled closer to the reeds, we could see Michael's high-beam flashlight waving in our direction. As I got closer to the reeds, I could see Michael in his boat, stuck just a few yards into the reeds. "Christ, how the hell did he get in that position?" I asked myself. Those few yards could have been a hundred yards. We were not going to get that boat out of there at night. Furthermore, there was no way Michael was going to struggle through those reeds and get to my boat in my current location. I had to find another entrance that would allow Michael to exit his boat and struggle through the shallow water where the reeds were not so thick. That location was on the other side of the point. That is where I told Michael I would have to go. He would have to walk out. Once I got to the closest point that would allow Michael an exit, he jumped out of his boat, sank chest deep in water and sludge, and then struggled ahead to make his way toward Jim and me. It took him some doing, but he made it. We got him into the boat safely, and back to camp we went.

Michael had somehow, at full throttle, run right into the center reeds. It had to have scared the shit out of him. Not only that, but those reeds are not deep. He was lucky not to have been thrown out of the boat. We were lucky to have him back in one piece. From Michael's account, he was on his way back to the resort from fishing on the bar in front of the totem pole. He said, "I decided to try one pass down the western shoreline as I came through the Narrows. When I decided to head in, I picked up the floodlights and knew I had to head east before I turned north toward the lights. I must not have gone far enough east! Before I knew it, at full throttle I went crashing into the reeds! At first I didn't know what was going on, until I realized where I was. So I decided to keep full throttle on and maybe I could churn my way out. I almost made it!"

He was right; only a few more yards and he would have cleared the far end of the reeds, but the motor simply gave out, and there he sat, stuck in the mud in the densest area of the bar. He had no phone, and we didn't have the two-way radios that in years past Michael had been adamant we carry in each boat. Michael told us, "When the engine stalled out, it was smoking like a steam engine. I started sending an SOS signal with my flashlight, hoping someone from the resort would see the lights. That was not working, so I started blowing my whistle." Luckily, a resident on the shore heard it, and Michael yelled out to call Whippoorwill and have someone come out to help.

Michael was noticeably distraught, thinking that he had ruined his engine. We would have to wait until the morning to rescue his boat. I doubt Michael slept well that night. He was lucky he didn't get hurt. That evening Michael called Paul, our friend that lives on Blue Lake just a few miles away. He would come down in the morning with his waders and help us pull Michael's boat out.

The next morning, after a nice breakfast, Paul showed up around 9:00 a.m. A dense fog had settled in over the lake. We could not see the boat docks from the cabin because it was so thick. We didn't want to wait for the fog to lift, so Terry, Michael, Paul, and I got into my boat and slowly made our way to the center reeds. Paul was all decked out in his waders. Michael had on his jeans. It would be cold in the water for Michael, but Michael is a tough cookie.

Once we noticed the reeds, the boat came into view. We had hit the location on our first try. I got my boat as close as I could to a depth where the bow just started to creep up the bar. At that point, both Paul and Michael jumped out of the boat and into the water, which was just a foot or so deep. They trudged their way through the dense reeds until they came to a clearing where Michael's boat had come to rest. They tied on a sturdy dock rope to the bow, and with Paul in the rear and Michael up front, they tried to pull and push the boat into a position where I could tie on and pull it out. (See figure 30.) Finally they broke through the front line of the reeds. The bow was out enough that Michael was able to throw Terry the tow rope. Terry tied on to my bow, and I started slowly in reverse. Before we got too deep, they both jumped into Michael's boat, and I pulled them clear of the bar. We moved the tow rope to the stern and began a slow return to the docks with Michael's boat in tow.

I thought I knew everything. At least that is the way I came across to everyone on our return trip to the docks. I just knew the direction I was going would take us right into our docks. In fact, I had thought I could see the docks way off in the distance, since the fog itself was lifting to some degree. Terry was the first one to question me about my direction. "You sure you're heading in the right direction?" he asked.

I answered, "Yup! I know where I'm going."

Terry, in his clever way, told me, "Well I can tell you one thing; you don't know where the hell you're going. The docks are to our left." Funny guy, that Terry!

I simply could not believe it. I just knew I was going in the right direction. Then Paul got out his phone and pulled up his compass. He was yelling back in Michael's boat that we were heading east, and all of us knew the direction back to camp from the center reeds was north. Could I possibly admit I had been wrong this whole time? Sure enough, by the time we all agreed we were heading in the wrong direction, the east shoreline came into view, and there I sat with my head up my ass. I was very embarrassed. It was a good lesson learned: not to have deaf ears. Anyway, I got a well-deserved ribbing, and we all had a good laugh about it.

When we finally made it back to camp, the first thing Michael did was get a charger on his battery. After a couple of hours, Michael was anxious to turn the engine over and see if he could start it. To his relief, he was able to get it running. That afternoon, Jim, Terry, and I went out to the sunken island in search of crappies. Paul had stayed for the afternoon and decided to go fishing with Michael.

It was such a beautiful day sitting on the island. We had caught about a dozen crappies that were beautiful fish, all thirteen to fourteen inches long. Terry caught most of them using the smallest minnows he could find.

Jim was fishing with chubs, looking for northerns. It is hard to explain his patience. He was watching Terry and me catch beautiful crappies, but he continued to fish with the chubs. His patience was rewarded when he tied into a thirty-five-inch northern with his cane pole. What a fight that was to see! When I netted the northern and got him in the boat, Terry took a picture of Jim and his northern that I believe turned out to be one of the best pictures ever taken over the years. (See figure 31.) Jim promptly released the big fella back into the lake. What a memorable moment that was for the three of us to enjoy!

CHAPTER 23

Michael's Journal—2016

O ur fiftieth trip north had come at last. Terry, Michael, Jim, and I decided upon another two-week stay. Rick opted to stay for the first week, so he drove over by himself from Washington. He would leave the next Saturday morning when the rest of the gang would show up, and what a gang it was. Doug, Wayne, Curtis, Charlie Brown, Wayne Junior (Wayne's oldest boy), and Wayne Kadavy, along with Terry, Michael, and Jim, would become the largest group we ever had for two weeks.

With only five of us in camp the first week, we were determined to enjoy some peace time before the bustle of activity that would hit the camp next week. I was looking forward to some quality time fishing with the guys that first week because I knew the second week would be anything but relaxing. We would have three boats for ten guys the second week. Everyone would be wanting to spend a good deal of time on the water in hopes of catching some fish, so Michael, Wayne, and I would be busy for sure. But it was a "good busy" and I would not trade it for the world.

The weather forecast for our first week was calling for mixed conditions on a day-by-day basis. Damn the smart phones anyway! They predict weather ten days out and are surprisingly good at it. There was no more guessing as to what the weather might be, which took a little bit of the excitement out of it. Now we could be disappointed many days in advance instead of disappointed just one day out.

We also wanted to try something different for one of our evening meals. At the wholesaler bait shop, we found out they sold crawfish. We decided to reserve twelve dozen crawfish for a Friday-evening crawfish boil before Rick had to leave the next day.

Besides catching a lot of bass, fishing was pathetic the whole week. We had spent a lot of time on the sunken island in hopes of catching some crappies, but even the crappies were not hitting. The walleyes in the evenings disappeared. For the week and into the next week, among all of us, we caught two walleyes.

A small note about my mental state regarding fishing. I was getting into an attitude where all I wanted to do was fish for bass in the mornings and then sit out on the sunken island in the afternoon and say screw the walleye fishing at night, which is what I did for the whole two-week stay. Even northern fishing was not turning me on as it had in the past. All we could catch were small bait-stealing northerns.

What could have been happening to our precious Bottle Lakes? The bass were in large numbers. The crappie fishing the last few years was as good as we had ever experienced. The bluegills were taking over the lake to such an extent that quality bluegills were hard to find. The northerns were small and in substantial numbers. The walleyes vanished. The perch were scarce. What northerns we did clean had empty stomachs. We had also started to notice a disappointing decline in the reeds. The reed beds were thinning out. Some beds simply ceased to exist. This was not the lake we had fished in 1967. If the DNR does not recognize these trends, I fear the Bottle Lakes will turn into unwanted lakes. I hope that never happens.

Friday had come with amazing speed. If it hadn't been for our staying another week, we would be heading home in the morning. It was at that time that I was grateful to have a two-week stay. Tomorrow, late in the afternoon, the rest of the boys would show up. It would be chaos for sure. Rick would leave early in the morning with plans to visit some old friends along the way back to Washington.

On Friday afternoon, Connie and Mike asked that everyone join them on the deck of cabin 1. About 3:00 p.m., we all gathered for a small celebration of our fiftieth trip to Bottle Lake. Connie and Mike brought over two bottles of a nice champagne. We laughed, talked a lot, and reminisced about some of our earlier years. (See figure 32.) After a lot of picture-taking, our small party broke up and we started to prepare for our crawfish boil that was going to be our evening meal.

We had ordered twelve dozen crawfish from the wholesale dealer during the first part of the week. It was time to go pick them up. They had them ready for us, contained in a mesh sack. Along with the crawfish, Michael was cooking sweet corn and potatoes in a galvanized milk can. I had never had a crawfish boil, so this was new to me. To keep all the crawfish residue contained on the picnic table, we used a plastic rain tarp Rick had in his car. When the corn and potatoes were done, all the contents were spilled out on the tarp. Then came the crawfish—all twelve dozen of them spread all along the table. We dived in, eager to scrape what little meat was buried in various hard-to-reach places.

The meal was not bad. The worst part of eating crawfish was the inability to find any sizeable chunks of meat; there were only tidbits buried in the tail. It took some doing to break through the extremely hard and brittle shell surrounding the tail. There was a knack to it I had not mastered. Also, they got cold right away. When we were done, we simply dumped the liner contents into a trash bag. That night we played poker. I think I lost.

In 2016, when we went to settle our bill Friday evening, Connie and Mike told us they were selling the resort. During the few years they'd had the resort, we could not have asked for better owners—especially Connie, who worked her butt off for her guests. We would surely miss them. They assured us they would sell to someone willing to keep the resort open. They had a potential buyer in mind. Again we were facing an unknown future. The following year would be our fiftieth year heading north. Would we have a place to go?

In the second week of 2016, we had a full house. Rick had to leave on Saturday. We took one group picture the next Friday evening before leaving the next day. It was the last large group picture we would take. (See figure 33.)

CHAPTER 24

Our Fifty-Year Anniversary: September 16, 2017

M y alarm went off at 5:30 a.m. I rushed out of bed and hit the shower. Curtis would be here in less than forty-five minutes. Curtis had decided to ride up with me on this trip, so he'd dropped off all his gear the night before. This would be Curtis's first time staying two weeks, but he packed enough junk to last him two months. By the time we were done packing, the truck and the boat were loaded to the gills. We were to meet Michael at 7:00 a.m. where our two-pickup caravan would leave for Park Rapids to rendezvous with Terry, Rick, and Jim. Wayne, Doug, and Charlie were scheduled to arrive the second week.

Reservations got a little turned around in 2017. Jim and Terry had decided to go one week earlier but still stay two weeks. Their second week would overlap our first week. That meant they would not get to see Doug or Wayne on our second week. It was too bad we could not have been all together for our fiftieth anniversary. Rick drove over from Washington for our first week. He would leave on Saturday.

Connie and Mike had found new owners: Jim and Jill. We would meet them for the first time this coming fall. Jill and Jim had sold their business to buy a resort. Whippoorwill came up, and they jumped at the chance. They are the friendliest couple. Jim is an avid hunter and fisherman. Jill is the brains of the duo. Together they are living in paradise and plan to keep Whippoorwill open as an active resort for as long as they can. This was good news to all of us.

Text message fishing reports from Jim and Terry were pouring in during the week before our departure. The fishing was crap! They caught only three walleyes the whole week. The small northerns were gulping down minnows so fast they thought they were starving. From what we had been seeing in their stomachs over the last few years, it was a real possibility. They had caught just a few crappies, along with a handful of bluegills. I hoped our first week would be different.

Our drive up to Park Rapids was relaxing. We pulled into town around 4:30 and made our normal stops, and then it was off to Whippoorwill to meet the new owners, Jill and Jim, with their dog Jackie.

The week's forecast called for cooler-than-normal temperatures with some threatening rain later in the week. I was not thrilled about going out at night to fish for walleyes—especially after Terry's and Jim's fishing reports from the week before—but I had to try. Sunday evening, Terry, Jim, and I went out walleye fishing. We got skunked. That was it for me for the week. Unless the walleyes started hitting or someone found a way to catch them, I was staying in and concentrating on bass fishing in the mornings and crappie fishing during the day.

I hadn't caught a walleye in 2016. I didn't catch a walleye in 2017 either, but we did catch bass. Lots of bass. This lake had turned into a bass lake and small northern lake. Michael caught one bass that weighed in at over six pounds. A six-pound Minnesota bass is nothing to sneeze at. They look like footballs, and those devils are strong. Michael also caught himself a nice smallmouth. What is up with Michael and his smallmouths? Nobody else catches them. Over the years, I suspect he has caught about a dozen smallmouths.

We decided to have another crawfish boil on Friday before the other gang showed up the next day. Will this be the start of another tradition? I think it will. With more practice, maybe I can find more meat on those crawfish and a technique to get it.

How fishing had turned around for all of us! I can recall from earlier years that all I wanted to do was fish for walleyes at night and northerns during the day. Crappies were almost nonexistent, except Jim and Wayne would pick up a few at night while still-fishing. When Leonard was still with us, I didn't go out after bass like Terry and Michael used to do. I suspect I missed some exciting times, but my time clock was all screwed up by staying out late and then trying to sleep the next morning. Now I found myself fishing for bass in the mornings and crappies in the afternoons. My evenings were now spent sitting on the deck, enjoying the evening air, waiting for nine thirty to come around so I could go to bed. I had turned into a dud.

I finally got to spend some time fishing with Doug the second week. He is the most easygoing person I know, with a personality that works well in his profession. Doug told me one time that he does not come up to catch fish but to enjoy friendship and camaraderie. Doug told me, "If I happen to catch anything, it is a plus." Doug had the answer! It is not about how many fish we catch or how much time we spend on the water; it is about enjoying our time together. Whether one is at dinner, playing cards, playing golf, or sitting on the deck, fishing should never get in the way of those precious times. Maybe if I looked at Doug's philosophy a little closer, I might not be such a dud after all.

How could fifty years go by so fast? It is almost unimaginable. Nobody ever got hurt. Aside from some episodes of constipation and severe colds, we had been incredibly lucky. We had cleaned hundreds, if not thousands, of fish over the years, and nobody had cut himself, as far as I can remember. A couple of times, Douglas managed to get himself wet by falling off the dock or while climbing out of my boat at the dock. But nobody ever fell in while we were out on the water. That is a minor miracle given all the time we spent on the water. We had all seen ourselves build good careers that took care of us and our families. We all had managed to move into our golden years in good health. So much had changed over fifty years. It was so much easier now to get from point A to point B. The roads had gotten better. The vehicles were more reliable. Communication became easier. The distances had gotten shorter by some alien way. The world had gotten smaller. However, even with our shrinking world around us, I still look at our yearly fishing trip as a great adventure—a time to catch up with the best friends I could ever imagine.

EPILOGUE

On the third day of May 2018, Leonard, Jim's dad, passed away. He was a great friend and fishing partner. We all miss him!

In February of 2018, we almost lost Terry to a blood clot in his lung. For weeks we were all on edge, hoping we would not lose one of our dearest friends and a great fisherman. The doctors say his survival was a miracle.

In 2018, Uncle Charlie, Terry's uncle, still lives on. He turned one hundred years young.

In September 2018, we headed north once again for another two-week stay. It was one of the worst trips we ever had regarding weather. We fought rain, wind, and cold. One morning we woke up to a coating of snow. Our boats had an inch of the white stuff in them. On another morning, our boats were covered in sleet. One afternoon, two boats decided to anchor on the sunken island. We were looking for crappies. There were storms in the area, and the clouds were low and ominous, but the air was calm with no wind. I had Terry and Rick in my boat. Wayne had Jim and Curtis in his boat. We all had bobbers on, fishing loose line. Suddenly I noticed my line slowly start to rise into the air, making a bow in the line that started at the rod tip and ended at the bobber. Everyone else was experiencing the same thing. Suddenly a bolt of lightning struck somewhere in the distant hills, and we heard the crack of thunder just a couple of seconds later. We noticed our lines fall back into the water. A couple of minutes later, our lines started to rise once more. We finally figured out what was happening. Everything around us was getting positively charged. We were close to initiating a lightning strike. Jim yelled, "We need to get the fuck out of here, now!" Up came the anchors, and we made a mad dash back to the docks. As we arrived at the docks, a bolt of lightning must have hit close, because the resultant thunder was as loud as I have ever heard.

One evening in 2018, we were so disposed from walleye fishing that nobody even considered it. Michael decided we would take out all the boats to the sunken island and everyone was going to fish for bullheads. Douglas had made us a beautiful brisket for dinner. There were a few pieces left over, so I decided to cut them into small chunks for bullhead bait. Around 8:00 p.m., when darkness had fallen, all our boats headed out to the sunken island. We found a spot in twelve feet of water. The three boats assembled around each other with all anchors buried in the weeds. I had Terry and Rick in my boat. We fished right under the boat on the bottom, using the brisket I had cut up for bait. We started catching bullheads one after the other. Interestingly, my boat was the only boat catching bullheads. Somehow we'd managed to locate ourselves between two large beds of reeds where we could get the bait close to the bottom. The other boats were not that fortunate and were struggling to catch a single bullhead. It was very cold outside, and after about one hour of fishing, it started to snow on us. The snow was heavy at times. Suddenly the wind changed direction, which changed our position just enough to take us off our location. The bullhead bite stopped that suddenly. When we went in, and we ended up cleaning over thirty bullheads. My boat contributed twenty-five of them.

In 2018, the DNR did impose a slot limit for northern pike on the Bottle Lakes. They finally realized something was happening that required immediate attention. They needed to turn the situation around quickly. The lake was full of small northerns. The same scenario was happening across all the lakes in central Minnesota. During our fifty years of fishing in the Bottle Lakes, the possession limit for northern pike was three per license, with no size restriction. In 2018 the possession limit went to ten northern pike per license. An angler could keep any northern up to twenty-two inches. All northerns from twenty-two to twenty-six inches had to be immediately released. Only two northerns above twenty-six inches could be in possession per license. This was the DNR's attempt to get the small northerns out of the lake systems within central Minnesota. We had noticed for years the steady decline of perch in the lake and the alarming lack of any perch in the stomachs of the northerns we did catch. We had also noticed a steady decline in our ability to catch northerns above twenty-eight inches. I hope this move by the DNR will once again revive the Bottle Lakes into a quality northern pike fishery.

A FEW REWARDS
Fifty Years of Fishing the Bottle Lakes

The Biggest Fish Caught: Terry caught a fifty-one-inch muskie. We nicknamed him Waldo.

The Biggest Bass: Michael landed a bass weighing six and three-quarters pounds. That big boy is mounted on his wall.

The Biggest Northern: Wayne and Doug each caught a thirty-nine-inch northern in the same year. We had larger ones hooked but never boated them.

The Biggest Walleye: Jim's nine-and-three-quarter-pound walleye at thirty-one-inches is one of the largest walleyes caught out of the Bottle Lakes. That walleye is mounted and sits in Jim's office. Along with his six-and-three-quarter-pound twins and many walleyes in the seven-to-nine-pound range, Jim is, without a doubt, the walleye king.

The Most Bass Caught: Michael and Terry must be the victors here. They spent as much time on the water fishing for bass as I did for northerns.

The Most Walleyes Caught: Jim and Wayne's timeless patience on the water while fishing at night yielded them many walleyes over the years.

The Most Northerns Caught: I suppose I will have to take this category. I caught so many northerns out of the Bottle Lakes that Lou would have been proud. There were times during our fish fries when everyone was eating the northerns I caught. One time I had thirteen northerns in my livewell. There were three of us in the boat. I caught eleven of them. What can I say?

Best Resort: I don't think anyone would disagree that we would all vote for Wambolt's as our go-to resort. It was truly a fishermen's resort. Maybe this was due to its rustic charm or its screened-in porches. Or maybe it was just the experience of sleeping with the mice that were constantly chewing on something. Whatever it was, Daryl and Rosemary provided us with many memorable years.

Worst Fishing Year: There is no question that this was 2006. Ten of us took home nothing except for a few crappies and a few northerns. The weather was cold and rainy. The conditions were hardly tolerable. It is hard to believe I took home three crappies to mount that year: a fourteen-incher, fourteen-and-a-half-incher, and a fifteen-incher.

Best Fishing Year: Our best year was arguably 2007. Five of us took home a limit of bluegills, northerns, and walleyes. Those fish didn't include the fish we had for our fish fry. Plus, we caught all those fish in one week. This was a feat not to be repeated. We came close but never matched it. If the crappies had been hitting that year, we would have had to go buy more coolers.

Most Fishermen in Camp at One Time: This occurred four times, in 1989, 2000, 2006, and 2016. Ten of us would make those trips.

Most Fishermen in Camp: This occurred in 2016 as part of a two-week stay during which Rick left in the first week. The total count for the two weeks was eleven.

ACKNOWLEDGMENTS

Thanks to Eileen for her patience, support, and encouragement. Her help with some editing and basic grammar was invaluable.

Thanks to Michael and Doug for feeding us. Our meals were precious times that could not be missed. It could not have been an easy task, but they made it look like one.

Thanks to Jim and Wayne and all the others that helped continue our tradition.

Thanks to Jim for my "phone call of all phone calls" in 1984. I will never ever forget that!

The hero award goes to Doug, who saved the lives of those involved in the I-29 accident.

A special thanks to everyone that ever made the trip for never getting cross with anyone. Nobody ever made a derogatory remark that I am sure would have been regretted. We had all managed to maintain our patience and temperament even during those stressful drives up north in the middle of the night. This is a testament to our friendship.

Finally, thank you to Rick and Leo from all of us. If it had not been for Rick's determination and for Leo providing us transportation, our first trip in 1967 might not have materialized, and I would not be authoring this book.

A special thanks to all involved at AUTHORHOUSE for helping me publish this book.

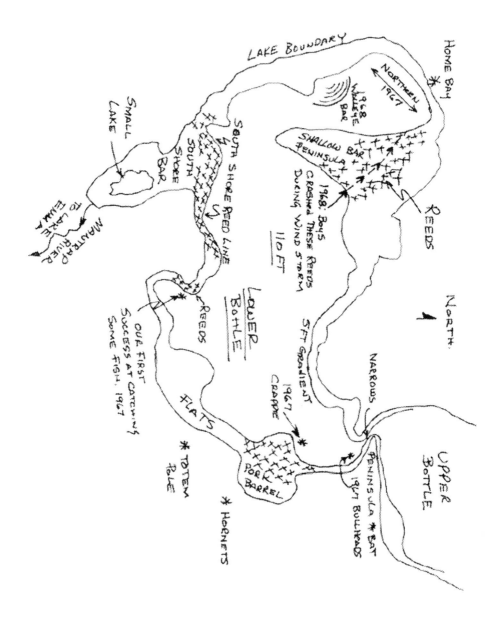

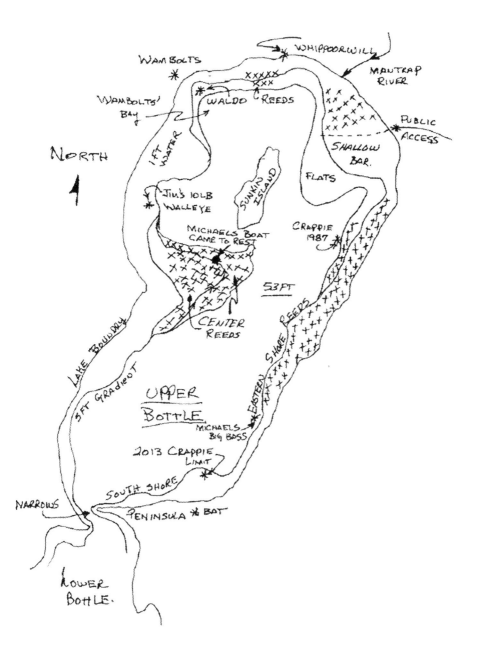

WAMBOLTS

WHIPPOORWILL

MANTRAP RIVER

WAMBOLTS' BAY

X X X X X
X X
WALDO REEDS

PUBLIC ACCESS

1 FT WATER

SUNKIN ISLAND

SHALLOW BAR.

FLATS

NORTH

Jiu's 10LB WALLEYE

CRAPPIE 1987

MICHAELS BOAT CAME TO REST

53 FT

CENTER REEDS

EASTERN SHORE REEDS

LAKE BOUNDRY

3 FT GRADIENT

UPPER BOTTLE

MICHAELS BIG BASS

2013 CRAPPIE LIMIT

SOUTH SHORE

NARROWS

PENINSULA ✳ BAT

LOWER BOTTLE.

313

Figure 1: Cabin 5, Home Bay Resort. *From left:* Rick, Jim, Doug in the doorway. Five of us made the trip in Leo's car, which is shown in the background. August 1967.

Figure 2: Jim walking in front of Don on the dock where the old green wooden boat with the five-horsepower motor is moored. August, 1967. Only half of cabin 5 is shown to the left. Directly back from the dock sits a single-room cabin tucked into the shadows, where in the spring of 1970, Wayne, Jim, and I stayed for one week, which would then be our fourth trip to the Bottle Lakes. That trip would be my last for many years to come.

Figure 3: Rick sitting on his throne in the bow of the heavy green boat. It was the most comfortable seat in the boat, and there was no dethroning him. August 1967.

Figure 4: Jim's northern caught on Friday, the day before we were to leave. Somehow the picture survived. August 1967.

Figure 5: Leo holding his northerns caught Friday afternoon. It's the only picture we have of Leo. August 1967. Somehow this picture survived.

Figure 6: August 1969. *From left:* Rick, Jim, Doug. Behind is the Pork Barrel. Beyond, hidden by the far trees, lies the Narrows. Shortly after this picture was taken, we had a run-in with some hornets. This was our third trip to the Bottle Lakes.

Figure 7: Wambolt's Resort. September 1984. After Jim decided against returning to Home Bay Resort, he started going to Wambolt's Resort, located on the northwestern corner of Upper Bottle Lake. The resort was truly a fisherman's resort dating back to the 1930s. There were ten cabins all in need of updating. The cabin on the far right was number 10. The cabin directly in the middle of the picture was the large community cabin. In 1984, Jim and I stayed in cabin 1 (not shown), located to the left of the picture.

Figure 8: Late September, 1984. Upper Bottle Lake. Wambolt's Resort is barely visible, hidden in the trees just right of Jim's head. Jim was in his element, all bundled up. The weather had turned cold and windy during the middle of the week. This was my first trip back to the Bottle Lakes since 1970. Jim would stay on for one more week.

Figure 9: September 1987. *Standing, from left:* Wayne, Jim. *Kneeling, from left:* Rick, Don. Taken on the Friday before we were to leave. This was our twenty-year anniversary of heading north. The crappies were found on the eastern shoreline of Upper Bottle Lake, seen in the background. These crappies represent the first "crappie bonanza" we ever experienced on the Bottle Lakes. It would take us till 2013 to find another crappie bonanza.

Figure 10: Late September 1999. Leonard showing off a very nice northern pike he had just caught. Whippoorwill resort is seen in the background. Leonard could outfish all of us. If he found someone to take him, he would fish till the wee hours of the morning, trolling for walleyes even after a full day trolling for northerns. Then he would repeat the whole thing the next day.

Figure 11: Our group in early September 1989. It was one of our largest groups ever to make the trip. *Standing, from left:* Brad (Doug's boy), Leonard, Terry, Rick, Dennis Wesely. *Kneeling, from left:* Don, Chris, Doug, Jim. Michael took the picture. I first met Terry on this trip. We became instant friends.

Figure 12: Late September 1993. *Standing, from left:* Leonard, Jim, Terry, Wayne. *Kneeling, from left:* Uncle Charlie, Larry. In 1993, Uncle Charlie made the trip with us. Unfortunately 1993 turned out to be one of the coldest trips we ever experienced. I took this picture just before we departed for home early Saturday morning.

Figure 13: September 1993. Jim's big walleye. Caught on Upper Bottle Lake late at night pulling a small walleye minnow in five feet of water. According to Daryl, it was one of the biggest walleyes caught on the Bottle Lakes that he had ever heard of.

Figure 14: Late September 1997. Our thirty-year anniversary. *Standing, from left:* Doug, Don, Leonard, Jim, Wayne, Michael, Terry. *Kneeling:* Rick. I consider this trip my most memorable. It was the first time all eight of us were together on one trip. The weather was favorable. The fish were hitting. We were all in good health.

Figure 15: Late September 1997. Our thirtieth-anniversary trip. One afternoon Jim went fishing by himself and caught these two walleyes on one minnow, one after the other. We called them Jim's twins.

Figure 16: Late September 1995. Wayne removing some of his tackle in preparation for our departure the next day. All three of Wambolt's rental boats were full of fishing equipment. It got so overcrowded we had a hard time moving from one end of the boat to the other. The next year, in 1996, I started a trend—bringing my own boat.

Figure 17: Late September 2000. Doug having a difficult time getting out of my Bluefin. The boat had steep sides, making it dangerous to get in and out of the boat. Later that week, one evening, Doug slipped while getting out of my boat and fell between the dock and the boat as it was moored. He didn't get hurt but got soaked. I vowed to get rid of that boat, and in 2002, I purchased a 1989 Lund Predator.

Figure 18: My 1989 Lund Predator moored to one of Whippoorwill Resort's boat docks. I purchased the boat in 2002 and still fish out of it today. In 2016 I put a new forty-horsepower Evinrude motor on it.

Figure 19: Late September 2011. Wayne had purchased a brand-new Lund Rebel, shown moored to one of Whippoorwill Resort's boat docks. The trees on the eastern shoreline of Upper Bottle Lake are in the foreground. What a beautiful boat—fast, stable, and equipped with everything.

Figure 20: Late September 2014. *From left:* Jim, unknown person behind the tree, Terry, Doug, Wayne, Wayne Katavy (*front, far right*). In the old fire pit was Michael, with back turned, cooking up fish for our traditional Tuesday-evening fish fry. Michael didn't start frying until Jim gave him the prepared fish. Everyone participated! Those not responsible for the preparation or cooking of the fish would help set up the table and make sure the proper amenities were provided. Our fish fry is one of our fondest traditions.

Figure 21: Late September 2002. *From Left:* Daryl and Rosemary, Leonard, Michael writing out a check, Wayne (*in front*). Daryl and Rosemary had just told us they were selling the resort. We were their last guests. That evening we drove a short mile to the east, where we visited Whippoorwill Resort and secured a spot for our next year's trip. When we arrived at Whippoorwill Resort in 2003, we were told that both Daryl and Rosemary had passed away six months after selling their beloved Wambolt's Resort.

Figure 22: Late September 1995. Terry arrived at Wambolt's boat dock with a beautiful largemouth bass he had just caught. After this picture was taken, Terry released the bass. Terry often went himself if Michael was not around. Terry is one of the best bass fishermen I know. He led us to using Senkos almost exclusively in the fall, fishing up against the reeds in the early morning. The reeds just left of Terry are almost nonexistent now. From the early 2000s to 2017, the Bottle Lakes were in the process of undergoing a drastic change.

Figure 23: Late September 2002. Michael with his largemouth bass. Michael decided to mount this very nice largemouth. This one was caught on a spinner bait. This was Wambolt's last year to be open. Years later I started going out bass fishing in the morning with Terry and Michael. On my first outing with them, I got skunked. Between the two of them, they caught and released over fifteen largemouth bass.

Figure 24: Late September 2012. Jim tangling with a northern using his sixteen-foot cane pole, fishing out of Wayne's boat. It appears they were still-fishing on the sunken island located in Upper Bottle Lake. The eastern shoreline is visible behind them. Those two guys could sit for hours fishing in this manner. Nobody has more patience. Both these guys are masters with the cane pole.

Figure 25: Late September 2008. *From left:* Wayne, Doug. Wayne caught two of the three in one outing, in the same place, all alone in the boat. One measured thirty-nine inches, and one thirty-seven inches. Doug caught the third one, thirty-nine inches, fishing out of my boat. Later in the week, Doug caught another, at thirty-seven inches, in Lower Bottle, also taken out of my boat. These were the largest northerns we ever caught over the years. We hooked many that were larger but never boated them. These three northerns were also the last northerns we would ever clean over thirty inches. Anything bigger got released. We labeled 2008 "the Year of the Big Northerns."

Figure 26: Paula and Paul in front of their house on Blue Lake, which is just a few minutes' drive from the Bottle Lakes. Paul and Paula were great friends to Michael and over the years became great friends to all of us.

Figure 27: Late September 2013. Our first week of a two-week stay. *From left:* Michael, Jim, Terry, Don. This was our first and only time we were able to catch a limit of crappies. Sitting next to Michael's right knee in the bag was his electric fillet knife. Normally Michael and I would fillet fish. For me it was part of the experience of fishing. We never objected to cleaning fish, no matter the species. For this picture, the camera was on a tripod.

Figure 28: Late September 2010. I'm holding the great muskie Terry had just caught, which we nicknamed Waldo. The muskie was bleeding from the gill where Terry's number-six walleye hook was imbedded. We left it alone, figuring this massive fish could deal with a small walleye hook once back in the lake. The fish measured fifty-one inches long. We had no scale, but using just length, we estimated him or her to be around forty pounds. Soon after this picture was taken, I carried Waldo to the shoreline for a couple more pictures. Shortly after, we would be in a life-or-death struggle to pump life back into this impressive fish. Whatever we did worked. With one swish of this massive fish's tail, he or she left Whippoorwill's dock.

Figure 29: Late September 2010. Terry kneeling in front of the muskie he had just caught. Time was running out on us, as we were anxious to get this fish back into the lake. We had no time for posing. A few quick pictures were taken. The fish was too big for Terry to handle because of his bad shoulders. I feel that if we had kept this great fish out of the water for another five to ten minutes, we would not have been able to save it. Shortly after this picture was taken, I cradled this impressive fish back to the dock, where we spent anxious minutes trying to save it. It responded, and with one great swish of the tail, the muskie left the dock to rule its kingdom once again.

Figure 30: Late September 2015. Paul pushing the rear of Michael's boat. Michael in front, trying to pull his boat out of the deepest confines of reeds in all the Bottle Lakes. The morning was foggy. After they cleared the boat of the reeds, I hooked up and started pulling it back to the dock only to get lost in the fog.

Figure 31: September 25, 2015. Jim caught this nice thirty-five-inch northern on his cane pole while Terry and I were fishing for crappies. The crappies were hitting. Jim, in his infinite patience, continued to fish for northerns. He was rewarded with this beautiful fish. After this picture was taken, Jim promptly released this big guy back into Upper Bottle Lake.

Figure 32: Late September 2016. Our fiftieth trip to the Bottle Lakes. *From left*: Connie, Michael, Paul, Terry, Mike (in front of Rick), Paula, Jim (*far right*). I took the picture. Connie and Mike had prepared a little celebration for our fiftieth trip. They brought over a few bottles of champagne that we all polished off in good fashion. This also represented the last year Connie and Mike would own Whippoorwill Resort. They were both fantastic to all of us. We will miss them.

Figure 33: Early October 2016. Our last large group picture we would take. *Standing from left*: Terry, Charlie, Wayne (with back toward us), Wayne Junior (Wayne's boy), Jim, Wayne Kadavy, Doug, Michael, Curtis, Don. Connie took the picture. The following year was our fiftieth year of going to the Bottle Lakes. Reservations got a little overlapped, so a large group picture of our entire group could not be taken.

Printed in the United States
By Bookmasters